Stories from the Household of

CM
&
CMW

Mary Ann Yutzy

Mary Ann Yutzy

7484 Shawnee Rd

Milford, DE 19963

maryannyutzy.wordpress.com

Ordering Information:

Quantity sales. Special discounts are available on quantity purchases by corporations, associations, and others. For details, contact the publisher at the address above.

Orders by U.S. trade bookstores and wholesalers. Please contact Mary Ann Yutzy: Tel: (302) 422-5952; Fax: (302) 424-4370 or visit www.lulu.com.

Printed in the United States of America

Yutzy, Mary Ann

Stories From The Household of CM & CMW / Mary Ann Yutzy

p. cm.

ISBN 978-0-615-86498-3

1. Family Life —True Stories —Life in a young and thriving family. 2. Humor —Funny Stories with a point. 3. Anecdotal.

I. Yutzy, Mary Ann. II. Stories From The Household of CM & CMW

HF0000.A0 A00 2010

299.000 00–dc22 2010999999

First Edition

14 13 12 11 10 / 10 9 8 7 6 5 4 3 2 1

CONTENTS

Dedication

I am grateful to Daniel Yutzy, my husband, known here as "Certain Man" for being the kind of husband who has lived out what it means to "lay down his life" for those he loves in tangible ways over the decades of our lives together. The stories of Certain Man will show a man who is truly one of a kind. I have a deep respect for you, Daniel, and beside that, I surely do love you!

After that, there are those five Offspringin's who have come to light up our lives in a thousand ways. Eldest Daughter, (Christina Bontrager) Middle Daughter, (Deborah Yutzy) Eldest Son, (Raphael Yutzy) Youngest Son, (Lemuel Yutzy) and Youngest Daughter (Rachel Yutzy). I've told you a thousand times, but I will tell you again: I am so glad that God chose to send you to our house.

As the years have passed, they have added to and improved our family by marrying some really wonderful people. Christina's husband Is Jesse Bontrager (Beloved Son-in-law). Raphael's wife is Regina Yoder Yutzy (The Ohio Heart Throb). Lem's wife is Jessica Lee Yutzy (The Girl With a Beautiful Heart). Our family would be so much the poorer without these three, and I cannot imagine our lives without any of you or the wonderful grandchildren that you have brought to our family.

But of all of these, I truly am most indebted to Beloved Son-in-law. Jesse, without you, this book would never have been. I know that as truly as I know that you have done a lion's share of the work to getting it to where it is today. Thank you for your faith in me, for prodding, for keeping on the project and for being the brains and energy to bring this dream to a reality. It's been a surprise to me in a whole lot more ways than a heavy box with my name on it at Family Christmas, 2012. Thank you!

Along the way there have been people who have inspired me and encouraged me. I would begin a litany here of gratitude, but I would leave someone out and they would feel bad.

But I do want to recognize the one person who first said that I could write. Henry Michael Shank (1943-1983) my eighth and ninth grade English teacher at Greenwood Mennonite School graded my essays with a red pen and a strict eye, telling my parents that he was hard on me because he knew I could do it. I didn't know what it was that "I could do" but I knew that I loved putting a pen to paper and crafting words into something that people could (and maybe *would*) read. He gave me confidence and encouragement.

My heart gives grateful praise for each and every one.

CM/CMW and the Disastrous Shopping Day

Now it seems that a Certain Man (hereafter referred to as "CM", or "Daniel") and that Certain Man's Wife (hereafter referred to as "CMW" "me") have lived in rather peaceful monogamy for over 26 years. One would think that such a thing as SHOPPING would never ruffle the feathers of CM. One would be wrong.

It came to pass that on the very last day of November in the year of our Lord, 1999 that CMW had planned a shopping trip with Eldest Daughter, Christina, now married to Beloved Son-In-Law, Jesse Bontrager. Christmas was coming, and there was much to be accomplished, and since there were very few free days in the life of CMW, the trip had been carefully planned. Old Gertrude, who lives at the house of CM and CMW, was at home every day except Tuesdays and Thursdays because of ill health. Thursday mornings there was an in-house Bible study, so this particular trip HAD to be on a Tuesday.

Youngest Daughter had worked a day ahead in her schoolwork, so she was going to spend the day at her Grandma Yoder's house. CMW did not know it at the time, but this was perhaps mistake number one.

Eldest Son and Youngest Son were staying at home to work on their schoolwork. CM was going forth to hunt for the Almighty Dollar. In an unselfish mood, he offered to send his cell phone with the womenfolk, but in an equally unselfish mood, CMW declined, saying that he really needed it more than she did and besides, she would stop several times and call home so that if she was needed, the two sons could relay that to her. This was mistake number two.

Middle Daughter was away at Sharon Mennonite Bible Institute, and there was a way to send a box to her that day, so the morning hours were spent getting brownies baked, getting items left behind packed, and tucking in some last minute surprises. It was after 11:00 before the box was packed, loose ends wrapped up and CMW and Eldest Daughter were finally on their way to the great shopping grounds. Evelyn Swartzentruber had been hired to meet the bus of Old Gertrude at 2:45, and when she queried about "How long?" CMW replied that she hoped to be home around 6:00 PM. This was mistake number three.

3

Dover was full, but the shopping was great, and since CMW very rarely gets such an opportunity, it seemed glorious indeed. Much was accomplished, and when she finally found a phone at 3:00, she found out that everything was fine, there were no messages, and that CM was even home at that moment. That was nice. This day was going better than expected.

Perhaps this gave her a false sense of security. Perhaps it just caused her to not think, but she remembered that she had Friend Evelyn there to watch over Old Gertrude, and that CM was going back out to his previously stated purpose, so she thought that she would just continue a while yet to finish some NEEDFUL things. (Mistake four.) Along about 7:00 PM she breezed into the kitchen of a very quiet house to find a very quiet CM on the La-Z-Boy with his Sunday school book and Bible on his lap.

"Where is everyone?" said CMW, very cheerfully. (Mistake five!!!)

"Well," replied CM carefully, "I had planned on going with Dad to the auction tonight to buy Eldest Son a car, but you didn't come home, so I sent the two of them along without me."

"Where is Evelyn?"

"You told her that you planned to be home at 6:00 so I sent her home when I came in around 6:00. I told you to take my phone this morning, but you said that you were going to call home every couple hours *(did I say that !!????!!)* but you didn't call, and there was no way to get ahold of you, I had no idea when you would come home, so I figured I might as well just send them ahead."

CMW didn't say so, but a great foreboding arose in her heart. She dearly loves her father, the highly regarded Mark Yoder, Sr., but the idea of Eldest Son at the car auction with his grandpa without the steadying influence of CM caused her considerable alarm.

Youngest Daughter, who had gotten a ride home with her dearly beloved Grandpa offered this nugget, "Grandpa says I have a Bad Mama if she went shopping at 9 o'clock this morning and stayed until 6 o'clock tonight!!!!" (THANKS, Daddy!)

CM had thoughtfully fed Old Gertrude and himself and Youngest Daughter. Hot dogs and biscuits and such, so they were content, and CMW was careful to be grateful, but CM was clearly not pleased with the situation in general, CMW in particular.

Not much pleasant conversation was had, until The Grandpa returned from the great car auction with Ecstatic Eldest Son. They had procured a Jeep Cherokee of great age and many miles for the wonderful price of only 1500 dollars. CM was careful to hold his feelings in check as he listened to the great exclamations of Eldest Son. This wasn't his fault, anyhow, it was clearly the fault of CMW, who had not come home on time . . . something that didn't escape the mind of The Grandpa who also came into the house and scolded CMW for wasting so much time abroad upon the face

4

of the earth. This did not particularly please CMW, who was feeling badly enough as it was.

After the house was quiet and everyone was in bed, CM explained that he had warned Eldest Son about getting a Jeep several months ago, saying that they were high maintenance, costly repair vehicles, and that he really didn't think it was the kind of vehicle he wanted.

Also troubling to CM was the fact that the Jeep was at the auction, without a tag, and he was going to have to take off the next afternoon to go and pick it up, take it to the Division of Motor Vehicles, get an insurance card, and he was probably going to end up beside the road somewhere, because Mark Yoder had bought vehicles before that didn't even get him home. Probably it wouldn't pass the emissions test, and how was he supposed to drive it down there anyhow without a tag? He allowed that, if it did run, and if it did pass inspection, it was a good price, but it was so "iffy."

Just about the time CMW was asleep, she remembered a service call that CM was supposed to do.

"Hon, did you remember to go and wrap Rodney Mulligan's pipes?"

"No, I didn't get there. I came home and then you weren't here and I had to take care of things here, so I didn't get there."

It was 20 degrees and a mean wind was blowing. These particular pipes were under a new double wide trailer with no foundation in place yet. CMW worried. She refrained from mentioning that he was going to the auction if she had been home, or that she had been home at seven o'clock. Some things are better left unsaid.

The night passed, and morning came. Rodney Mulligan had no water. The new pump had frozen and busted. This was clearly CMW's fault.

Though CM had thoughtfully fed Old Gertrude, CMW had thoughtlessly neglected to ask if he had given her the evening medications. He hadn't. CMW's fault.

In talking with The Grandma, it was discovered that The Grandpa really didn't think that Eldest Son would be happy with that Jeep, either, but CM wasn't there to intervene. CMW's fault.

The Jeep was nicer than expected, but it does drip oil on the floor of the garage. CMW's fault.

Somewhere, over there, someone is oppressing somebody. CMW's fault.

Oh, well, it will even out again. In fact, it already has! (Except for that oppression business. CMW needs some more time to get that one settled.)

And that's the news from Shady Acres, where CM is still the boss, CMW still keeps the house and all the children are growing up far too soon.

CMW's Sweet Mama and her Time of Trouble

Now it came to pass that the Sweet Mama of Certain Man's Wife had endured very much pain and trouble upon the face of the earth to the extent that her spirits were very low, indeed. This caused great concern among the sisters because it did seem that perhaps the problem was becoming that of the tears and discouragement more than that of the wretched knee. The knee, admittedly, did HURT, but it was progressing quite well according to the professionals who had replaced the old knee joint with one that had the advantages of modern technology.

So the sisters took it upon themselves to make sure that someone went in every day, and they combed her hair, though there was nothing wrong with her arms, and they made her bed and did her laundry and cleaned her bathroom, and swept her floor and loaded her dishwasher and spoke cheery words even amid the tears. And prayed for the Lord to help for they knew not what else to do. And the days went by, and the days went by and the days went by.

Now, behold, the one thing that Sweet Mama did show interest in was the fact that spring was coming and the Purple Martins would soon be returning to the land of Delaware and the Martin boxes were not yet ready for their return. This was the job of Our Daddy who is the husband of Sweet Mama. So after much prodding and pleading on the part of Sweet Mama, he donned his bib overalls, and performed his obligations. And the Martin boxes were put up, not only cleaned out, but also painted. This pleased Sweet Mama to no end, since she could observe the activity from the kitchen window.

Now it came to pass, on the Monday of this present week, that the oldest sister, known as CMW, went forth from her house to Sweet Mama's house with her own Eldest Daughter and Youngest Daughter, to do the duties that needed doing. Sweet Mama was not in good spirits, but was struggling to stay on top of things as she maneuvered herself about as best she could. CMW noticed that there was present in the kitchen a very sharp-looking 22-caliber rifle, and she wondered if Sweet Mama was considering using it. Indeed, Sweet Mama was. (Do not panic. She was not suicidal.)

As the morning progressed, Sweet Mama could often be seen peering out of her kitchen window in the direction of her Martin houses and commenting on the activity there. And a hapless pair of sparrows was frolicking about in the throes of young love, making a nest in the most logical place they could find -- Sweet Mama's Martin house. Sweet Mama was not pleased. She was heard to mutter threateningly under her breath things that are not altogether proper for a retired Mennonite minister's wife to say.

Now the sparrows were only following the call of nature, but they were very friendly with each other, and this also displeased Sweet Mama, for it meant that surely, more sparrows would follow. She put her hand upon the gun and stealthily crept to the window. With great quiet and caution, she opened the window and positioned her gun against the casing. At this very moment, the sparrows happened to fly down to the ground to further their relationship, and Sweet Mama took this sacred moment to pull the trigger. And behold! Both were sent into eternity with one single shot of the gun. Everyone came to stare in astonishment and exclaim.

Eldest Daughter said, "Grandma, that is rude! Grandma, that is mean! You should never disturb something like that!!!"

Sweet Mama replied very grimly, "I did not like what they were doing!"

And the hapless sparrows lay where they fell. Every now and then Sweet Mama would steal to the window to reassure herself that they were really dead, and still there. As the morning progressed, she was heard to confess, "I do sorta' feel sorry for them." Unfortunately, her grin was not repentant, and her sympathy sounded insincere.

However, it soon became clear that there was a side benefit of the morning's activity. Sweet Mama experienced a dramatic turn around. She became more optimistic and cheery. The wretched knee did not hurt so badly. The days were more interesting, and she became itchy to get out of the house. On Thursday, she dressed herself in a pretty dress, combed her hair, and went forth with neither walker nor cane to her doctor appointment, and asked when she could get rid of the ugly white support stockings. On Friday, the physical therapist told her that he would not be returning, that she was doing so well, she really didn't need any more therapy. He told her that she could do anything she wanted, including driving a car.

And that's the news from Shady Acres and the extended family, where Certain Man still works too hard, Certain Man's Wife still tries to keep the house, all the children keep growing up too fast, and Sweet Mama is more herself than she has been in a loooooooooooong time.

CMW's Family Does Corn

If anyone thinks that they have done corn this summer, let me tell you an "absolutely true, been there myself, hardly believable" account.

On Monday, Sarah, Alma, (my sisters) Polly, (my brother, Mark Jr.'s wife) Sweet Mama and I were at Alma's house to do corn, and we did corn for Alma and Sarah. On Tuesday, we were at Polly's house and we did corn for Mama, Polly, and Diane (She is the wife of Bobby Aycoth who lived with Mark and Polly for years. We feel like they belong to the family.) and on Wednesday, we were at Shady Acres (our house) and we did corn for our family, some more for Sarah, some more for Polly, some more for Diane, and some for our very own cousin Twila, who came to help us. Our cousin James' wife, Karen, also came to help us in our great distress (It was the biggest day, and we were tired!) so we gave her some, and also did some up for some other people we love.

Now the Yoders of the Mark Yoder kind make the doing of corn almost a religious rite. There are certain rituals that need to be gone through. The corn is never as good if it is picked by females. Females are not gifted in this area. They have been known, under greatly unusual circumstances, to sally forth into the patch and to appear later, greatly befuddled, thoroughly tired and ready to quit. This is not good, as their work is only beginning at this juncture. So the men make it their business to pick it, and they haul it by the pick-up load back to civilization.

Then all the children of available age descend (some under great coercion) upon the loaded pickup truck to husk the small mountains. There is an arbitrary number of baskets (4) that usually need to be husked before the mothers begin to silk. Now Certain Man took it upon himself to invent a wondrous gadget which we call a "cow" (so named because of the four liquid producing outlets which it possesses). This is an ingenious gadget made of pipe that is like a large "X" on a stand that has a spigot at the end of each of each pipe.

Four women can sit facing each other while they brush the corn under running water. This practice of silking under water is something that was brought into our family by our dear Polly, and we can sit and talk and silk corn with amazing dampness and efficiency. It is best if the four ladies working at this job are good friends. There has been much laughter, even tears and solving of the world's problems around this particular circle. If it is a sunny day, Certain Man has a large canopy that is lightweight and can be put up and then moved when necessary. This brings some comfort (of which there is precious little on corn days) if there are no suitable shade trees.

The one extra job of the mothers in this circle is to monitor the progress of the husking crew. It is necessary to stop now and then and hurl instructions towards the direction of the truck or silently listen to the snatches of conversation -- such as follows. (Actual quotes, here.)

"Now listen. I want to either see you putting a husked ear into the basket, or picking one up from the pile."

"You all are doing terrific! Keep it up!"

"No, DO NOT THROW THAT WORM ON ME! MOM! MAKE HIM STOP!"

"You can't husk to an advantage up there on the roof of the truck. Get down."

"That's a long hard job. What would we ever do without you all?"

"Watch it, you are throwing the silk back into the husked corn!"

"Can someone please get us another wash basket?"

"Come on, over there. Make your fingers fly!"

"Are you sure that you are doing your part? It doesn't appear to me that there is much activity in your corner."

"Mom, can I stop? I'm sick and tired of this job."

"Well, what do you suppose would happen if we all stopped when we were tired? Do you want corn to eat this winter or not?"

"NOT!!!!!"

"Are you children almost done?"

"Is it okay if I have 3 (or 4, or 5) Mountain Dews today? When a guy has to work this hard, he should have 'unlimited sodas' for a day."

"I'm so sick of corn, I refuse to eat corn for lunch. Can't we have some REAL FOOD?"

. . . And on and on and on.

When there are sufficient numbers of large wash baskets full of corn that is silked, the discussion begins as to who is going to cook. We have two large outdoor cookers that we fire up, and this is a hot and dangerous job. We found out this year that pillowcases are wonderful things to have when you are cooking corn in outdoor cookers. We loaded 22 or 25 ears of corn into an old pillowcase, and when the water was boiling sufficiently, lowered the pillow case into the cooker, and flung the long end up over the lid.

(Well, usually we did. One time we forgot and there was great excitement about the flames that were licking their way up the side of the pot. There was much outcry and motherly admonition).

10

When the pot comes back to a full rolling boil, the whole pillow case is hauled out, and the pillowcase contents dumped into the first of three cooling buckets. For several years now we have been using the big "muck buckets" that you can buy at Walmart. They are larger than a bushel basket, and are sturdy plastic. These have worked exceedingly well in the cooling corn process, but we always spent lots of time fishing the corn out of one bucket and putting it into the next.

Certain Man came to our rescue again in this little problem, and fashioned a wire basket kind of thing that he made from plastic coated chicken wire. It fits snugly down inside the bucket, so all we need to do is pull the "cage" full of corn out of one bucket and plop it into the next one. By the time the ears of corn reach the third bucket, it gets an ice-water bath and is ready for draining and cutting off.

This cutting off operation is also done outside. We set up a table, and the people who are cutting line up with their various weapons of warfare. Polly likes hers all cut off by a knife. Sarah and I like ours all cut off with a creamer/cutter. Mama and Alma like a mix of the two, though Mama would take all creamed before she would want it all cut off with a knife. Then we have Diane and she is not fussy about either way. She likes it however we want to do it.

Our husbands all play a different role in this complicated process. Jerrel (Alma's husband) plants the corn and gets it sprayed and keeps it growing. (It was simply wonderful this year.) Mark usually engineers the picking, though Bert (Sarah's husband) also often gets his hands in this part of it, as well as sometimes helping to cook. Daniel, my Certain Man, is our encourager, thinker up of new things, cooker, and sometimes cutter-offer. He does not like to pick, and isn't very good at it, and I am quite suspicious that he doesn't like to husk because he is seldom there when it is being done. But often, as the day is getting very long, and the gals are getting quite ready to stand out by the road and give the corn away, here comes the familiar brown work van, and the favorite guy of all (yep, that's him!) jumps in to help us to victory. Mark also lent his hand to the very end a time or two this week, and this masculine effort is very much appreciated.

This corn business really is something that we all do together. It is not my project or Alma's or Polly's or Sarah's, although corn is something that Sarah is really into. We can't all of us always stay for the whole day, but often we can and do. And our efforts and labor saving devices proved well worth it this year. We did over 6,000 ears (if our calculations are correct) and froze 477 QUARTS of corn. Now that is some kind of accomplishment, though I am not sure how much we did besides that this week. Even today, I didn't much feel like setting the world on fire. I think there might be a clinical name for this such as "post corn trauma" or "too much corn syndrome" but I am too tired to care.

11

I promise you, all of this is true. There are witnesses among this gathering who have been with us in the midst of our labor. So there!

CMW, Mo'eisha and Missions Retreat

She was loud and black and poor.

CMW was fairly confident of the first two by her voice on the telephone when Mo'eisha called and begged to be allowed to go along on the church's mission retreat weekend. She couldn't tell the latter. CMW had never seen her, never talked to her before, but her voice was pleading.

"Lupé says ya'all is goin' on this here church thing and I was wonderin' iffen I could go along with ya'alls." CMW is a sucker for poor, fatherless children, and after very little debating or thinking, she said Mo'eisha could come.

Mo'eisha's clothes were inadequate and ripped, and she didn't smell very clean. She was boy crazy, too. These were things CMW couldn't tell over the phone, but it didn't take too long in close quarters to find out. Mo'eisha was one of those children that you had to work at to love.

But Mo'eisha has been the strongest defender of CMW's "own" little Lupé-girl, who meanders in and out of Certain Man's house and whom the whole family loves with a fierce and protective urgency. Lupé invited Jesus into her heart one late, hot summer evening after struggling with more grown-up questions about Christianity than many adults ever think to voice. She was only 12, but the issues were real to her.

Lupé went to an extremely volatile public school where drugs were rampant, talk was vulgar and humanistic theories were touted with authority and vigor. She had begged CMW to homeschool her because she was so afraid of this new, big, middle school. She was tiny for her age, two grades behind, and the child of illegal Mexican immigrants. She remembered coming across the river on an inner tube, being left alone as the protector of her three year old nephew, hiding in a border restroom, waiting for the signal that said all was clear, and then carrying him to safety.

CMW very much wanted to say "yes" to her request, but the laws in Delaware were such at that time that she hardly felt like she could. And so Lupé entered the big rough world of middle school. Things were tough. One of her classmates, an honor student, died suddenly mid-year from what appeared to have been a suicide. Though tiny, Lupé was extremely attractive and mature, and there were sexual issues and insinuations that make CMW want to go in there with a baseball bat.

So when Mo'eisha, with her big mouth and large frame suddenly took little, vulnerable Lupé under her wing, CMW felt kindly towards her. Mo'eisha attended her own church, and often, when someone was hitting Lupé up with "There are many gods. You can get to heaven any old way" kind of talk, Mo'eisha was frequently there with her "Wha's a mattah wif you? Dey ain't no God but one. Ain't you smart enuff to know dat?" She had some wild theology at times, and non-resistance wasn't a single part of her experience, but CMW loved her for the way she stuck up for our "Little Latin Lupé Lou" (Certain Man's household's pet name for her).

But now, CMW was at the Missions Retreat with this boisterous girl who was getting on everybody's nerves, and regularly getting mad at Youngest Daughter, as well as Lupé, and the other two children, Ari and Vicente. She especially didn't get along with Youngest Daughter, who was getting increasingly vocal about her aggravation.

I would hasten to add that being Black at Missions Retreat was not a drawback. This is an especially integrated group, with Blacks, Hispanics, Mid Easterns, and Caucasians all gathering together to worship and fellowship and be renewed. It is a wonderful experience (usually), but Certain Man was in Missouri at an Amish family reunion, and CMW was tired. She really didn't feel like dealing with the dynamics of the relationships, and she didn't know why she always put herself into situations like this.

"Jesus loves the little children.
All the children of the world.
Red. Brown. Yellow. Black. And white.
They are precious in His sight.
Jesus loves the little children of the world."

The song was rolling around in CMW's subconscious all day. It was Saturday evening, and the Holy Spirit had been prompting her to talk to this dynamo, to find out more about what made her tick. CMW started with her family. A mother who has no job and doesn't drive. . . A little sister who is three years younger. . . No father present. And, no, she didn't want to talk about him.

And then CMW said, "Mo'eisha, you have talked a lot about church and going to church and all of that, but I wonder if there was ever a time when you invited Jesus into your heart?

"Yeah," she said. "I done dat."

CMW said, "Mo'eisha, I think it is important for us to know when that happened, and where. Can you tell me?"

"Yeah," she said, "Lass yeahr, at my church."

CMW said, "That's wonderful, honey. Can you tell me what that means to you?"

14

"Oh," she said, "Hit means everthin' to me."

Said CMW, "What I meant was, how has that made a difference in your life? Why did you do that?"

She ducked her head and her voice was quiet for once as she almost whispered, "Because I want to go to Heaven."

CMW's heart gave that sudden lurch that she has learned is from the Father saying, "Sit up straight and pay attention! You are on Holy Ground."

You know, she wouldn't want to miss moments like this for anything. No, it isn't always convenient and children aren't always fun or easy or clean or gentle with our hearts. But is it worth it? A thousand times "Yes!" And if someday in Heaven, CMW sees these children, it will be more than worth it.

"Lord Jesus, may it be so!"

CMW's Mama and the Errant BB

Now it came to pass that the Youngest Sister (whose name is Alma) was cleaning the house of Sweet Mama, following the surgery to replace her second troublesome knee in the spring of the year of our Lord, 2000. And whilst she was cleaning the cabinets in the kitchen, lo, she came upon a very deep hole in the woodwork in which a BB pellet lodged at a very great depth.

"Mama!" said Youngest Sister. "What happened here?!?!?!"

And when Sweet Mama came to look upon it, behold, her eyes filled up with tears and she did not wish to discuss it. "That happened a long time ago" she said. "It's none of your business."

Being blessed with the tenacity that is typical of the Mark Yoder tribe, Youngest Sister was not deterred from her intent, and eventually she wormed the whole story out of her reluctant parent.

Scarcely any time had elapsed before she called her eldest sister, Certain Man's Wife. "Mary Ann, did Mom tell you what happened in her kitchen and why that BB is in the wood of the cabinet beside the table?"

CMW was uncomfortable. Sweet Mama had confided in her some time previously, only after swearing her to secrecy and silence under dire threat. So even though she knew the story, she knew that it was not something Sweet Mama wished to have broadcasted about.

"Uh, yes. I guess I did."

"Mary! Do you realize how serious that could have been? That could have been terrible!"

"Well, it wasn't. For that we can be grateful."

"I know, but--!"

This morning, faced with the fact that the story is spreading far and wide, Sweet Mama gave permission for it to be told. And so, you see, this is what happened.

Sweet Mama generally kept a 22-caliber rifle on hand to do business with the sparrows and starlings that invade her Martin houses. However, she has sons and grandsons who were worried about the close proximity of the houses around the nursing home. They have made warnings to her urging her to be cautious about using the higher powered gun. So, heeding the concerns of her progeny, she laid her hands upon a gun that was a bit more suitable.

This gun, however, caused her no end of grief. First, she had to put this little tiny pellet into the gun, and then she had to pump and pump and pump until there was enough "OOMPH" to make the pellet fly.

When a gal is old enough to have celebrated her golden wedding anniversary, there are some things that are too inconvenient to be satisfactory. Sweet Mama was not pleased with this gun. She never got two birds with one shot (she often didn't get one). It was insult added to inconvenience. However, her love for the Purple Martins, and her zeal to protect them led her to persevere in her attempts to keep the sparrow and starling populations down.

On this fateful morning, there was unacceptable activity at the martin houses outside the kitchen window. It was a very busy time in the household. A particularly troublesome client, Lucia, was still living with the family. She needed assistance with her breakfast and Our Daddy was leaning over the table to help her. Sweet Mama happened to notice that there were unwelcome visitors invading the territory. Grabbing the pellet gun that she kept handy, she inserted the pellet, placed the gun firmly between her knees and began to pump it furiously. Now she was somewhat wrought up, and she wanted to be sure that the pellet would fly an adequate distance, so she gave it a few extra, vicious pumps.

Neither Our Daddy nor Sweet Mama quite knew how or why that gun went off, but suddenly, the air was alive with the sound of a gun discharging. And Our Daddy felt a very strange sensation. It didn't hurt at all, but it felt strangely like something had passed through his trousers. Now Our Daddy is not a man to fill out his trousers very fully, nor does he buy trousers such as would adhere to his person, so they often appear to be quite roomy. Whatever had passed through his trousers had gone in one side of the seat of said garment and out the other, conveniently missed any skin, and lodged in the wood of the cabinet on the other side.

However, Sweet Mama did not know this. She only knew the gun had gone off, that Our Daddy was in the line of fire, and that the pellet was even now probably lodged in his person. She dropped the gun and fled to his side.

"Mark, Mark! Did I hit you?? Oh, Mark, are you okay?"

By this time, Our Daddy had ascertained that he was not injured, and reassured her that no harm was done. She greatly peered upon his trousers and discovered a small hole on one side, and a small hole in the other side. Whereupon she burst into tears and wept copiously.

Suddenly, the whole thing struck Our Daddy's funny bone, and he proceeded to laugh and laugh and laugh. The more he laughed, the harder she cried. Behold, the mix of emotions ran quite high for some time. Sweet Mama was not amused. She was overwhelmed at the thoughts of all the "Might Have Beens".

18

So, Sweet Mama chose to swear CMW to secrecy (she "did not want it to get out" as she put it) and told her the whole sordid tale one day with a great guilty showing of the evidence and more tears. Apparently Our Daddy had no such need to tell, and the story was safe until the day that Youngest Sister made her discovery. However, then the story began to spread. Youngest Sister did not tell so many people, but it was amazing how this person told that person, and that person told that person and slowly, the story started drifting back to Sweet Mama. She was troubled that "people were talking."

Then the story started to change. This was even more troubling to the mother, but she felt helpless in her own defense. She had, after all, shot her own husband in the seat of his pants and there was no way she could say she didn't. And people didn't want to know the whole story. They just wanted to laugh and tell somebody else.

But one day, she was really, really cross. She had heard from some friends from New York, Allen and Carolyn Roth. Allen Roth had heard from his father in OREGON that Mark Yoder's wife had shot him with a SHOTGUN. Never has there been such an upset lady.

She said, "Whoever heard of a story like that going clear to West Coast and being so mixed up? If I hadn't caught it when I did, they would probably be saying I shot him with a CANNON. It wasn't a bullet. It was a BB. It wasn't a shotgun or even a 22. It was a pellet gun. And I didn't shoot him. It accidentally went off. And, most importantly, I didn't hurt him. It missed."

CMW does not recommend discussing this with Sweet Mama. CMW heard her tell her much loved sister, Aunt Gladys, to "Shut Up!" (actual words) when the innocent lady was enjoying a chuckle about it this morning.

So that is the whole story. And the facts are the facts. If anyone tries to tell you a different version, you can tell them that you know the truth. This is the **truth**, the **whole truth** and **nothing but the truth.)**

And that is the news from Shady Acres and the Home of Our Daddy and Sweet Mama where all the women are tenacious, all the men are known for their determination, and all the children (and grandchildren) have a healthy dose of both.

CM/CMW and the Great Toilet Disaster

Now Middle Daughter of Certain Man and his wife often comments about how her household has many things that her friends think are weird, and she often looks upon life at Shady Acres and it's happenings with a sigh, and the words, "Welcome to my crazy world..."

Now the entire week, Old Gertrude hath been ill. And the sickness was not unto death, but it did cause her to cough and snort. The coughing and snorting often disintegrated into upchucking and many dismal noises that sounded like the death knell. This might have been okay in the confines of her boudoir, but she got very lonely in there and insisted upon being ensconced upon her favorite chair by the fire in the family room. Behold, great was the protest of the children.

But she got to stay home from Center on Monday and Tuesday, and she was improving with the medicine that the good doctor dispensed and it looked as if she might recover. For which CMW was just drawing a great sigh of relief. It was about four o'clock, and the other two individuals were due in from their respective day programs and it looked as if there might be a somewhat peaceful evening ahead. Supper was cooking, classical music was playing, and none of the children were fighting. There was to be cantata practice at the Yutzy house that night, and so a measure of order was expected.

Behold, at 4:15, the doors burst open and in came Timmy. He was walking arrogantly and carrying a large plastic bag. He was not attired in the clothing with which he had left the house. Anyone who cares for intellectually disabled adults knows what this means. It means there has been a major potty accident at the center. Depending on the individual, you suspect the wet stuff. Depending on the individual, you know it is the other. Timmy NEVER wets himself. CMW knew what was in that large plastic bag.

"Hey, Tim! Why don't you just leave that bag down here in the downstairs wash box?"

The snub nose went in the air, and there was a great, independent toss of the head as he went right on as if nothing was said. CMW did not feel like arguing with him. He had access to two wash boxes upstairs. He is generally very meticulous about his dirty laundry. He would be sure to get it to where it belonged, and then the smell would not greet everyone who walked into the house.

This was important with the evening meeting.

Tim disappeared up the steps to his room. Occasionally, CMW thought that he was taking pretty long up there, but Certain Man had come home early, and was on his La-Z-Boy, and the household was relatively quiet, so she held her peace.

Behold, after a space of time, another bus pulled up, and Linda was home. CMW went to fetch her. She was carrying a large plastic bag. She was not attired in the clothing with which she had left the house. CMW sighed, and brought her in and took her to the bathroom. About the time she had her on the toilet, there was the sound of pouring rain. In the house. In the kitchen, specifically.

There was a great roaring noise from CM as he leaped up from his La-Z-Boy and bounded up the steps. CMW dashed out of the bathroom to see great volumes of water descending from the ceiling. Upstairs, Timmy was flushing and flushing and flushing the toilet into which he had put many lengths of toilet paper. In addition to the other stuff.

Now it just so happens that there is a background story here. Timmy has been known to do this same trick repeatedly on Saturday Mornings. The toilet in the bathroom that he uses is a water saving toilet without a very big flushing hole. It clogs very easily. CMW has often implored her plumber husband to replace it with a more reliable model. CM has countered that Timmy must learn. And if he can't learn, then he has to use the downstairs bathroom. CMW has said that it isn't very convenient for Timmy to use the downstairs toilet because there are two handicapped ladies using it as well as all the downstairs traffic. CM has stated that Timmy just needs to learn. CMW has said that just one time of cleaning an inch of water off the bathroom floor when it is accompanied by Timmy's donations and floating bits of toilet paper would help to change his mind. CM has countered that it is too expensive to just change that toilet. What does CMW think he is made of anyhow, money? CMW gave up this argument some weeks ago and has tried to "learn Timmy."

By this time, Timmy was happily downstairs on CM's La-Z-y Boy, clean clothes on, listening to his radio. When CMW came around the corner into the bathroom, CM was on his knees with two large towels, almost done mopping up the mess, and muttering specific threats under his breath.

"We are just going to turn the valve off going to this toilet. It will be a dreadful inconvenience, but ONE flush is all he is going to get..."

"Maybe I should just go down to Penco and get one of those power flush toilets. They make a dreadful noise, and everyone in the house, clear down to the basement will hear it when it's flushed, but at least it would flush..."

"It will cost $300.00 but maybe that's just what I ought to do...."

"If we aren't careful we are going to have to replace this floor, there is water getting under the linoleum and you know what a mess that is..."

"I just can't see why he can't get it through his head to stop flushing when it is running over..."

CMW murmured affirming words and tried to help, but the adrenaline was flowing, and CM was quite industrious, and the floor was soon spotless.

And the water stopped descending. And Middle Daughter, helping to clean up the downstairs mess was heard to mutter under her breath, "welcome to my crazy world," and CM was heard to pledge to replace the toilet the very next day with a more reliable (but NOT that terrible power flush) one. In the meantime, his instructions are being followed and the water supply has been turned off in hopes of thwarting further flushing disasters.

And that is the news from Shady Acres, where Certain Man is still the boss, CMW is hoping he doesn't forget his promise to replace the toilet, and all the children are doing a splendid job of putting up with their "crazy world."

CM/CMW and the Sunday Moon

Now it came to pass upon the third Sunday in March, 2001, the Yutzy household had planned for guests for dinner. And Certain Man had it in his heart to invite some newcomers to the Fellowship to break bread with the family. So phone calls had been made, and two young families with their children had agreed to share the Sunday noon meal. Also sharing lunch was Beloved Son-In-Law, Jesse, with Eldest Daughter, Christina, as well as Kent and April, daughter and son-in-law of esteemed cousins, Dave and Ilva Hertzler.

Certain Man's Wife dearly loves a crowd of people, and she had made roast beef and mashed potatoes, fat lima beans and deviled eggs, tossed salad and corn. She had a jello salad and also homemade bread. Eldest Daughter had made a perfectly delectable blueberry delight, and the house was cleaned and ready.

Now the two young families were in the throes of recent departure from the Amish faith which can present special challenges, so CM and CMW wanted there to be as little distractions as possible from their conversations. This was also one of the reasons for the "more careful than usual" preparation.

Now it also came to pass that Timmy, the 37-year-old Down's syndrome male that resides at the household of Certain Man and his Wife has had an unusually hyper week. It was the week for his yearly physical, blood work, TB test, new glasses, and the excitement had put a real strain on him. There had been reports from the center about his lack of cooperation to the extent that he was not allowed to accompany them on a trip. Towards the end of the week, the new glasses disappeared totally from the face of the earth. This was not accidental. Timmy just doesn't "lose" his glasses. All of this had been accompanied by odd behaviors such as "chase Rachel and make her cry," "pat Mama on the top of her head when she is least expecting it," "hang socks from the curtain rod just to see what someone will say," "leave important belongings on the van since I broke them anyway" (anyhow, you get the picture). The good thing was that for the last two days, he had been doing better, and CMW had hopes that he was settling down.

Along about 2:30, all nineteen people had eaten and were filled, and the adults and young people were still sitting around the dining room table.

Conversation was pleasant and CMW was experiencing a sense of quiet relief. Timmy, having finished his second helping of everything, had made his way to the La-Z-Boy in the corner of the family room, observing and enjoying all the activity. He, too, was feeling pretty swell. He had been to church, all spiffied up, had come home and gotten into his well-loved, comfortable sweat suit, had eaten a dinner of monumental proportions, and now, here was all this excitement going on around him. How much better could a guy have it?

Well, you could ask for a little attention, I guess. There was an unusually funny story told in the dry humor of one of the guests, followed by much laughter, when suddenly, Timmy leaped to his feet, whirled around to face his chair, and locked his thumbs in the sides of his sweat pants and underwear. CMW felt as if she were in a trance as she watched in shocked disbelief. In one quick move, down went the sweat pants AND the underwear, and there was Timmy's backside, as bare as the day he was born.

"TIMMY!" shrieked CMW. "STOP THAT THIS MINUTE!"

Timmy never does anything except in his time and his way, so he proceeded to give a few decided wiggles for emphasis, then regained proper possession of his garments and sat back down as if nothing had even happened. There was a brief, shocked silence around the table, then the humor of the situation hit with force.

CM tried to keep a straight face as he went around the end of the table and took Timmy gently by the hand. "Come on, Buddy. I think you had better spend some time in your room." Guilty party went willingly, and stayed out of sight for a very long time. CMW seriously doubts that he has learned his lesson. She has taken steps to give his beloved sweat suit to Salvation Army or other needy cause.

The full impact this had upon the guests has yet to be seen. It happened so fast that one of the men missed it. He appeared disappointed. The others seemed to be forgiving, if not amused.

And that is the news from Shady Acres, where Certain Man is still the boss, CMW tries hard to keep the house and its inhabitants in some resemblance of order, and all the children put up with a lot.

CM & CMW and A Valentine's Story

Now it came to pass that on Valentine's Day, in the year of our Lord, 1971, there was a Certain Young Man who was taking a Certain Young Woman upon a date. This was a first date for that particular seventeen year old damsel, though the Certain Young Man was on his FOURTH "first date." (Uh-huh!!!)

CYW was not altogether sure of this CYM, having eluded his pursuit for a great many months with careful tactics that involved hiding behind the seats of cars, ducking into convenient doorways and declining proffered friendship with calculated coolness. However, when the Heavenly Father set out to impress upon her heart the need to at least give the young man a chance, she obeyed -- albeit with reservation.

On this particular Sunday in 1971, they set forth to hear the Gospel Echoes team sing at the Plain City Elementary School Auditorium. It was term break from Rosedale Bible Institute, and special permission had been given by Willard Mayer, the principal, no less, for a single date. The age of both mandated that it should have been a double, but Brother Mayer, bless his heart, was an old romantic, and he was willing to allow that since it was between terms, he would bend the rules and permit a single date (this once).

CYW had found a new pair of shoes for this occasion, classy leather Hush Puppy heels, and she felt quite well dressed for the occasion. It had snowed over the weekend, and it was cold. CYM had a Ford Fairlane of antique origin that had a habit of stalling in the middle of intersections. It had a console in the middle that kept young people a respectable distance apart. This was not a problem, though, since both young people were very well aware of protocol. They arrived safely at the meeting place.

The program went well. (There was that one situation when the emcee called for all the men in the auditorium to reach over and take the hand of that loved one by their side. CYM looked in one direction very intently whilst CYW looked in the other, but otherwise, it was good.)

When the concert was over, the crowd pressed out of the building, into the February cold. The parking lot had lots of glare ice, and it was quite treacherous. CYW was finding that the soles of her new shoes were extremely slippery. Visions of crashing down in great disarray and disgrace began to float through her mind. Weighing the options carefully in her mind, she decided that it would be proper to take CYM's arm that was so conveniently beside her. So she steadied herself with a hand lightly on his suited elbow, and they continued on their trek across the parking lot. She stole a sideways glance at CYM and was surprised to see a perplexed look on his face.

Then he spoke, "Uh, Mary Ann. Now if one of us falls, we BOTH will!"

Well, she could take a hint. She laughed, let go of his arm, and continued her journey.

She did take it upon herself to ask him one morning, many years later, if he was avoiding bodily injury that day or temptation. He thought that was a terribly dumb question. Of course he was worried that they both would fall. Oh, well. Self-preservation really is the strongest instinct, I guess.

And that is the Valentine Memory from Shady Acres, where CM has often steadied CMW in treacherous places (both real and imagined) and the many years have been well worth the journey.

CMW and the *VERY BAD* Day

Now it came to pass that the Monday of this week was a *VERY BAD* day for Certain Man's Wife.

It all started before five o'clock when Certain Man's dog took it upon himself to bark. And bark. And bark. This was not your "Come quickly! Something is intruding!!!" kind of bark, but more "I'm bored...", "Yes, I'm bored...", "I'm sure I'm bored, I know I'm bored, I'm bored, bored, bored."

This went on whilst CM turned over several times and muttered threatening things toward the window which the dog could never have heard even if he tried. CMW was trying to get a few more minutes of sleep when suddenly, up from the bed with great purpose arose CM, and pulled on his coveralls with great urgency.

Says CMW from her pillow, "Sweetheart, where are you going?"

Not so sweet heart answered savagely, "To shut up that dog!"

In what seemed like a very short time for him to travel the distance between the upstairs bedroom and the dog kennel, there came a sudden short surprised noise from the dog and great silence reigned. Very soon the foot of the conqueror was heard upon the steps and CM returned to his slumber. CMW was quite wide awake by this time and decided to get up and get the laundry started.

Now it also came to pass upon this Monday, that CMW and Sweet Mama had to take a medication class to retain the license which they have with the state of Delaware to provide foster care for intellectually disabled adults. This class was to begin at 9:00 AM at a destination about a half an hour away. There are three intellectually disabled adults at CMW's house. They all ride different buses. They go to three different day programs. Mornings, at best, are very scheduled and need to be kept well under control. However, the last bus leaves at nine, and CMW needed to leave at 8:30. This meant that she really needed to plan well.

As the minutes slipped away, it became apparent that every contractor and every person with any sort of a plumbing problem had kindly waited until Monday morning to call the plumber. And so CMW gave showers, made breakfasts, packed lunches, and answered the phone. And attempted to get everyone ready for their respective buses on time. Besides staying cheerful. For a while at least.

Then she and Sweet Mama ventured out to the class where her intelligence was insulted one more time. The beginning of the class was sweetened by the promise of a "surprise" to come at the end of the class, so CMW and Sweet Mama settled in to wait it all out. The class was the same as every other year. The same material was covered, and essentially the same test given. It took an inordinately long time. The participants were a motley crew, some of whom were barely literate. It tried the already taxed patience of CMW sorely.

Then the "surprise" the instructor had for this particular group was to tack an "infectious waste" class on the end of the "medications" class. CMW was not impressed.

Finally, all was done and CMW was home again. However, the afternoon was such that Youngest Son proceeded to ask "Are you having a bad day, Mom?"

A bad day? Well, come to think of it, things weren't too swell.

The wonderful homeschooled children forgot the "wonderful" part of their description and fought and dallied and didn't understand their algebra and didn't want to learn their times tables and didn't want to write their sentences and wanted an hour and a half for lunch.

Against the rules of the house, there was a very fresh, very tall glass of liquid refreshment set on the edge of the computer desk by Youngest Son. Youngest daughter's elbow just happened to come around and hit it squarely and there was Mountain Dew all over the desk, the fax machine, the carpet and possibly important papers. There was loud and indignant outcry from Youngest Son.

Youngest Daughter and friend, Lupé, decided to take the fairly new card table to the patio to do extensive art work with paints and paper. When taking it down again, one leg wouldn't fold properly, producing a determination that does not work well with hollow metal legs, and there is a very strange crease in it and the angle at which it hangs is interesting indeed. CMW instructed patiently that when something does not go easily in desired direction, it is prudent to ask for help, not force it. Sigh.

Within 15 minutes, CMW opened the drawer in the kitchen which holds pens and pencils and markers and crayons and scissors and such. Probably because the day was creating a very deep desire for order, or some other Freudian disorder, she decided that cleaning said drawer would prove to be a good job for two little girls.

However, when she went to take it out, it would not come. When she got it out to a certain point, the little clips are supposed to lift up, and the drawer is supposed to slide out. Well, guess what? It was not gonna' happen. Then the stupid drawer would not go in. Nor out. Nor in. CMW jiggled up and down. She wiggled back and forth. Got screw driver and tried to move little clip. Not a good idea.

CMW was just about to wrench that rebellious drawer apart from its moorings when a little voice inside her head said, "When something does not go easily in desired direction, it is prudent to ask for help, not force it." So the jiggling continued until the drawer could be eased back into its closed position. Contents were transported to the table via a large cake taker and sorted and discarded and replaced, and that job was done.

Then the bus bringing home the first client of the afternoon proceeded to run over the hind end of the favorite little kitty. There was much noise and wailing. The kitten was injured, but not dead. Yet. CMW was sick in her stomach and very troubled, but needed to take the role of chief comforter.

About then Middle Daughter decided to take Offending Dog for a walk since she felt sorry for him and the rough treatment of the morning. Offending Dog HATES cats, and happened to spy the injured kitty. He got away from Middle Daughter and took great steps toward putting small kitty out of her misery. The injured kitty rose up with all her might and latched a claw into Offending Dog's cheekbone and did mighty damage to said territory. There was much screaming and tears and shouting, causing CMW to need to run towards the window to see who was being killed now. Offending Dog was restrained. Injured kitty was tenderly protected. CMW wondered if now would be a good time for the long walk on the beach.

And then there was one other matter.

Bank One sent a VISA statement. CMW knows that she needs glasses, but can usually make out okay without them. However, when she pulled the statement from the envelope to see what the damages were, she nearly had a heart attack. Over a thousand dollars!!! What? She took the statement into better light to examine the purchases. One time at Wal-mart and one time at Salvation Army. Her breath was coming in short gasps, and heart was going quite rapidly. Who was using CMW's card? More importantly, what was CM ever going to say? How could such a thing ever happen? So she got her glasses and peered more carefully upon the face of the statement.

Oh. Well. Anyone could have made the same mistake. You see, the due date was 10/21/00. It WAS right there in the space beside "Balance Due" and could CMW, after such a day be blamed for seeing that as $1021.00? I hardly think so.

But now supper is over, the laundry is mostly done, the beds are made and CMW is ready to get everyone settled in for the night. The relief over the VISA bill has caused the other things to not look quite so bad. Tomorrow she will bake bread and take out any residual frustrations on twenty pounds of bread dough. The effort will quiet her frustrations and the smell of it baking will soothe her soul . . .

And that is the news from Shady Acres where Certain Man will make sure the dog doesn't bark, Certain Man's Wife will try to control the credit card, and all the wonderful home schooled children will still have to learn their times tables and their algebra and write their sentences.

CMW Learns a Lesson

Now it came to pass that Certain Man and Certain Man's Wife went forth upon the face of the earth to attend the wedding of niece Bethany Zehr in the Croghan-Lowville area of the great New York state. The day before they left was full of adventure and uncertainty as the snow fell greatly and the roads were very slippery. CM was heard to proclaim as that he did not know whether he would venture forth or not to attend this wedding.

However, CMW arose early on the morning of their intended departure, and observed that the snow had stopped and that the forecast was for the weather to clear. Knowing CM as she did, she reasoned within her soul that nothing would keep CM from this wedding, as he had purposed in his heart (yea, and had promised his multitude of nieces and nephews) that he would not miss a single nuptial celebration. His record was impeccable to this point, and he does like impeccable records.

So she called the various care providers (her sister Sarah was keeping Timmy, the Country Rest Home was keeping Old Gertrude, and Blind Linda was to go to her birth mother, Mrs. Squibb) and arranged everything, packed suitcases for the weekend, sent everyone to their respective abodes, and the family finally ventured forth around 11:00 AM.

The weather was pretty fair in DE, and though the roads showed much evidence of carnage from the day before, they were actually in pretty good shape. The trip proceeded pretty well with the usual potty breaks and starvation breaks. Eldest Daughter and Beloved Son-in-law were accompanying the family in the large maxi van that belongs to The Esteemed Daddy, Mark Yoder, Sr.

(CMW hates this van because there is approximately four feet between the ground and the first place to put a foot when one tries to get into it. It would be easier to mount a horse of large proportions. Unlike the horse, however, an entire family can ride in this van with room to spare, so the van is the usual vehicle of choice).

After entering the fair state of Pennsylvania, they determined that the state was not so fair after all. There were large, unexpected snow squalls which made roads hazardous, driving treacherous, and visibility quite challenging. But they safely came at last to their destination. The

33

temperature, however, was close to zero, and the old New York houses had much trouble keeping the poor southerners warm.

The next day was clear and sunny, but still very cold. The wedding went well, and the family enjoyed very greatly the fellowship. There was one thing that was irritating CMW, however. Beginning Thursday morning, when it first started to snow in DE, every time the family went to cross a parking lot or gravel lane or sidewalk or lawn, there were people hovering at her elbow with such instructions as this:

"Hon, watch it. This is really icy!"

"Mom, be careful. We don't want you to fall!"

"Shall I hold your hand to help you across this ice?"

"Watch your step right there, it's really icy."

And the one that really caused her to be surprised, "Watch this overhanging roof right here. It's low, and you might bump your head on it."

She really didn't think that had anything to do with the ice, and was ready to be done with the solicitous talk. She knew she was overweight. And she knew that she had a trick ankle, but she rarely has trouble when she is paying attention, and believe me, she was paying attention. So she started to protest loudly whenever they started their "help."

"You guys quit worrying. I'm alright. I'm being careful. I can take care of myself." She even quoted CM's statement from their first date when they wanted her to hold on to them, "Now if one of us falls, we both will." They were good sports, but they continued to offer assistance.

Saturday night after the wedding, CM went with one of his nephews to see to some matter of business, so it was CMW's duty to drive the van the several miles from one house to the other. (They were going to the one with that offending overhanging roof, no less). CMW was feeling pretty smug because she had managed to bring this big old van all that way without mishap. Picking her way across the frozen yard, she had her hands full of food that they were taking to the family gathering. As they were going across the lawn, Middle Daughter started her litany again.

"Mom, be careful. It's slippy!"

"Deborah, I'm just fine. Don't worry!"

"It's really slippy, Mom. Do you want to hold my arm?"

"Deborah! I am not 80 years old! Will you please not worry?"

"'Two are better than one, for if the one shall fall, the other shall hold him up.' That's Bible. Even works for suspenders. Are you sure you don't want me to help you?"

In the middle of CMW's next words, (mighty potent protest) she felt her head come into contact with that overhanging roof and the next thing she knew, she was flat on her back, banging her head with great force on the ice. It happened so fast that she really didn't even know it was happening. One minute she was motoring along with all her faculties and the next she was seeing great amounts of lights circling her head while she lay in a most undignified manner upon the ground.

Now the bump hurt, and the head was really ringing, but CMW hates for people to buzz about with great anxiety asking foolish questions, (Are you hurt??? Did you FALL??? Are you okay??? Can you get up???) even worse than she hates unsolicited offers of help, so she leaped to a standing position immediately, grateful that everything worked and that there were so few witnesses.

But the story was too good to keep a secret. Later, telling the tale for the benefit of the many nieces and nephews she said, "Believe me, I really did see stars!!!"

One of the older nephews inquired innocently, "Aunt Mary Ann. Did you see the moon, too?"

This was a new thought. "No, I did not!" she said firmly. "And I hope no one else did either."

And that is the news from Shady Acres (and lands afar) where the family has finally made it home safely, where Certain Man begins a new job on March 1st as the PLUMBING INSPECTOR for the state of DELAWARE, KENT COUNTY, where CMW is nursing a rather sore shoulder and neck, and the children have managed to come down with the flu and insist on running temperatures in the range of 103.

This, too, shall pass.

And the moral of the story is: "Don't be too sure of yourself in slippery places."

CMW's Family Makes Potato Salad

Now it came to pass that the third Saturday of every May is the designated time for the Festival of the school that is housed at the Central Mennonite Church. And the esteemed aunt of Certain Man's Wife, whose name is Aunt Gladys, is the only one who can make the potato salad in a way that is acceptable. Aunt Gladys is the sister of Sweet Mama of CMW and she happens to be married to the brother of Our Daddy of CMW. Said man is known as "Uncle Jesse."

The fame of this couple (Uncle Jesse and Aunt Gladys) includes their love for people, their strength in sorrow, and incongruities that could be disastrous in other relationships, but somehow work for them. They are just FUN to be with and a study in balance and humor and faith. Their offspring and the offspring of their offspring are delightful and steady and colorful. And *numerous!* The double cousins have enjoyed (and endured) much togetherness over the years.

Now it also came to pass that the making of potato salad has evolved into a family affair. Aunt Gladys and her daughters and their families descend upon the house, as do the women folk of the household of Our Daddy and Sweet Mama, to lend their hands and tongues to the procedure. Sweet Mama has been helping for years now, and CMW and Eldest Daughter as well as the Middle Sister of CMW, (Sarah) have also been involved in the fray (or fracas, if you prefer). Over time, there have been other hapless souls which have been called upon to help, but seldom have they returned for a second time. Perhaps the telling of this story will explain that phenomenon.

There are certain traditions that have been followed in years past. Uncle Jesse has usually gone and bought the potatoes and cooked them the day before; all 200 pounds of them. This is no mean feat, for it bears noticing that there is WORK involved in getting potatoes ready for the pot. Especially if you get them cheap at a roadside stand or wherever. There are spots to be removed and there are cuts to get dirt out of and they need to be scrubbed.

He has done this year after year after year, and we want to acknowledge that he has been very faithful.

This year, however, Jesse Yoder had a bad case of BALK. He did not wish to do potato salad. It was time for someone else to take over the monumental job. There were some sad mumblings on his part concerning all the activity. The eyebrows on this Yoder man were somewhat down, and that is not a good sign.

Aunt Gladys wasn't teaching school. She gathered her energy and courage about her and decided to manage the potato cooking operation. She ordered nice baking potatoes. They were much nicer than other years. (They cost more, but they were supposed to be the top of the line.) She got the potatoes ready for the pot. There were considerably more seconds than she had bargained for. (She put some back into a pail to bring out to show the inferior quality). She cooked a pot. Oh, NO! PANIC!!! They were mushy. They were falling apart! These must be the wrong kind of potatoes. She frantically called her sister, Sweet Mama. Sweet Mama called CMW. CMW reassured her that they were perfect potatoes for potato salad. They would do wonderfully. The only thing that needed doing was to watch them carefully and take them out before they were overdone. Really. Baking potatoes were the best kind of potato to use for this sort of thing.

Aunt Gladys also talked to Becky, an esteemed cousin, who learned to cook under the careful tutelage of revered Aunt Mary Lois. Becky also assured her that these potatoes would be just fine. Her Mother always used baking potatoes for such things. She did recommend taking them out before they were even quite finished cooking. Aunt Gladys went back to her toil. She got to bed at one o'clock on Thursday night. But she finished her task and there was a great pile of cooked potatoes on the table, awaiting the hapless slaves of the morning.

Morning came, bringing with it the eldest daughter of Uncle Jesse and Aunt Gladys, Shirley. She and her husband, Maynard, and the four youngest children that reside at their house had come for the weekend. Sweet Mama showed up next. She had spent the day before hard boiling and peeling 30 dozen of eggs. Her fingers were very sore from her chore if the previous day, but she got busy immediately and started to peel potatoes. So the knives began to fly. Sweet Mama helped to peel until CMW got there, then she and Aunt Gladys proceeded with the grating of the potatoes, the shredding of the hard boiled eggs, the chopping of the celery and onions and the mixing and mixing and mixing that goes with it. Shirley, Eldest Daughter, and CMW were busy with the peeling and the peeling and peeling that goes with it.

A short time later, Aunt Gladys and Uncle Jesse's Youngest Daughter, Naomi, showed up. She took up the job of measuring out the Miracle Whip, the mustard, the sugar, and such, for the dressing. All hands were busy and the hours flew by. Much wonderful conversation was had and there was laughter and some tears and lots and lots of family "catching up."

This was also the time for Aunt Gladys to come over and look over the pile of potatoes reflectively and say, "I'm just not so sure that there are as many potatoes this year as there was other years. I'm afraid we won't have as much as we should."

This observation was met with much objection as the peelers assured her that there were every bit as many potatoes as other years, there would be enough potato salad. There was no need to worry.

This also was the time for calls to taste each batch as it was finished.

This procedure was accompanied by much discussion such as:

"Are you sure it is sweet enough?"

"Does it have enough salt?"

"I don't think it is mushy enough."

"Does it have enough mustard?"

"There's something just not quite right with this batch, but I don't know what it is. What do you think?"

There was a marked absence of men folk until close to lunch time. Along about 11:40, in strolls Uncle Jesse. The potatoes were almost all peeled by this time, as the girls were trying hard to be done with that by the Noon Bell. He nonchalantly asked what the plans were for lunch.

He need not have asked. This is also tradition. You order subs from a little shop nearby (Faulkner's) that makes some of the best. Much discussion was had around the table about who wanted what, who would share with whom, who wanted hot/sweet peppers, who wanted oil/mayo, who wanted dill/ sweet pickles, who wanted hot/cold subs. Then husbands had to be found, and children had to be planned for, and so this was finally resolved some time after the last potato was peeled.

Uncle Jesse did not want a sub. He had another idea. While everyone waited for the sub order to be ready, the remaining jobs got divvied out. Shirley took over helping to mix and stir. Naomi carried six-quart buckets of potato salad to the basement refrigerator. CMW grated potatoes. Sweet Mama chopped celery, onions and grated eggs. Aunt Gladys continued to mix and season and supervise. Eldest Daughter went to pick up the subs.

It was with great joy that the sub order arrived. This was the break everyone was waiting for. Hungry people gathered around that big oval table that used to be in the dining room of the David and Savilla household and divided up the order. There were hot steak subs and Italian subs, Naomi's wonderful garden tea and potato salad (of course). When all the food had been handed out, Uncle Jesse went and got himself some bread and salad dressing and made himself some tomato sandwiches. That was okay, maybe, but some of the group felt sorry for him. He refused offers of part of the subs of others, and happily munched on fresh tomatoes and bread.

When the lunch was finished, the laborers returned to their chore. Now was the time to say such things as "How many more batches do you think we have?"

"I think we are going to run out of eggs."

"Where are you keeping the onions/canned milk/celery/sugar /salad dressing?"

"Is this batch all ready to be mixed?"

"Hand me that stack of buckets, will you?"

"Are we ever going to be done?"'''

"What time did you get to bed last night?"

It was also the time to say, "I believe we have MORE potatoes than last year."

Along about the middle of the afternoon, some of the children came in and were headed up to Naomi's house. After they left, there was quite a ruckus heard in the basement. It was a muffled call for "Mom! MOM!! MAMA!" Now there were no little children around, and most of the children had gone up the lane, so we didn't pay a whole lot of attention. All the mothers that had children there knew where they were.

Well, the noise persisted, so finally someone opened the door at the top of the steps. "Does someone need help down there?"

Back came the desperate voice of Naomi, "Yes, HELP!!! I have to have some help down here NOW!"

CMW flew down the steps to see Naomi standing by the refrigerator, struggling valiantly to hold in fifteen 6-quart buckets of potato salad. That she had been mostly successful was evidenced by only two buckets on the floor, but some shelves had collapsed under the weight of it all, and she really was in a desperate situation. With some effort and some assistance, things got righted again, and the buckets got returned to their proper place and the disaster was averted.

"Whew!" said Naomi. "Don't tell Mama that one bucket came open!"

And so the project was finished. When the last potato was shredded, the last dressing mixed and the last bucket filled, it was with satisfaction that the Queen of the Potato Salad noted that there had been 23 buckets filled for a total of almost 35 gallons. This was one solitary bucket less than last year, but all concerned agreed that they were going to just let it go.

And the only accident of the day that produced blood came during the clean-up. While Eldest Daughter was busily washing up all the dirty dishes, she sliced her finger open on the sharp edge of a cake pan, and did bleed prolifically all over everything. Otherwise, there were no mishaps.

There was a very serious issue that still needs to be noted (and resolved). In the midst of the afternoon, the man with the lowered eyebrows was heard to say, ""If Aunt Gladys does potato salad one more year, I'm leaving her!!!"

(She's really going to miss him...)

And that is the news from Shady Acres and the extended family, where the Festival is now over, and if there wasn't enough potato salad, it doesn't matter anymore.

Old Gertrude and Youngest Son

Now, it is no secret that Old Gertrude is not particularly attractive. She is old and stoop-shouldered, has a prominent nose, wears coke bottle glasses, has hair that is just a mess to do anything with, and has these teeth that somewhat defy description. They are protruding. And brown. And sorta' falling out, like. They are the things you notice first about her (if you don't notice her breath). The fame of her looks is such that there was a time when CMW was trying to convince her youngest sister of something and Youngest Sister protested vehemently, "If that's true, then Gertrude is beautiful!!!"

But anyone who really knows Old Gertrude knows that she thinks quite the opposite. She enjoys her looks. She's young. Her teeth are white. Her hair is perfect. Don't say nothin' about her glasses. Sometimes when CMW comes in to give her a shower, she is standing in front of the mirror, stark naked, admiring the scenery, and murmuring appreciation to herself.

All of this has not been lost on adolescent Youngest Son, Lemuel. It has been a source of amusement, yes, but there has also been an element of concern over the integrity of the situation. If it isn't true, why does she persist in believing it? CMW hasn't really been aware of just how much this situation has been being mulled over in the young man's mind until last week. After all, Old Gertrude has been a part of the family since Youngest Son was five weeks old, and she has always believed in her great beauty. It just isn't a new or seldom mentioned issue. But this week, Youngest Son came up with something that set CMW back on her heels and caused her mother's heart to do much pondering.

In the middle of a perfectly ordinary day, he said, "Mom, I've been thinking about Gertrude and you know how she thinks she so beautiful? Well, I've been thinking. Maybe she sees herself the way God sees her."

CMW's puzzlement must have shown on her face, because he continued. "You know, her mind is like a child, and wouldn't it be neat if her faith was just childlike enough that when she looks at herself, she actually sees what God sees. There really is no one who has a sweeter spirit, and who has a more childlike faith than she does, and I was just thinkin' that it would be neat if she had a faith that caused her to actually see herself like God does and that would be beautiful."

CMW looked at this tall man-child that she loves so fiercely and who sometimes causes her great consternation. She said, "That's a beautiful thought, Lemuel. It just might be so..." and she tucked it away in her heart to bring out when the rappin' and the jammin' and the tappin' threaten to drive her to distraction.

But she has continued to think about his words this whole week. What would happen if we had enough faith the see other people the way God does? What would happen to our hearts, our relationships, our homes, our neighborhoods, our churches? And how do we develop that mindset?

One of the ways we work on it is to be reminded that things aren't always the way they seem, and if we can take the reminders on ordinary days from unexpected sources and ask God to birth an awareness in our hearts, it can begin to happen.

And that is the thought for the day from Shady Acres, where CM hath gone forth to Columbus, Mississippi to manage a week of MDS with the youth group, CMW remains at home with a very quiet house, and all the children except Youngest Daughter (including Eldest Daughter and Beloved Son-in-Law) are with CM in the sunny south.

CMW Gets Perspective

CMW has had lots of time to miss her family in these last few days. Right now, she feels like if she sees one more chicken lying dead upon the litter, it will be one too many. Stupid chickens contracted dermatitis and are dying like flies. Some allergenic reaction has caused much coughing and congestion in CMW's lungs. She's been wearing a mask faithfully to keep from getting too much dust, but she is just pretty miserable. Makes her think in terms of "incurable," "terminal," "debilitating," and other woeful words. (Can a human "bean" get dermatitis of the lungs???!!!!???)

The events of this week have brought some things to Certain Man's Wife's attention that are not the nicest to notice. Have you ever noticed how children (and the rest of the world) can conspire together to keep you humble?

EXAMPLES:

The other night CMW was out in the chicken house picking up the dead when Allen Beachy came early for the evening check. He's been helping out in the absence of Certain Man -- and what a lifesaver he is. His timing is usually predictable, but he came early, and caught the 'lady' out there. Now there is a certain outfit that a gal wears for such stuff and it isn't made for beauty. She had a big white cover up on her head, was wearing a stained, ugly frock, and dirty, old chicken house shoes. It was not a pretty sight. She didn't smell very good, either.

The first chance she got, she made good on an escape, and went into the house. Youngest Daughter was in there and CMW lamented to her that it is perfectly detestable to be caught in the chicken house in chicken house garb.

Intoned CMW with great feeling, "It's not that I'm trying to impress Allen Beachy or anything, but to be caught looking like this??? Don't you suppose he thought me a raving beauty?"

Youngest Daughter chuckled and said very cheerfully, "Well, Mom, he'd have to have a GREAT imagination!"

OOPS!

But that isn't the half. The other day, CMW was sitting on her La-Z-Boy and Youngest Son was sitting beside her on the hearth. He is an affectionate child and he had reached over and was holding her hand while he talked to her.

She noticed that he was rubbing the back of her hand thoughtfully and then he said, "Mom, your hand is just so, I don't know, just so..."

Grinning CMW said, "So work worn and old?"

"No," he said, "I wasn't thinking that. He paused, then said, "It's just that the skin on the back of your hand looks kinda' like the skin on a chicken that's been dead for three days!"

It is time to bring on that Mary Kay skin regimen!!!

But I am not done yet!

There was that fateful day in the Salvation Army Store. CMW was at the checkout counter and the clerk was busily ringing things up. CMW noticed that she was giving hefty discounts on everything, and it was not a discount day. CMW's conscience began to bother her.   "Uh, excuse me, but I don't think those things are discount items," she said hesitantly.

"Oh," said the clerk airily, "You'se a senior citizen, ain't you?" "Uh, no," said CMW, a bit haughtily, "I'm not."

"Oh, well," says the clerk, unconcerned, "No matter. If they looks it, I gives it to them."

I tell you people. Something is going on here, and CMW doesn't much like it.

And that's the news from Shady Acres where it is high time for the family to return from lands afar. CM needs to tend his own chickens, CMW needs a long vacation and all the children (but especially the two youngest) could be a little more tactful.

CMW is dealing with that Salvation Army business by not going there much.

CMW and the Times that Be

It was Monday, September 17, 2001. The events of the last six days had been weighing heavy on the heart of Certain Man's Wife (CMW). On the sad, sad Tuesday before, she had been listening to the program "Morning Edition" from National Public Radio as she drove Old Gertrude to an appointment. At nine o'clock, as they finished out their broadcast they came back on to say, "This just in. We have a report that an airplane has just crashed into the World Trade Center in New York City."

Now CMW is pretty much "Slower Lower Delaware." It just didn't register at first. But the reports kept coming, and the sadness began to wash over her in ever increasing waves. When the news flashes became two airplanes, then the Pentagon was burning, then there was another hijacking, it became too big to assimilate.

From the very first, there was talk of WAR. And the draft. On that morning, as she drove home from the appointment, the implications and overwhelming possibilities put their stitches on every thought like a sewing machine with the tension too tight.

"Lord Jesus," she prayed, "what of our Country? What shall we do? How shall we respond? And I have a nineteen year old son. Whatever will become of him? And all the other young men who find themselves in a position of peace and nonresistance?"

No answers, except the freeing sense of peace that none of this was out of the hands of the Father.

And so the days passed. The family talked and talked and talked. Middle Daughter wept much as she thought of her Muslim family in Bangladesh, some with family members stateside. Certain Man articulated strong feelings and Mennonite doctrine that didn't always reconcile to his satisfaction. Eldest Son was often pensive, not discussing things with anyone, listening over the edge of his book with a thoughtful eye. Youngest Son was fierce in his passion that evil had been done, but struggled with his sense of justice tempered by a head commitment to nonresistance and his compassionate heart. Youngest Daughter discussed much with her Hispanic friend just what had happened and what it meant.

CMW pondered and pondered and pondered. Especially troubling to her was the treatment that innocent people were receiving at the hands of American zealots. Over and over her heart cried, "It isn't right!"

But on this Monday, she had an appointment in Dover. Eldest Daughter was going along, and as they started out, she said to CMW, "Mom, do you need gas?"

CMW looked at her gas gauge with puzzlement and said, "Not particularly. Why?"

"Well, Mom," she said. "There is a gas station in Dover run by this man that looks Arab. He wears a turban and ever since this happened, no one is buying gas from him, and I think we ought to go up there and fill up."

CMW looked in respect at this adult-offspring. "Christina, that's a wonderful idea! Let's!!!"

CMW knew about the gas station. It is called US Gas. It is a full-service station on Route 13 that does healthy business as a rule. They have competitive prices, and still fill your tank for you. The owner is a big man. With turban and flowing locks, he has always seemed pretty foreboding and invincible to CMW. She has even fancied that he walked with a swagger, and she has NEVER bought gas there before. She never felt a need to. The gasoline bays were usually full, and she has a perfectly useful gas station just a mile from her house.

But on this day, she made the decision to do as suggested by Eldest Daughter. It seemed right to, somehow. So she pulled up to the unusually empty gasoline pumps and waited. A fresh-faced young man of Middle Eastern descent came out to pump her gas. He made no conversation and did not clean her windshield, but dutifully stuck the nozzle into her tank and then disappeared. The gas totaled up and stopped at $18.78 or some such odd number. CMW took a twenty dollar bill from her wallet and waited.

"Mom," said Eldest Daughter, "aren't you going to give a tip?"

"A tip? No, I'm not going to give a tip. You don't tip when you're buying gasoline."

"Yes, Mom. You need to give a tip. When it is full service, it is nice if you give a tip. I think you should."

Now CMW does not agree with this. She never has, and still doesn't. But it seemed as if the Lord spoke to her heart and said, "No change, Mary Ann. Just give the twenty and don't take change." And so she agreed in her heart that she would take no change.

But the fresh-faced young attendant was nowhere to be seen. Turbaned Man walked back and forth in front of his gas station. He did not swagger. He walked old and tired. His shoulders spoke of burdens. He finally walked over to the car, and topped off the tank at $19.00. He came up to the window, and his face was guarded. CMW smiled into his bearded, brown face and handed him the twenty.

48

"No change." she said, and began to close the window. He didn't understand and began to fumble with his roll of money.

She smiled her best at him and said again, "No change. Just keep the change" and averted her eyes and closed the window and left.

Now Turbaned Man did not dance a jig or swagger. He did not thank CMW nor did he act grateful. (It was, after all, just a dollar.) But the incident has rolled around all day in her heart and she has come to realize something very important in the hours since then.

It has nothing to do with dollars or tips or even gasoline. It wasn't for Turbaned Man that she needed to do this. It was for her own heart. To delineate where the allegiance really lies. To clarify what obedience to the Father truly means in (yes!) Slower Lower Delaware. You see, it is all well and good for us to debate what should be done to the terrorists. We can argue the abilities of our government to make good decisions or bad decisions. We have the intelligence to see where given choices might lead us, and to determine whether they are worth the risk or not. We have the right to chose our opinions and responses to the situation.

But any of these things will be just that-- our determinations, our opinions, our choices. The chances of that affecting how this tragedy is played out in the rest of the world are minimal.

But before God, the thing all of us should do is to figure out how we can live fearlessly and lovingly in a world that has gone so wrong. We need to determine what we can do to stop conflict and injustices that occur under our noses every day. We need to watch for opportunities to exercise our hearts in ways that go beyond the hurts and fears and agony of these days and brings healing and restoration in our corner of the world. We need to seek to be Jesus with skin on to those who see us every day. That's a lot harder to do than to have an opinion on what the government should do about terrorism (at least it is for CMW). But something hard is no less right.

And that is the news from Shady Acres, where CM's job has brought him face to face with this crisis in ways he never had to think of before, where CMW needs to get off her soapbox and practice instead of preach, and where all the children will someday wake up and realize that they have lived in times that will be forever stamped in history.

50

CMW has a Disaster

Now behold, it hath been a very busy time at Shady Acres since the day of Christmas. And there has been laundry that has never quite gotten finished. There have been rooms that the doors have been discreetly closed to the public eye. There have been dishes that stayed on the counter for numerous days because they had to be hand washed and would not fit into the dishwasher, and of course, no one took the initiative to wash them. The days went by on wings, and there was never enough time to get things done.

Now Eldest Daughter and Beloved Son-in-Law were packing out their house for the anticipated move to their new abode, and having much experience in the art of packing, Certain Man's Wife went forth to help. This caused additional shortages at home, but everyone held on to the hope that after the fifth day of January, when the move was complete, perhaps some degree of normalcy would return to the house. Certain Man was patient and did not complain over the lack of proper diet or folded laundry or swept floors. Behold, he held his peace and smiled whilst CMW went about with a furrowed brow and sometimes short patience.

(Having read an anecdote in the "Readers Digest" about hot flashes and forgetfulness and irritability being symptoms of menopause, he did make one unfortunate utterance, but was quickly repentant, and thus avoided bodily injury.)

Now upon the Thursday before said moving day, CMW determined to spend the whole day at the Eldest Daughter's house and accomplish as much as was possible for her (and said offspring) to do in one day. The day was profitable and there was much finished, for which great thanks was given.

Along about six in the evening, CMW made her way home. Once there, she started a load of laundry, put some chicken on to cook for later use, caught up on everyone's day, and did general household maintenance. Thinking that she needed to prepare some supper for the starving natives, she finally settled upon some tomato soup from the can, and some toasted cheese sandwiches on homemade bread. (You see, the "homemade bread" bit was to make up for the "soup from the can" bit and that assuaged her guilty conscience somewhat.)

She proceeded to get everyone fed, and then it was time to dispense the medicines and make coffee for the ladies who live at her house. There is something about mixing up coffee and dispensing medicines that always has a peculiar effect upon CMW. For some reason, it always makes her think that she should visit the restroom. This strange sensation usually passes if she just waits a minute or two, and so that is what she proceeded to do. Unfortunately, this was one time when the sensation did not recede as anticipated. It was not a false alarm.   Too much bottled water and too much coffee had been consumed in the course of the day to be ignored, and CMW realized that she really had better head for the restroom NOW. Well, Old Gertrude's table was on the way to the restroom, so CMW paused just long enough to set down her pills and coffee before making a beeline for the desired destination.

Flying into the restroom, she had just pushed back the edges of her sweater when she heard a most distressing noise . . . that of something falling into the porcelain convenience. She paused and looked in disbelief as her cellular phone sank quickly to the bottom trailing an impressive line of bubbles. She had forgotten that she had it in her sweater pocket. That was bad enough (though the toilet was miraculously clean) but does anyone remember at this juncture why she was in such a hurry in the bathroom? Does anyone know what happens when you put your hand into cold water when you have to go to the bathroom so badly that you almost can't hold it anymore?

Yes, well. Not only did she fry her phone, she also wet her pants. This is not funny. And this is not the way a woman of her age and(*ahem!*) social standing should be treated. Yes, she knows. Incontinence is probably another sign of the bad "M" word.

And that is the news from Shady Acres where Certain Man thinks it is funny, CMW knows that if you don't laugh, you cry, and all the children are expected to provide creative ways of explaining to Atlantic Cellular what happened to the phone.

CM/CMW's Youngest Son Learns to Drive

Now it came to pass in the year of our Lord, 2002, that the Youngest Son of Certain Man and Certain Man's Wife reached the age of sixteen, that magical age when the law of the fair state of Delaware gave permission for a young man or woman to take the wheel of several tons of lethal weaponry and go forth upon the roadways and byways, giving mothers no end of trouble and anxiety.

And Youngest Son betook himself to pester his parental authorities concerning the proper classes that he needed to procure, seeing that he was homeschooled and not automatically given the opportunity through his educational facility. CMW was certain that it couldn't be time for such an endeavor, but when the calendar could not be brought into her submission, she reluctantly gave her consent for him to pursue his ambitions. So he rallied about him a gang of like-minded ruffians, namely Gabriel (son of Youngest Sister of CMW, Alma), Christopher (Son of Youngest Brother of CMW, Mark Jr.), and Andy (Son of Esteemed Cousin of CMW, Joan Mills), and they descended upon the Adult Education Division of Sussex Technical School for the express purpose of fulfilling the prescribed Drivers' Educational Course. (Said institution will never be the same again. Neither will the hapless parents who took turns driving this inimitable quartet to and fro.)

In spite of raucous noises, burping contests, heated and affectionate discussions, very adolescent male humor, and emergency food stops and bathroom breaks, they all managed to finish the classroom work, finish the required notebooks, finish their observation time, and finish the required time behind the wheel. They won the right to obtain the coveted blue certificates that would allow them to obtain the much dreaded (by Mom) DRIVER'S LICENSE.

Now these blue certificates are usually mailed to the individuals, but Gabriel, having an earlier birthday than the other three, and already being sixteen, wanted to obtain his at the first possible moment. Youngest Sister of CMW called down to the office to see when it would be ready and learned that she could pick it up at the office on a given afternoon. So she called CMW to inquire whether she should also pick up Youngest Son's and take both boys forthwith to the Department of Motor Vehicles and get the license.

CMW thought that this was a wonderful idea, but wondered if a parent would need to be present. She called the DMV and discovered that she or Certain Man did, in fact, need to go along. This only added to the fun of the situation, for there are few things that CMW likes better than going somewhere in the company of one (or both) of her sisters. The joy was somewhat tempered by the fact that there were two of their male offspring that were going, too. But it had to be.

Much discussion was made about who should drive and where they should meet, but finally they were on their way in the minivan that belongs to CM and CMW, with the two sisters in the front and the boys properly ensconced in the back. It is a rather long road to Sussex Tech, and there was good conversation and laughter and even time for some motherly admonition. (There was some question as to how much it was heeded. At one point in the discussion, CMW intoned one of her favorite laments that went something like, "You need to remember that we only have ONE of YOU," and Gabe, with his droll sense of humor said very perplexedly, "But Aunt Mary, there's TWO of us!" Lo, and behold, there were!!!)

As the miles went pleasantly by, Youngest Sister happened to mention that the Driver's Ed office was holding Gabe's blue slip for her and that the others were being mailed out.

Said CMW, "Did you have to ask them to hold it?"

"Yes," said Youngest Sister, "Didn't you call them and tell them to hold Lem's?"

"Uh, no," said CMW. "I didn't know I had to!"

"Oh, Mary!" said Youngest Sister. "They probably mailed them out in today's mail."

"Nobody told me!" wailed CMW.

"What time is it?" Asked Youngest Sister.

"3:25," said the Adolescent Males.

"Oh, dear," said Youngest Sister, "the Driver's Ed office is closing at 3:30. They said if we came after that, the blue slip would be at the main office. You probably can't get Lem's after that."

"Well," said CMW, "maybe we can make it. We are almost there."

So a very hurried, harried group of people pulled up to the entrance of Sussex Tech, and three of them hurried in while CMW parked the car. As soon as she could, she joined the others in the school. Oh, wonderful miracle! The troupe had gotten to the office with hardly a minute to spare to find that the blue slip for Youngest Son was in the envelopes prepared for mailing when the office closed at 3:30. They were able to retrieve it (as well as Gabe's) so it was off to the Department of Motor Vehicles for the embattled crew. Which is not a good place to go when you already feel battle weary. But buoyed on by their own private miracle of the blue slip, they forged ahead.

54

The DMV office was full and running over. They took a number and settled in for a very long wait. The room was full of people who had come to get their license reinstated after arrests for speeding, D.U.I., and other unfavorable crimes. There were those who were there to take the test for the first time, others who had come to renew their license, and then the noble few who were there with blue slips in hand to obtain the restricted license granted to people such as these two that CMW and Youngest Sister called "sons." (Believe me, in that company, the two young men with the Yoder genes looked very fine indeed! This was not a gathering of the wise and beautiful.)

After a very long wait, their numbers were finally called, and CMW and Youngest Son advanced to the desk where CMW needed to sign more important documents than Youngest Son did. There was one in particular with which she was pleased where it said that the "sponsoring parent could at any time, and for any (or NO) reason, restrict the privileges of the driver until his/her 18th birthday." CMW liked that. She pointed it out. Youngest Son was not impressed.

Youngest Sister and Gabe finished about the same time as CMW and Youngest Son, and they were literally herded into this roped off area to await the great picture taking machine-- which proceeded to break down. So they waited and waited and waited. Finally, it was fixed and the line started to move again. CMW and Youngest Sister decided that they could wait in the car since their pictures weren't going to be on these licenses anyhow, and they exited the crowded room.   Their sons were about next in line for their pictures, so it was surprising to see that the boys were not forthcoming.

Finally Gabe put in his appearance and shortly thereafter, a somewhat disgruntled Youngest Son. It seems that the camera started misbehaving again after Gabe's picture, and when the cameraman came to Lem's they used the old picture from his original Delaware ID.

This was especially troubling to a young man who really didn't want to look 14 on his driver's license. There were braces and contacts since that picture, and it was demeaning to have such a fresh-looking face. Albeit, since it was the only way that he was going to get his license that day, he decided to hold his tongue.

There had been rather animated discussion about whether one of the boys would be allowed to drive home. Since the van belonged to CM/CMW, it was thought by Youngest Sister that it should not be her son. Since Gabe wasn't going to be allowed to drive, CMW was of the opinion that it wasn't really fair for Youngest Son to drive, either, and so she had claimed the driver's seat when she and Youngest Sister had returned to the car. It was a rainy day, and Youngest Son stood in the drizzle outside the van, pleading with CMW to be allowed to drive.

"Please, Mom, please! Can't I PLEASE drive home."

"It's not fair, Lem. Gabe just got his license, too. He wants to drive as badly as you do."

"No, Mom, he said he didn't care! Honest. Please!!!!"

"Aunt Mary, I really don't," came a voice from the back seat. "I'll get time to drive. I don't mind at all if he drives home."

"See, Mom! He doesn't care. Please can I drive home!" Youngest Sister was chuckling in the seat beside CMW, and Youngest Son was prancing about on the pavement outside of the car. CMW was clearly caught in the middle.

"Alright," she agreed reluctantly. "You may drive home."

"No!" said Youngest Sister, rather quietly and belatedly beside her. Youngest Son was already doing his victory dance. CMW had, after all, said "yes" Now what to do??????????

CMW tries not to be too changeable in her word. She had already changed her mind once. Much as she hated to, she decided to give Youngest Son a chance. Youngest Sister climbed into the back beside her son, behind the driver's seat. CMW took the passenger's side of the front seat. Youngest Son clambered in and took possession of the wheel. He gently started the car, and eased out of the parking space.

"Where do I go, where do I go???" he asked anxiously.

"Turn here, turn here," chorused the three victims.

"How do I get out of here, where do I go?"

"Son, don't you even know how to get out of the parking lot at the Department of Motor Vehicles?"

"I've never been here before and I wasn't paying attention when we came in."

"You're going to have to start paying attention."

"Mom, I know, but where do I go? I have to know how to get out of here."

With the combined efforts of the entire cabin crew, they finally made it safely out onto the highway.

Then. "Mom, I'm really hungry. I haven't had hardly anything all day. Could we please stop at Taco Bell for something to eat? I'm starving." This suggestion was met with quite general approval. Both Moms thought it would be okay to celebrate this momentous occasion, so the plan was to stop at the Georgetown Taco Bell/KFC that was right down the road. It was, unfortuitously, on the other side of the road.

The litany started again. "Mom, how do I get over there? Where is it, I don't see it. What do I do?"

Again, the cabin crew leapt to the occasion with instructions being hurled at the poor head of the novice driver.

"It's over there, on the left."

"You need to get over."

"You need to get over NOW."

"You need to get all the way over into the turn lane."

"Right here, right here!!!!"

Youngest Son manfully struggled to keep his head, to check the mirrors and to change the lanes and to do so gracefully. As he finally pulled into the turn lane, the light turned green for his line of traffic. He eased into the accelerator just a bit. Pandemonium broke loose.

"Watch it, Lem! Slow Down!"

"The cars aren't moving yet!"

"Slow down, Son, slow down."

The feet of CMW were furiously pushing an imaginary brake pedal on the passenger's side of the car, and she was holding onto the dash with all her might. A zillion thoughts were dancing through her brain with rapid fire brilliance.

"The pavement is wet. He's not used to driving a minivan. He doesn't know how to compensate for the added weight and volume. Minivans are bad for slipping on wet surfaces. That car is not moving fast enough. We are gonna' crash, we're gonna' crash, we're gonna' crash!"

From the back seat came a frightened, anguished "A-h-h-h-h-h-h-h-h-h-h-h-h-h-h!!!!!!!!!" from an unusually perturbed Aunt Alma. Youngest Son was plying the brakes, (but not nearly effectively enough in his Mama's estimation) and gradually getting the speed down (but not nearly quickly enough for the elderly in his car--who by this time were considerably more elderly than they had been previously).

"Mom, I got it under control." (One of Youngest Son's favorite lines, by the way.) And in fact, he did. He got it stopped a good six feet from the back of the slowly moving vehicle ahead of him. But he had succeeded in thoroughly scaring both Mamas beyond any reason. Gabe allowed that it had been pretty close, but for the most part maintained that he wasn't "scared a bit" and both boys protested that it was worse for all the "screaming that was going on." Anybody knows that it is a cardinal sin for a passenger to "scream" at a driver. If Youngest Son had run into the back of that car (which, in case you didn't know, he was in NO danger of doing but if he had--) it would have strictly been because of the hollering going on in the car.

CMW brought up the clause that said the "sponsoring parent could at any time, and for any (or NO) reason, restrict the privileges of the driver until his 18th birthday" and reminded Youngest Son that she was the boss in this situation and that the boss was saying it was too close. Great weakness in the knees and shaking of the hands proved that CMW had not come through completely unscathed. There was very little appetite on the part of the elderly, but both Moms realized the potential to retrieve control of the steering wheel, so the group proceeded to Taco Bell. When they came out, CMW took the keys, and CMW drove back home. Much protest and discussion was made concerning the situation, but neither side was inclined to move from their position.

At small group meeting that evening, Youngest Son had the audacity to request prayer for his mother and her adverse reactions to his driving. He thought she really needed help to have the right attitude. This was met with amusement on the part of almost all present except CMW. She requested that those present be witnesses to the fact that the accidents that her offspringin's have been involved in have happened when she has not been along to help prevent them. This was met with general indignation on the part of the children of CM and CMW. They resent her role as Guardian Angel. Besides, where is her faith in God? (So now it's a Spiritual issue.)

And that is the news from Shady Acres, where Certain Man is far better at helping young men learn to drive than his Addled Frau. Where Certain Man's Wife has decided that Driver's Education wasn't meant to be even a minuscule part of a Mama's job, and all the children are growing up much too soon. (It seems like it was only yesterday that she held this youngest son on her shoulder and was glad to hear a burp!)

Youngest Daughter Gets Her Tonsils Out

The big question at the house of Certain Man and Certain Man's Wife these days is, "Were my tonsils cut out or cut off?" Does anyone have an answer to this question?

Youngest Daughter came through surgery on Monday with an "A+" according to her anesthesiologist who also happens to be a favorite neighbor. She seems to be doing well, but is still pretty anxious for something for pain after some hours have elapsed. She has been blessed with friends that come, bearing gifts, bringing company; books, videos, and craft projects that will take her attention for at least a segment of the time that is heavy on her hands. She is so used to activity and entertainment, that it seems like any quiet time is a real burden.

When The Wounded first came home, she wasted no time in getting into her favorite vanilla bean ice cream. She ate more than CMW thought was good for her, but the medical profession had said to encourage her to eat. Youngest Daughter followed this exercise by a rather prolonged session on the La-Z-Boy in a reclining position.

Along about 2:45 in the afternoon, the phone rang, and it was one of CMW's friends, Robin. Just as CMW answered the phone, the driveway monitor went, and there was Old Gertrude, home from the center. Cradling the phone on her shoulder, CMW went to fetch Old Gertrude. (State regulations mandate that an adult must be present when a client is disembarking from a state vehicle.) Speed is not one of Old Gertrude's more prominent attributes, and it was a bit of a time stretch until CMW was back inside the house, allowing Old Gertrude with her ever present walker to take her sweet time to come up the ramp and into the house.

CMW made it into the house a full lap ahead of her. The first thing that greeted her was a most distressing noise,, and when she investigated, behold, Youngest Daughter was kneeling upon the floor of the family room, vomiting profusely. The puddle was impressive.

CMW terminated her phone call and went to assist. Youngest Daughter was very sad, indeed, about the mess, and was wailing things about being sorry, and not being able to help it, and other heart-rending cries. CMW reassured her greatly, and helped her regain composure and when it seemed that surely there was nothing left to come up, sent her on her way towards the bathroom.

There are things in this world that are just inexplicable. Old Gertrude has always had a habit of taking her walker to the smallest place possible and standing there while she surveys the countryside. It is an aggravating habit, one for which she has often been gently (and sometimes, not so gently) chided. There is nothing as frustrating as coming to the only doorway there is to get where you want to go, and there find an immovable object-- which is pretty much what Old Gertrude is when she has parked her carcass. And she doesn't like anyone to tell her to move. Her standard answer is, "Don't rush me! You'll cause me to fall!"

What CMW cannot understand is how Old Gertrude just happened to be parked in the doorway that leads to the necessary room just when Youngest Daughter was on her way there in a big hurry. CMW was busy cleaning up the mess, or she may have been able to prevent what happened, but suddenly there was another great commotion at the doorway, and Youngest Daughter was again wailing about being so sorry, and Old Gertrude was as cross as an old broody hen. Being in the way, and refusing to move did not work out in Old Gertrude's best interest this time. Youngest Daughter was not finished with her up-chucking after all, but she could not get past Old Gertrude. Old Gertrude was in the direct line of fire, and caught the full load on her prized blue jacket. Which she had not yet removed from her personage.

When it was too late, of course, she moved. Youngest Daughter got by and into the bathroom. And finished her job in there. But Old Gertrude was as aggravated as the family has ever seen her. She came across the kitchen floor much faster than her usual speed, face red and cross.

"Well," she huffed. "Can't ever use that coat again!"

It was just too funny. CMW had to laugh. Which, incidentally, wasn't appreciated by either party. So she gathered up all the offending articles that were reeking and put them into the washer. She wiped Youngest Daughter's face and calmed her down. She reassured Old Gertrude that the prized blue jacket would be good as new after it had a trip through the washer. And she got out her carpet scrubber and cleaned up what was left of the impressive puddle.

She couldn't help taking the opportunity to remind Old Gertrude one more time that standing placidly in a doorway is not always a proof of power.

And that is the news from Shady Acres. Where Certain Man is the one who most frequently has to tell Old Gertrude to move, where Certain Man's Wife could really do without all this excitement, and all the children are complaining that a certain area of the family room still smells offensive.

CM Brings Down a Tree

Tonight Certain Man decided that the old Mimosa tree just wasn't going to make it back to life this year. He had been working in the fence row, weeding the hedge roses as if his life depended on it, and making really good progress, too. Every time he turned the corner, though, there stood that stately old tree, devoid of any leaves, in sharp contrast to the greenery around it. When Certain Man's Wife came out to weed the front flower bed, he must have decided his time was better spent than weeding the fence row. He brought his little tractor out with a chain and a loader on it and harnessed the old tree up like he thought it might get away. CMW watched out of the corner of her eye to see how this was going to progress, but kept on weeding.

Now Certain Man has a friend down the road named Gary Burlingame, and the two of them have been partners together in many different escapades. Said friend owns a very loud and powerful chain saw and the two of them made a pretty impressive production out of leveling a towering maple that grew in the backyard of CM and CMW a few years ago. As CMW watched CM's preparations tonight, it became evident that CM had no intentions of calling his friend. She wondered why, but held her peace until she saw Certain Man produce a tool that looked somewhat like an overgrown hacksaw. He began sawing somewhat ineffectively at the base of the tree.

"Sweetheart, why don't you call Gary to come down here with his chainsaw to help you cut that tree down?" (Gary lives less than two miles away.)

"Shoot, I can saw this thing down in less time than it takes for him to get down here." (Saw, saw, saw, saw.)

"I know, but it looks like a hard job. You'll be forever sawing that tree down."

Wrong thing to say. A challenge. No answer. More determined sawing.

"Besides, think of how much fun Gary would have sawing that tree down."

No answer.

"You know he would love it."

"Nah." Much vigorous sawing. "I'll get it."

CMW went back to her weeding, but kept an anxious eye on the progress. Which wasn't very much, it seemed.

After a while, Certain Man left his sawing and got on his tractor. He put it in gear and started backing up. The tree was still firmly chained to the loader. The left rear wheel came off the ground. CMW refrained from shouting and jumping up and down. She thought of everyone she knew who had perished in tractors overturning and was relieved to see that Certain Man did not overextend his efforts.

Yet.

He got off and went back to sawing.

CMW's garden was getting weeded with less attention than it needed. She frequently needed to go back and redo some of the areas but it was obvious that Certain Man needed her to keep watch. He sawed a while longer, then tried the tractor trick again. The left rear wheel came off the ground. Certain Man turned the front wheels and kept on tugging. Left wheel went back down to solid ground, and right wheel took its place spinning in mid-air.

By now, Eldest Daughter had come to see what Certain Man was up to. CMW left her weeding so as to be there when first aid and CPR were needed. She also needed to be in closer proximity so that her softly given instructions could be heard over the noise of the tractor motor. Eldest Daughter added her voice of dismay to the fracas. Between the frantic looks and softly given instructions of his wife and daughter, CM was convinced to stop trying to snap the tree off at the roots. Suddenly, he threw the gear into forward and slammed into the trunk of the tree with a great force, greatly startling poor CMW and Eldest Daughter, who were directly on the other side.

The tree did not budge. Not a single bit. The cut was on the wrong side, anyhow, so CMW wasn't sure what that sudden attack was all about. She really was showing considerable restraint, but Certain Man was not impressed.

"You go weed your garden!" he said, more sternly than was necessary, and pointed in that direction to make sure she knew which one. By then, Beloved Son-in-Law had shown up to see what was happening and he was clearly in sympathy with Certain Man. CMW realized that her wise words were being deliberately spurned, so she resolutely turned her back and went where she had been told to go.

Surreptitious checks showed the Beloved Son-in-Law (who maybe should be more careful - lest he lose his adjective) with Certain Man, in the thick of things. They connived together to turn the tractor around and put pressure on it from the other side, while Son-in-Law cavorted in the branches. CMW was not sure, but thought that this was to add weight to the tree, causing it to give in to the pressure upon the trunk. The tree did not budge.

Certain Man returned to his spot on the ground, with his oversized hack saw and started to saw again. Son-in-Law got on the other side of the tree and like an old pioneer, grabbed the other side of the saw. Back and forth, back and forth they sawed. All operations were being watched and noted by Eldest Daughter who was doing a reputable job of making enough noise so as CMW's absence was scarcely noticed. Youngest Daughter and two of her friends were also climbing nearby trees assisting in the operations with feminine instruction and appropriate warnings. Then CMW saw that they were going to try the tractor trick again. CMW held her breath (from afar).

There was a sort of tearing, cracking sound as the tree splintered and bent, but did not break. Having managed to saw the trunk a bit over halfway through, they had actually been able to put enough pressure on it to bring it down. They still needed to saw through the rest of the trunk, but now the end was in sight, and their enthusiasm was renewed. They sawed and encouraged each other and actually did get the tree separated from its roots. Ah, sweet victory for the pioneers. Ah, blessed relief for the spectators. No one perished, no one was even injured. In fact, to hear Certain Man's version, there was never any danger.

"If it was only half as bad as you thought it was," he said, "then you maybe could have worried."

They made a big production of hooking onto the tree with the chain and dragging it through the streets. (Well, actually, they just pulled it down the shoulder of the road to the chicken house lane, then back to the brush pile, but CMW thought that there was a little more celebrating than was necessary. She refused to watch.) She finished weeding her garden, even though the sprinkler was making her wet during the last foot or so and decided to call it a night. She tried terribly hard to beat Beloved Son-in-Law at a good natured game of tetherball, but finally gave up and let him win. She was so relieved that everyone was safe and sound that it just didn't seem right somehow to ruin his evening.

And that is the news from Shady Acres. Where Certain Man has triumphed as usual, Certain Man's wife seems to have some ant bites that she never realized she had, and all the children have once again seen firsthand that the Daddy at Shady Acres will most often accomplish what he sets out to do.

CM/CMW'S Eldest Daughter and the Spider

Once upon a time, before Eldest Daughter was married to Beloved Son-in-Law, CMW betook herself and all five of her wonderful children on a Brave Expedition to the Great Shopping Grounds. It was the season of Christmas, and the traffic was very heavy. The children were agreeable for the most part, and the usual sparring conversation was enjoyable.

It was a rare occasion for the family, as Eldest Daughter was employed as a mother's helper for a homeschooling family that had seven children, and it was hard to coordinate everyone's schedule to include all the children of Certain Man and his wife. The one thing that was not so nice on this day was that Certain Man was not along, as he was forth upon the land searching for the almighty dollar. (This was a necessary thing for him to do, however, as the family was on a Brave Expedition to the Great Shopping Grounds!!!!)

Now it came to pass that Eldest Daughter often used the family van to go to work, as there were errands for her to run, groceries for which to shop, and other things for which her employer depended upon her. One of the errands that she often did was to fetch the shirts of her employer's (businessman) spouse from the laundry. It was very convenient to carry them in the back of the minivan on an appropriate hook situated there, and so it was not unusual for the shirts of Keillor Hudson to reside in the Yutzy family van.

So it was that as the family was making their way homeward, one of the younger siblings of Eldest Daughter asked, "Who bought a shirt today?" There was much puzzlement on the part of the family, as none of the male children had made such a purchase, and CMW had not bought a shirt for CM. But there was a spiffy looking shirt on a hanger, kinda' smooshed under the back seat.

"Oh," said Eldest Daughter. "I wonder if that shirt might not belong to Keillor. I picked up the laundry for Jenna this week, and I wonder if one of the shirts might have fallen down, and I didn't notice."

There was much back seat investigation of the shirt and discussion about its quality and its ownership until Eldest Daughter said, "Throw that shirt up here and let me see it." (She was residing in the front seat as befitted her status as Eldest Daughter and also as the direct result of her having shouted "Front-Way-Home!!!!" the loudest and the soonest before the crew left home.)

CMW was watching the heavy holiday traffic. She was in the left hand lane of Route 113 South, somewhat hemmed in by the myriads of vehicles that were all wanting to go somewhere quickly. However, out of the corner of her eye, she saw the garment in question come flying through the air, landing somewhere in the vicinity of Eldest Daughter's territory. Eldest Daughter picked up the shirt and examined it. "Yup," she said, "It's Keillor's, alright."

CMW looked down at the rich plaid, and caught sight of something that made her blood run cold. Crawling very nonchalantly up the sleeve of this garment, totally out of sight to Eldest Daughter was a Black Widow Spider. Now Delaware had a scourge of these intrepid crawly things over the past couple years, and the area of Shady Acres Farm had been especially hard hit. The winters had not been severe enough to squelch the population, and the spiders multiplied happily and vociferously. A Black Widow Spider has a specific kind of look that is just scary, but CMW had seen enough of them in her time that she usually just squashed them (thoroughly) but without much fanfare. They really are not as aggressive as the Sugar Creek Gang books from CMW's childhood made them out to be.

However, Eldest Daughter does not, even to this day, tolerate spiders. She has been known to scream loudly in her calmer responses to being in the same room as such things, and to flail wildly and do other potentially dangerous things when confronted with them unexpectedly. CMW was not thinking about the reaction to unexpected confrontation. All she could think of was not alarming Eldest Daughter about the species of spider that was even now, crawling towards her.

So she said, very calmly, "Uh, Christie. There is a spider on that shirt."

"B-L-E-A-H-H-H-H-H-H-----." Shrieked Eldest Daughter, flinging the offending garment across the front of the car directly toward CMW. "A-H-H-H-H-H-H----- MOM, I HATE SPIDERS!!!! AH-H-H-H-H-H-"

CMW was clearly in a fix. She had no idea where the Black Widow Spider was at this particular moment. She had to watch traffic. She had this ballistic daughter in the front seat, flailing about, and the shirt was now on CMW's lap.

"Chris! That was a BLACK WIDOW SPIDER!!!!!! How could you just fling that over here? I have to drive. What am I supposed to do?"

"MOM, I CAN'T HELP IT. I HATE SPIDERS!!! I'M SORRY!!! I'M SORRY, BUT I REALLY HATE SPIDERS!!!"

CMW wasn't feeling especially in love with them at that moment, herself, but she stole a quick glance down over the shirt and found nothing there. She checked traffic, and glanced down to the floor board. There, still

66

nonchalantly crawling along was the Black Widow Spider. She took her eyes off the road, and her foot off the gas long enough to squash it. Thoroughly. Then proceeded with the sermon that consisted of instructions that reminded Eldest Daughter of the need for maturity, and calmness and self discipline and trust in the Lord. It was a waste of breath and time.

"Mom. I can't help it. I just hate spiders!"

And that is a memory from Shady Acres, where the years have taught CMW that there are character and personality things that just can't be legislated. Where CM has been more understanding of the feminine hatred for crawly things than most men, and where all the children (But particularly Eldest Daughter) still HATE SPIDERS!!!

A Christmas to Remember

It was Christmas in our home that long ago day. Three little boys and one little girl were as excited as four children could be. It really didn't matter that we were living in a basement with the only convenience being a sink in one corner, and a pail behind a curtain in the other. We didn't notice the tired lines around our Mama's eyes or the struggle she had to keep her spirits up as she awaited the birth of a new baby.

Daddy was a farmer. All that meant to us was that he could usually be found somewhere on the grounds when we needed him, and that he smelled like cows most of the time. There were smiley lines around my Daddy's eyes that never stopped, it seemed. The harder he worked, the more he smiled, and that was all the time.

We all had our dreams in that basement. I, for a new doll. The boys for the usual things that little boys want. Our parents were hoping for the day that the house above us would be livable, and for a healthy baby. The year before, a pregnancy had ended in a miscarriage for my mama, and it was difficult not to worry.

We never knew that money was tight. They put the four of us into the old green and yellow Chevy, and drove us to town. We were seldom allowed into the stores, but on this particular night, they let us go inside for a few minutes to look (and perhaps give some ideas).

My five-year-old mind was boggled. I had never seen so many dolls in my life. The old W. T. Grants store appeared to have dolls from floor to ceiling. I looked frantically down the rows and there, to my relieved surprise, I found the exact same rubber dolly that I had a home.

"I want that one!" I said decisively.

My parents were surprised. "You have one just like it at home!" They objected.

My mind was made up. They didn't try too hard to change it, as I recall. Maybe they understood me better than I knew myself at that point. (Maybe they were just relieved at the price tag!) Anyhow, when the presents were handed out that Christmas Eve, I got a new dolly -- just like my old one. They both slept with me that night in my old iron bed on a bare cement floor, and I felt loved, secure and very, very blessed.

A lot of Christmases have come and gone since that Christmas in 1958, but I think of that Christmas every time I think about special Christmas memories and "Christmases to remember." I smile a bit, and sometimes I cry, too. I see so many elements wrapped up in that Christmas that have never changed as I've come on down the road of life.

Christmas will always be the love of parents, making joyful days for their children when their own hearts may be heavy. It will be families together, even when the floors are cold, and the rooms are divided by curtains on a string. It will be love, and the joy of the familiar taking precedence over the new and better. It will be the humble ways that families who love the Lord and each other share their hope and faith for a brighter tomorrow.

We didn't know then that there were brighter days ahead for our family. The long winter would be over. Our blond-haired, blue-eyed, beautiful and healthy baby sister would come to brighten our home and to fill our finally remodeled house with wonderful baby sounds. How thankful we all were!

But even more, how thankful I am for parents who had the faith and hope to make wonderful memories for us at a time when they had no way of knowing that everything was going to be alright.

Old Gertrude Causes a Ruckus

It seems that Old Gertrude has fallen and broken the bone between her shoulder and her elbow. Why the medical people insist on calling this the "humerus," I will never know. There is nothing funny about it. Especially since they sent her home straight from the emergency room with instructions to "Be careful how you handle her."

Now Certain Man's Wife has done quite a bit of personal care in her time, and she got things arranged with the help of Certain Man and Eldest Daughter and Youngest Daughter. (Middle Daughter was inconveniently in Papua, New Guinea). They even set up a hospital bed which was a big help. But Old Gertrude was not inclined to get out of that bed once she was in it, and she was not about to put any weight on her one leg, and she was not going to roll over, and she was not going to get out on her wheelchair.

After a few days of hollering and protesting and complaints of pain beside "the cat" (which is what she delicately calls her bottom area) the emergency room was prevailed upon to take an X-ray of her hip and pelvis and they determined that she did, in fact, have a fractured pelvis. They sent her straight home again from the emergency room with instructions to "try to get her to exercise as much as possible. But be careful how you handle that arm..."

Now Medicaid is a bad word to most people who are involved in health care of any kind. Sometimes it seems like when you need them the most, there is some regulation that will prevent them from providing the needed assistance. This was one of those times.

Certain Man's Wife stood in the Emergency room and pled for some in-home health care to take care of just a daily bath. There were going to be bedpans to contend with, and 22 hour a day duty even with the two hours of help for which she was asking. The kind doctors shook their heads.

"Unfortunately, there is no way. If her hip was broken, we could do it. If she needed dialysis or insulin we could do it. But we can't do it for a broken arm, and we can't do it for a fractured pelvis."

"Even when you compound profound mental retardation, walking with a walker and both fractures?"

"Sorry. Nope. They just won't approve it."

Old Gertrude has walked with a walker for years, and used a wheelchair when there was any amount of distance involved. So now, she had a broken arm that prevented her from using her walker. She had a fractured pelvis that made it difficult to put any weight on her already trembly legs. And she had a stubborn streak that caused her to strongly resist anything that might even remotely cause her discomfort. (This is an old lady, here, who will boo-hoo like a baby over a hangnail.) And she was picky about who did what for her.

It was possible for CMW to hire some help, which was greatly appreciated, indeed. However, it was difficult to find anyone who wanted to come for just two hours every day, so CMW began a daily juggle of schedules and family needs and such so that she could accomplish all that she needed to do, (usually!) and still take care of Old Gertrude adequately.

The one thing that was exceedingly difficult to manage was time away to get groceries and supplies. There was always a crisis or a last minute occurrence that held her captive. Sometimes she prevailed upon sisters or mother or daughter or husband or sons to procure necessary things, but the list of things that she needed to get for Old Gertrude and the list of things she felt she had to shop for herself grew longer and longer.

Then one day, Eldest Daughter, who loves Old Gertrude and is usually quite good with her, but who does not do personal care, offered to stay at the house long enough for CMW to run into town for some much needed items. So CMW put Old Gertrude on the bedpan (and got her off again) and situated her comfortably in her beloved bed, listening to a CD, and then she sallied forth.

It felt wonderful to be out. It was a Wednesday afternoon, CMW's house was clean, and she had some time to get the things she needed. That morning, CMW had tried on a dress that her Sister-in-law, Polly, had given to Middle Sister, Sarah. It was too big for Middle Sister, so she passed it on to CMW. When CMW looked at it she was aware that it wasn't a perfect fit, but decided it was okay, so she had left it on all day. It was sort of a greenish thing with leaves on it. CMW didn't particularly like it, but she could wear a back brace under it while she was helping Gertrude, so it was pretty comfy as well as practical.

Before leaving for the store, she stood in front of Eldest Daughter and asked, "Is this okay to wear to town?"

Eldest Daughter looked up briefly from what she was doing, and said, "Sure. It will be fine." So, CMW trotted off to the Medical supply store. She shopped carefully and was very pleased with her purchases. Of course, there are some things that just seem to not be available anywhere else, so-- it was on to Wal-mart!!!"

While CMW was in the Health and Beauty aids section, she was pleasantly surprised by Middle Sister's voice. It isn't very often that the two of

72

them see each other in the store, so they chatted for a brief minute. She had come in to get some medicine for Sweet Mama's client, Kathy, as Sweet Mama had had gallbladder surgery the day before and was quite indisposed.

Said Middle Sister to CMW, "Oh, you're wearing that dress. I thought it was so pretty."

Said CMW "I don't really think it is pretty, but it works..."

Said Sister Sarah (kinda quiet and off to the side) "Did you know it wasn't hemmed?"

Yelped CMW, (in a loud whisper) "WHAT???" She peered down at the hemline -- or where the hemline was supposed to be, and, lo and behold, not only was it not hemmed, it had frazzles hanging off of it all around. CMW was mortified! She craned her head around to look all around it and then discovered another thing that was not as it should have been.

You see, some weeks ago, CMW had purchased a black, rather long slip. It was for wearing under some of her Sunday dresses which were rather dark and rather long. For some inexplicable reason, she had been wearing it when she tried on the dress. Now, this particular dress was longer than the slip, but the long, full slip had prevented CMW from ascertaining that there was a very hefty slit up both sides of this dress's skirt. BIG SLIT. So big, in fact, that whenever she took a step, a full eight inches of very black slip showed where CMW NEVER shows underwear. All CMW could think of was "Get HOME. NOW!" But there were things that had to be gotten, so she prayed she would not see anyone else she knew and quickly rounded up her necessities and escaped.

When she got home, she asked Youngest Daughter and Eldest Daughter why someone hadn't bothered to tell her that her dress was in such disarray. They insisted that they hadn't noticed it.

"Besides," said Youngest Daughter, "Everyone has fringes hanging off their clothes these days."

Sez CMW, "NOT ME!!! And I for sure don't hang a black slip out the sides of my dress for all the world to see!!!"

And that is the news from Shady Acres where Certain Man was unnecessarily amused, CMW has put that dress with the Salvation Army collection, and all the children are adapting-- as they usually do.

CMW and Blankets and Feet

The phone rang on Saturday morning at nine o'clock. It was before the sons of Certain Man and his wife had bestirred themselves from their reclining positions. It is the one morning they have to sleep till their hearts' content, and CM and CMW have noticed that today's youth are always on the short side of sleep.

This is obviously the fault of CM and CMW, who insist on such things as MORNING CHORES before school for Youngest Son, and that Eldest Son has to WORK at a JOB (of all things!!!). Both of these things have been found to make it impossible for young people to get enough sleep, and parents could never expect them to get to bed early, for Pete's Sake.

"After all," said Youngest Son, one of the times that CMW was gently suggesting that maybe the problem lay with the bedtime, not the arising time. "I have to have some social life."

So the Sons of Certain Man and Certain Man's Wife have gotten into the habit of "catching up" on Saturday mornings. Of course, these plans go awry with great frequency when there is a garage to sweep, or chicken house work, or any of a number of things for which families find young men quite useful.

The caller on Saturday morning was Friend Matt. He wished to speak to either of the young men, and since it was of the time that young men should be up, Certain Man's Wife climbed the stairs to take the portable phone to the victims.

Because of both sons' length, CM and CMW bought extra long twin beds to place in their room. Both beds broke when rather unexpected burdens descended upon them suddenly, so the sons removed sideboards, foot boards and rails and put the box springs directly on the floor. This was accomplished after removing everything that had been hiding under the bed and delegating them to other places around their room. (When Eldest son was young, he could not go to sleep if anything was out of place in his room. While CMW was not watching, he became immune to that little idiosyncrasy, and behold! It is now hazardous in there!!!) Because of the broken beds they now sleep rather low to the floor, sort of among the rubble. To come into their rooms while they are sleeping is an adventure of faith (especially if it is more than 24 hours after the weekly cleaning.)

Now these two young men have very different personalities, and they sleep in very different positions. Eldest Son burrows. When CMW takes it upon herself to make his bed, it takes him "several days to get it back to comfortable." He likes lots of blankets, and if he is sleeping, all an observer can see is this long, round hump. It reminds CMW of a horizontal silo. Youngest Son sleeps on his back, sprawled out, with his feet often sticking out of the bottom of his blankets. He, too, likes lots of blankets, but he uses them differently.

On Saturday Morning, when Certain Man's Wife knocked on the door and gained admittance, she waited at the door for a minute to see if the conversation was going to be short enough for her to take the phone back to its place in the kitchen. Eldest Son took the phone call, while Youngest Son languished in that half asleep state that is so sweet when they are babies. Certain Man's Wife looked down at the foot sticking out from under the covers and was taken aback at the size of it. It was huge! And hairy! She fought a sudden lump in her throat as she thought of the many times that she had covered that foot up and it was little, and pink and chubby. Sometimes it was grubby, as its owner has only developed a penchant for showers in recent years, and sometimes it was tanned from running barefoot, with stubbed toes and calluses. It used to be that she could determine where that foot went, and when it went there, but the last several years have changed that as things such as driver's license and sports practice and youth group and friends have made their inroads into his life.

Her eyes traveled up the line of the blankets and were suddenly stopped at another sight that caused her heart to lurch. Draped across his chest was his beloved blanket. When he was the littlest child in the house, CMW had made knotted comforts for each of her children. His blanket was just a bit smaller than the others, as HE was so small, but he stayed pretty much attached to it through the years. Not in a "Linus" sort of way, but he usually had it on his bed, and often slept with it. The years had taken their toll and some time ago, he had come to CMW asking if there was some way to "fix it." The binding was pretty much worn through to the flannel backing, and the stuffing was coming out. CMW had studied on it and finally bought a wide satin binding that would cover the old binding, catch the loose edges and make a durable finish. Several weeks ago in a burst of energy she had finally gotten it finished and returned to him. At times she almost had to laugh when she saw that new satin binding against the faded old blanket, but it never seemed to bother Youngest Son, and he had been quite grateful for her efforts on his behalf.

So there he was; big manly foot sticking out of a thick soccer blanket, and a blanket with baby blue satin binding and rocking horses and drums,

76

covering his heart. Half asleep, half awake. So much a man, so much her little boy.

Certain Man's Wife had seen enough. She had quite enough to think about. She descended to kitchen without her phone. The boys could bring it down later. She felt suddenly tired and very, very old.

Why should a big foot and a baby blanket cause her to cry?

And that is the latest from Shady Acres. Where all the children are growing up much too soon.

CM Smells a Dead Mouse

Now Certain Man grew up milking cows by hand and gathering thousands of market eggs daily on a little farm in Central Ohio. He always said that he would not gather eggs or milk cows when he had his own farm, and he has remained very unswerving to his vow. There have been many times when CMW has entreated him for a milk cow for the family's milk supply, but he has remained adamant.

"NO MILK COWS. They tie you down too much. Besides, who is going to milk them?"

"The boys can learn. Even Youngest Daughter could learn to milk a cow. She loves to be outdoors and she--"

"Look, I'm nobody's fool. You can say what you want. That kind of stuff gets old really fast, and then it would be 'good old Dad' out there milking. I ain't gonna' start, then I won't have to keep on. NO MILK COWS!"

Even though CMW suspects that she will never prevail upon him for even just one little old easy-milking Jersey cow, she still likes to dream. (Have any of you gals ever noticed the muscles on a guy who milks by hand morning and evening? They're pretty incredible! Believe me, I know! See first paragraph!)

Anyhow, even though Certain Man does not gather eggs, he has become a chicken farmer, sending thousands and thousands of Del-Mar-Va-lous chickens yearly to the shelves of the grocery stores. And even though he does not have a single female bovine on the premises, he does keep some slightly altered male creatures around to supply his grill and his Sunday dinner table and the many opportunities for hamburger that present themselves at Shady Acres. He prides himself on these animals, feeds them "Sweet Stock" which is a horse feed, and takes two years to grow some of the best beef around. He found a butcher shop a great distance away that does butchering that is truly "a cut above the rest" and believes that the extra miles and slightly higher fees are worth it to have the quality that he wants.

Usually, around the first of February he will give a call to Sudlersville Meat Locker and set up a time for them to come and get the two steers that are two years old, and then waits for the call that says it is time to retrieve his finished, frozen meat.

One Saturday, several weeks ago, it was the time for him to bring home all his hamburger, filet mignon, steaks and roasts. He delivered out the meat that he had sold and was giving away, then brought the rest home. With the help of his tall sons, he carried it down to the basement and arranged them in the meat freezer.

Now CMW usually helps to clean out this freezer and then repack it so that she knows what is going on and where he has put things. This is not because he is not organized. It is because he is far more organized than she ever has been, so it behooves her to watch where he put stuff so that she can find it when she goes to cook. He is a conscientious and faithful provider, and meticulous about quality as well as accessibility, so on this occasion, when he got it all finished before she got down there, she was more than satisfied with the job he and his two sons had done.

Now this particular meat market packs the finished product into large, heavyweight, waxed cardboard boxes with tight fitting lids. These boxes are splendid for many different jobs over the year, and CMW is always happy when her supply of useful boxes is replenished with the yearly butchering. Certain Man was somewhat uncertain about what to do with these boxes, so he left them standing in the basement where they were when he unloaded the meat, and there was a veritable mountain of them. He checked them thoroughly, though, before closing the freezer to make sure they all were empty, and when they were, he congratulated himself on getting everything in.

It is no secret in the household of Certain Man that the nose of his wife is very inclined to smell things that are not the way they ought to be. The family and even the cleaning lady have been dispatched on wild goose chases to find "something stinky" when CMW happens to catch a whiff of something that doesn't agree with her. It may be a towel on the upstairs rack, or someone's unchanged underwear, or mildew in the wash basket, or even just the smells that go along with caring for intellectually disabled adults. There is nothing she hates worse than a house that smells bad when someone walks in the door.

And for several weeks before the meat was brought home from the meat locker, she had been proclaiming, "This house STINKS! What is it? Do you kids have any idea what smells so bad? Sweetheart, can't you smell that smell?"

The family would dutifully stop and sniff and no one seemed to think anything was out of order except Eldest Daughter who would sometimes say, (without being asked) "Mom, what stinks in this house? Something smells when you stand right here in the laundry room." So CMW did everything she knew to get rid of the smell. And it didn't get better. It got worse. And after bringing home the meat, it started to change. Instead of being in the laundry room, it appeared to be emanating from the basement. And instead of a musty, mildew smell, it was smelling like compost. Or worse.

CMW was getting more and more concerned. One by one she was enlisting the assistance of the offspringin's to help her discover the source. By now some of them could smell it, too.

Said Youngest Son, "Mom, you know it is the kitty litter box down there. Rachel NEVER empties it, and it has been MONTHS."

Said Youngest Daughter, "It is NOT! Tatters NEVER uses that kitty litter box when she is in the basement. She only uses the one upstairs!"

"That's a bunch of crap!" said Youngest Son. "Just go look at it. It's full of cat poop!"

CMW hastily intervened at this juncture and said, "The litter box does need to be cleaned out, Rachel, but Lemuel, I investigated that possibility and the smell is not coming from the litter box."

Eldest Daughter came in one day and said "Whoo-ee, Mom. Somethin' is really rankin'!"

So CMW went again to the basement to discover the source. She shook or kicked every single box that had come from the meat locker and they all were empty. She looked behind the freezers and between them because there was one time when a package of meat had gotten dropped back there. Her search uncovered nothing. She carefully shut the door at the top of the basement, lit candles and refilled potpourri and worried. Once again she appealed to Certain Man.

"Sweetheart, I can't believe that you can't smell this smell. It smells awful!"

"Hon, I know you say there is a smell, but I just don't smell anything!"

Said CMW, "Well, I am comforted by the fact that if I don't smell good, you won't know the difference, but I wish you would just stand and the top of the steps and sniff. Something really smells BAD!"

Later that evening, when Certain Man was engrossed in something else she mentioned it to someone that there was a terrible smell that Certain Man could not even smell and he looked up long enough to say, "I did smell it. I opened the basement door and I can't believe that you don't know what stinks!"

Certain Man's Wife looked at him dumbfounded and said, "Pray tell. What is it?"

"Oh," he said, matter-of-factly, "It's a dead mouse."

"A DEAD MOUSE? Daniel, maybe a dead CAT, or MOOSE, but that smell is way too big for a dead mouse."

He looked at CMW with a most condescending manner. "A dead mouse," he explained patiently, "has a particular 'mousy' smell. You can tell when it is a dead mouse. It SMELLS like a dead MOUSE."

If the truth be told, CMW was really in no position to argue with him. Mice have been terrible this year, and she HAD put out mouse poison in very hidden places. But she thought quietly to herself that this smell, if it was, in fact "mousy," had to be a whole army of mice, slaughtered and dumped into an uncovered mass grave. So she said no more, but decided that when it was morning, she was going to find that dead mouse and deal with it.

So the next day, she started at one end of the basement and sniffed into every crack and cranny. Nothing rewarded her quivering nose until she got over to the pile of boxes from Sudlersville Meat Locker. Methodically, she started stacking boxes and lids onto a table that was beside the meat freezer. When she had moved an entire stack, she stopped short. There on the floor under the bottom one was a single hamburger of the sort she buys from Sam's Club in a ten pound box to use for quick grilling. It smelled very bad. Puzzled as to how it got there, she flipped it into a trash box, and continued to move another stack of boxes. Suddenly there was a terrible smell. It was quite "mousy," indeed. She was startled to find nearly a whole box of Sam's hamburgers on the floor behind the stack of boxes. It was on its side. It was open. Hamburgers in different stages of decomposition and decay were spilling from the plastic packaging. It was all she could do to keep from gagging as she cleaned up the mess and got it into a box with a lid tightly upon it.

She drug it up the basement steps and out into the sunlight of the great outdoors. And called Certain Man. "I found your dead mouse."

"Oh, Yeah? What was it?" (To his credit he did NOT say "Where was it?")

"It was a box of hamburgers. It must have gotten set out when you were putting meat away, and somehow overlooked when you finished."

"Oh, Man! What do they cost, anyhow?"

"It's not that big a loss, Sweetheart. I think I pay eleven dollars for the whole box, and we had used some out of it. I'm just glad to have that smell out of there."

"And I'm glad it wasn't a big box of hamburger from the meat locker!"

And so the peace and the atmosphere were restored.

A week later, CMW picked up another ten pound box of hamburgers from Sam's Club to use for quick grilling. Certain Man was helping to put the groceries away.

"I see," he said solemnly, "that you bought some more 'mouse'."

And that is the news from Shady Acres, where Certain Man's ability to laugh has saved many a marital spat, where Certain Man's Wife never did find out what the first smell was, and where all the children are not in the least deterred from their favorite meal of grilled hamburgers.

CM and CMW go to the Big Apple

Now it came to pass that Certain Man and Certain Man's Wife traveled to the fair City of New York to attend the graduation of the daughter of dear friends, Daniel and June Pollard. And Renee, being the bright, bouncy, beautiful and intelligent teenager that she is, had invited Certain Man to bring the commencement address for this special and momentous occasion.

New York City is a wondrous place, indeed. However, it is not the sort of place that CM and CMW would normally go excepting that there is a long family history that has taken them there on numerous occasions. For many years, The Daddy of CMW held the position of overseer to the vibrant, variegated and versatile Mennonite congregation meeting there. He and Sweet Mama have spent countless days and nights in situations that have greatly enriched them and stretched their capacity to relate to many different people of many different races and cultures. Out of their relationships have grown many rewarding and stimulating friendships for CM and CMW.

CM and CMW have found that the city is an exciting and challenging place to be. The first time that they spent a night in the Pollard's house, CMW could scarcely sleep. There was noise of disturbing quality that went on and on through the night. Car alarms went off with great regularity, shouting, sirens, and even gunshots made her sleep very uneasily. In the morning sun, the walks that she took with Certain Man could almost cause her to weep. Beautiful children, beautiful people, sad and happy, pensive and animated, passed by them in a never ending river of humanity.

"All these people," she would think. "Where are they going? What are they thinking? To whom or to what have they given their hearts?"

On the numerous occasions that she has been to New York, she has usually enjoyed the experience immensely, but unfortunately, this time, it rather looked like there was going to be an exception. On the way to New York, she had slept in the front seat of the van for an hour or more, while they bobbed along the many roads that took them to their destination. And when they disembarked in the city, she realized with dismay that she was experiencing great discomfort down the left side of her neck and into her shoulder.

"H-m-m-m!" She thought, "I must have slept on it funny, somehow." She tried rubbing the area but it didn't seem to help. So she got ready for graduation and tried not to think about it. She almost managed to not think of it, in fact, while she listened to the interesting and well-done activities of graduation. The Homeschoolers of the church handed out family awards, the children sang, and Certain Man did a splendid job on his address. However, as the day wore on, the pain became worse and worse. Her neck was not stiff. She could turn her head in either direction, but the pain was relentless, no matter how she turned her head.

She finally asked Sweet Mama (who, along with Our Daddy, was also present at the celebration) if she had some pain pills. Sweet Mama, in fact, did, and CMW took them in the hopes that it would help. It didn't. Except that it served to worry Sweet Mama quite muchly.

Now CMW has very heavy eyebrows. They will lower into a very frowny look without her even trying, but when something hurts, it takes a concerted effort to even keep her eyes open, and the hours passed with her trying hard to be cheerful, but not really succeeding. It was clearly an "eyebrows down" sort of day. One of the young friends from the congregation came by their table at the graduation party, and learning of the problem, spent some time doing a very helpful massage. It was greatly appreciated, but unfortunately, the effect did not last. There was just something pulled very tight that would not let go.

CMW decided that there was nothing to be gained by moping about, so she helped to clean up after the party, and she and Certain Man toted things back to the Pollard's house from the church and looked forward to an evening spent in very wonderful company. The Graduate opened her presents, and there was much laughter and conversation, but CMW's heart was not in it. She decided to go out and retrieve some things from the car, and while she was out there, a parking place opened up that was much closer to the front door of the Pollard residence, so she decided to move the car. And while she was in the car, Certain Man's cell phone rang. She was astounded to hear Sweet Mama's voice on the other end. (She and Our Daddy were staying several blocks away at Allen and Carolyn Roth's house.)

"Mary Ann," said Sweet Mama, "I was telling Carolyn about how your neck was hurting and asked her if there was anyone in the congregation who could possible help you. She said that there is an elderly lady named Tashmeni who is from the Caribbean who could maybe help you. Do you want to try?"

Did she want to try?!?!

"Oh, yes, Mom! I will try anything that Carolyn thinks might help. I don't know how I will ever sleep with this."

"Well, then, we'll stop over around 8:15 for you and take you over there."

"And I will be watching for you."

So, around 8:15, Carolyn and Sweet Mama stopped over and CMW clambered aboard their van for another interesting exposure to New York traffic and New York culture. In a neighborhood where all the windows and doors are barred and the lights shine from naked light bulbs in the foyers, and children of all races play and shout in the street, they pulled up in front of a house and parked on the street.

In the darkened doorway, Carolyn rang the bell, and a brown skinned, slender young man with smiling eyes let them in. He watched in pride as his daughter, a little, round, brown, curly-haired girlie cavorted on the floor, and he spoke of his little boy. When formalities were over, Carolyn guided her two friends to another doorway leading to a basement apartment. There are no wide and generous stairwells in this section of New York. Each one that CMW has seen has been narrow and steep and challenging. But she followed dutifully down a scary stairs to a surprisingly cheery basement room, where Tashmeni waited with her smiling eyes and (what CMW hoped were) skillful fingers.

There needed to be more formalities, and then Tashmeni asked questions in her Guyana style English. "Was the neck stiff?" "Could CMW turn it?" "Where did it hurt?" When the questions were answered to her satisfaction, she determined that what CMW needed was a deep muscle massage. That sounded good to CMW, for she really wasn't too sure that yanking around on her neck was going to do much good.

"Yanking around" may have hurt less.

Tahshmeni got busy at her task. She was not a woman to do things halfway. She had fingers that appeared to have steel tips on them. And she knew which muscle hurt and she was going to give it a reason for complaining. Sweet Mama sat upon the plastic couch and worried. It appeared to her that Tashmeni was going about this with more enthusiasm than was necessary. She held her peace for some time, then tried to give some helpful suggestions.

"Sister Tashmeni, you are really working hard. Are you sure that you won't be too tired after all this?"

"Oh, no. I am not tired." More vigorous rubbing. She brought out a tube of something that was for an arthritis rub. It smelled suspiciously like the kind of thing that would really burn if it got into your eye. She spread it all over the offending muscle, and rubbed it in with great determination. CMW's loose hair at the bottom of her bun kept getting in her way. Tashmeni would gently smooth them up, and they would come back down again. She finally got a clip to hold them out of the way, and returned to her task unhindered.

After massaging the muscle for probably a half an hour, she got out her vibrating heat infusing instrument and thoroughly vibrated and heated the area. CMW could tell by this time that Sweet Mama was anxious indeed.

Her eyes were worried and the things that she said were meant to give Sister Tashmeni an easy way to say that she thought what had been done would be sufficient. She told stories of times when she suffered at the hands of over enthusiastic people who were trying to help. CMW suspects that she prayed.

And finally, Sister Tashmeni deemed that it would, in fact, be sufficient. She put away her vibrating heat tool, and her arthritis rub. She gave instructions that the treatment should be repeated, and she insisted that Carolyn Roth, Sweet Mama and CMW all drink a refreshing potion of carrot juice. It was fresh and surprisingly good.

The round, brown girlie and the beautiful little boy were grandchildren of Tashmeni, and after they were properly admired and more formalities exchanged, the threesome climbed the steep steps back to the dark street and headed back to the Pollard's abode.

The shoulder was tender, indeed, but the terrible pain was gone. CMW was greatly relieved, and Sweet Mama was very pleased to have been able to find someone to help. Certain Man had been sure that CMW would not return before ten o'clock, and he was pretty much right (again!). When CMW got into the house, she found that the young people had gone bowling, and the older folks were settling in for the night. So after some pleasant conversation with her friend, Sweet June, she and Certain Man decided to retire for the night.

CM and CMW had the nicest room in the house. They had two windows, and an electric fan in the one gave wonderful relief from the relentless heat. There were crisp, clean sheets on the bed, and the bed was comfy and wide. CMW sank down with gratitude into the cool darkness and thought about the day. It had certainly been interesting!

Certain Man collapsed on his side of the bed. He had driven the whole way to New York, and he had brought the message at the graduation. He had helped clean up and he had made new friends. He was quite weary as well, but pretty much satisfied with his day, and glad that CMW was feeling better. Just before turning over to go to sleep, he suddenly grabbed CMW in a bear hug and kissed her very fiercely. CMW was not surprised, as he is given to this sort of behavior, but she didn't particularly like it that some of her disheveled hair came between the lip lock and caused a distraction. So she pulled it out of the way, and was suddenly surprised by a very strange sensation. She is quite accustomed to intense kisses from her husband but this was giving a new meaning to the words "hot and burning." Her lips felt like they were on fire!

"Uh, Sweetheart," said CMW, "does your mouth feel funny?"

"Yeah, it's kinda' burning-like!!!"

"Mine is really burning, too. I wonder. . . Whew, this is really strange.
. . Oh, I bet I know."

86

"WHAT?" He leapt out of bed to get a drink of water from the bottle on the dresser.

"Tonight when Tashmeni was rubbing the arthritis salve on my shoulder, my hair kept getting in the way, and she kept putting it up. There must have been some on my hair, and when it got in between the kiss, that stuff must have come off on our lips." It was suddenly too funny, and CMW dissolved into helpless giggles.

Certain Man could not keep a straight face, either, and CMW could hear his voice smiling in the dark. He did not try to kiss her again, but professed to still love her and bade her a sweet good night. They both slept like babies, oblivious to sirens and car alarms and shouts and even gunshots (if there were any).

Some people go to New York to see a show or to have adventure, or to see the sights or to just have fun. But not CM and CMW. No, no. They have to go and experience all the things that make for a good show. Pain and suspense and barred windows and basement apartments and strangers and even hot burning kisses. The sweet thing is that along the way they have lots of adventure and lots of fun.

And that is the news from Shady Acres, where Certain Man has driven everyone safely home again, where CMW's shoulder, though actually bruised from the enthusiastic ministrations of Sister Tashmeni, is still feeling great, and where the children stayed home and made this whole trip possible.

CMW and Eldest Son's Car

Now it came to pass that Certain Man had gone to lands afar (well, actually, to Indiana) with the youth group for a week to do a service project. Certain Man's Wife had stayed behind to mind the house and the ladies and the chickens. She had good help from Youngest Son and Youngest Daughter, but there were many challenges to the week. Things like a broken water line in the chicken house; a stubborn feed line that required the attention of Brother-in-law, Bert; running out of feed at midnight, and even a mouse dropping down on her head when she opened a door to go into the chicken house. (There was no one there to rescue her, so she did not scream. Actually, the mouse was running frantically along the floor when her eyes adjusted to the darkness enough to realize what happened, and by then, screaming seemed a little belated). In spite of everything, optimism did not fail her. However, she was exceedingly grateful to see her spouse and adult children return to the family fold on Saturday past, so that she could get on with everyday living.

Yes, well. Everyday living did not present the tranquility that she had hoped for.

It seems that Eldest Son's VW Jetta was having problems. Certain Man and Eldest Son had cast about for a reputable repair shop for this foreign baby, and finally found Carey's Foreign and Domestic Car Repair in Georgetown who agreed look at it.

Certain Man's Wife is aware that Eldest Son is very fond of his car. She would not think of saying anything negative about it. Except that she really does not like driving it. It sits very low to the road. When she is in this particular vehicle, she feels as if she is sitting on the road, scooting along on a skateboard with a steering wheel. It makes weird buzzes and beeps for no apparent reason. It has a stick shift in the floor. She feels as if she can never quite reach the gas and clutch pedals. And the thing that was taking it to the shop was especially disconcerting. It had no dash lights. It was impossible to tell how fast you were going when it was night unless you turned on the dome light, and then it was an approximation, especially with CMW's middle age eyes.

But, as I said, Eldest Son is very fond of this car. He even put in a "sweet" stereo system that makes bumps that CMW can hear inside the old farmhouse at Shady Acres with the windows closed and the air conditioning on. (However, that is another story which we shall not divulge at this point.).

The appointment for the Jetta was for first thing, Tuesday morning. Since every single driver in the family except CMW has a job, the decision was made to take it down on Monday evening. Certain Man wanted to move some chickens in the chicken house with the assistance of his sons, and then he was going to go with Eldest Son to take the car to Georgetown.

This story cannot be told without placing some blame on the shoulders of CMW's Eldest Brother, Clint. If he had stayed out of it, everything would have been cool, but sometimes people just complicate things. He called in the middle of the morning.

"Mary, someone gave me two tickets to the Shorebirds Game tonight, and I was wondering if your two sons would like to have them."

Certain Man's sons are usually quite ready to go to the Shorebird's game, and especially when the tickets are free. There was also that chicken house thing that might be avoided if they were not present when it happened. CMW wasn't sure if this was a good night for them to go. She suggested that maybe Eldest Daughter and Beloved Son-in-Law would want the tickets and, if not, then maybe The Sons could use them.

Beloved Son-in-Law had quartet practice, and Eldest Daughter was having the quartet for supper. They couldn't go. Certain Man thought it would be fine for The Sons to go to the game. He would move chickens another night. CMW or Second Daughter could help him take the Jetta to Georgetown.

And so, thanks to Uncle Clinton, The Sons headed to Salisbury and the game. As they were preparing to leave, they thought of TRANSPORTATION.

"Mom, can we take the mini-van? We can't take Raph's car because it needs to go to the shop." CMW considered this. She really wanted to keep it home..."in case," but they were taking Cousin Gabe with them, and Lem's two door vehicle made things a bit unhandy. She decided that there was no real reason to say "no," so she gave permission. They left celebrating.

Scarcely a half an hour later, the phone rang, and it was CMW's Daddy. The Honorable Uncle Monroe's were at their house, and Our Daddy greatly desired that CMW and her siblings would feel free to stop in for a little bit, as the rest of the evenings of their sojourn were already full. CM thought that CMW should go. He would stay home with the ladies and Rachel, and she could go and enjoy the evening. When CMW's Middle Sister called and was going, it was especially appealing. CMW agreed to pick her up on the way, and they could ride together.

"Sweetheart, what about Raph's car?" queried CMW as she was considering what needed to be done that night.

"Why don't you drive it out to Greenwood, then call me when you are ready to leave, and I will meet you at Bert's or the light in Ellendale, and we will just take it down from there."

"But the dash lights don't work. I can't tell how fast I am going!"

"Just be careful. It's not dark now, so it will just be the trip home that you need to worry about."

CMW thought privately that maybe she would return home while it was yet day, and decided to follow his wishes. She thought of taking his pick-up, but he needed it for what he was doing, so she got her purse and went out and got into the car. It was low and uncomfortable. She adjusted the seat. She went to start the car. No keys. So she clambered out, and went in and searched until she found them. She went back out to the car, and climbed back in. She turned on the ignition.

Oh, for crying out loud! The radio was blaring. And she could NOT find how to turn it off. Frantically, she punched this button, then that. She succeeded in turning the beat to disco (which did not help) and finally found the volume control. Good. At least, she could turn it down. She did. All the way. And she got the Jetta successfully out onto the road and on the way to Greenwood.

As she was scooting along the road almost on her bottom, she happened to notice the gas gauge. Oh, Dear. It was on empty. This seemed very strange, for Eldest Son was usually conscientious about such things. She calculated the distance to her sister's house, to Greenwood, and then to Georgetown and came up with a very dismal conclusion. She had to stop at a gas station somewhere. She was not pleased.

She stopped at Middle Sister's house, and Sister Sarah came out and seated herself most graciously. She is used to cars. She did not complain about such things as skateboards with steering wheels. She did not even complain when CMW said that she needed to stop for gas. CMW always finds her company most agreeable, and her spirits lifted with the pleasant conversation.

There seems to be only one gas station that is in business in Greenwood these days. It is a big Shore Stop Mobil station just south of town between the north and south bound lanes of Route 13. So that is where CMW aimed the infamous Jetta, and pulled up to the gas tanks. The place was, thankfully, not overly busy.

The first order of business was to determine how to pay for the gas purchase. CMW remembered that she had NO CASH. Most of the gas purchases that she makes are made with a gas card which she keeps in the minivan (which was at Salisbury with The Sons). Recently, she had cleaned all credit cards out of her wallet except her Discover Card, which she used only in an emergency. Except that, for some reason, it was not there. She had taken it out to record some numbers at home the day before. Great discussion with

Middle Sister produced no help. Middle Sister had come without even a purse. Then CMW remembered that she had a PNC Check card, and that the account had about 14 dollars in it. That would get ten dollars worth of gas, so she fetched out her PNC card, and sallied forth to the gas tanks.

The ridiculous foreign car had the gas tank on the wrong side. Every single vehicle that CM and CMW own has the gas tank on the driver's side, but this pretty little Jetta had to be different. So CMW got back into the car and tried to maneuver it around in the right way. There were great goings back and forth in the parking lot. The Greenwood Police happened to pass at that very minute and gave her quite a start.

"As far as I know," she said to Middle Sister, "I'm not doing anything wrong, but the way this is going, I probably AM." She avoided looking at the police officer, as she was sure there was a guilty look on her face that would cause questioning if noticed. The Greenwood Police officers are not known for their reasonable and compassionate behavior, especially on that section of road. She finally got the Jetta turned around with the gas tank facing the service bay. While making this change, she remembered that tucked away in her billfold was a MAC card from Discover Bank, and that the account there had considerably more than the PNC account. So she decided to fish that out and use that instead of the PNC card since she was uneasy about the solvency of the latter account. This also took some digging and rooting to procure. Middle sister sat patiently while the card was found (Endurance wears well on her).

CMW again sallied forth to the gas tank. She inserted her MAC card and prepared to dispense gas. Oh, yes. This was not a credit card. A PIN number was needed. Thankfully, CMW remembered what that was, and finally got everything processed and approved. The little blinking sign read, "Please lift nozzle, choose grade, and dispense gasoline."

CMW lifted the nozzle, chose the grade, and went to insert the nozzle into the gas tank. Oh, dear. The little door was not open. She frantically tried to get it open, she pried and wiggled and jiggled the door. It would not budge. There must be a lever in the car.

"Sarah! Hey, Sarah! Can you reach over there and pull the lever to release this gas tank door?"

Sarah looked around, surprised. She had just been sitting there, cowering from the spectacle and thinking things were somewhat quieted down.

"What?" She was buckled in her seat, but she dutifully tried to unbuckle her seatbelt and was peering over to the driver's side with no success whatsoever.

"Wait a minute. Here--" CMW opened the door on the passenger's side of the car. "Here, hold this nozzle. If I hang it up, I will have to go through the authorization process all over again." She stretched the hose out long, and thrust the nozzle into the surprised hands of Middle Sister as she sat on the front seat. "I'll go over there and try to get it, because I think it is down there by the door."

CMW flew around the car to the other side of the Jetta, and flung open the door. There was NO LEVER. She looked beside the seat. She looked in front of the seat. She looked on the front of the dash, under the dash, on top of the dash. She looked under the seat. She started the process all over again, and looked for a button to push instead of a lever to pull. NOTHING. Great mutterings were going on beside her, and she got more and more anxious.

Suddenly she heard Middle Sister say from somewhere in the distance. "How much gas do you want in this thing, anyhow?"

"What?!?!" She pulled her head out from under the steering wheel somewhere and there stood Middle Sister with the gas door open, and the nozzle in the tank.

"I got it open!" She said with more glee than was appropriate.

"How did you get that open? I tried and pried and ---"

"All you needed to do was push on the back of it and it would have come right open," she said calmly. (CMW would like to interject that the husband of Middle Sister knows pretty much everything there is to know about cars, so she SHOULD have known how to open that door. It makes sense that she would know such things.)

Ten dollars and two cents later, they were finally on their way.

"I feel," she said gloomily to Middle Sister, "Like Laurel and Hardy!"

"Except," said Middle Sister brightly, (probably thinking about the particular builds that belong to CMW and Middle Sister) "We are two HARDIES!"

And that is the News from Shady Acres, where Certain Man made another a whole story before the Jetta was safely in the car lot, where Certain Man's Wife's life is surely shortened because of it, and all the children were able to enjoy this episode from afar. Behold, they are glad.

A Love Story

They were both young. He was 16. His family was poor. One of ten children, he was born almost at the end of a long line of boys, November 24, 1929, exactly a month after Black Thursday. It was the beginning of THE GREAT DEPRESSION. He had the great blessing of being born into a warm, loving family. The oldest of a set a twins, he was blessed with dark wavy hair and a ready smile. His wise and Godly mama called him her "Little Sunshiney Man." His kind and gentle Papa taught him God's word and to work hard. Though times were tough, he was protected and loved.

She was 17, and new to the Mennonite community at Greenwood, DE. Her prayer veiling material wasn't thick enough, and her nylons weren't black enough. Her gently curly hair was blond and her face was pretty. Though her scruples were impeccable, the other girls would sometimes talk. Back home, in Pennsylvania, she had a brilliant papa who was teetering on the edge of violent mental illness. Though her family loved each other with a fierce loyalty, it was, after all, the depression, and their school-teacher papa struggled mightily to make ends meet. She had been put out to work at ten years old and she had made her own way for many a year.

Some people thought she would never look twice at this fresh-faced young man, but they were wrong. Older, taller, and more sophisticated young men tried to change her mind, but their efforts were in vain. She saw that there was something called potential and security in him. She knew that he was kind to his mama. She decided to say "yes" when he asked her out in August of 1946. Besides, she liked black hair and smiling eyes.

Three years later, on October 16, 1949, at a Pennsylvania mountain church in a little town named Cocolamus, they were married.

Most of this story I know by heart, because they were, and are, my precious Daddy and Mama. I can hardly believe it, but for half a century I have been privileged to observe this ordinary, but incredibly beautiful, love story. The young do not know how deep and rich and intrinsic love can be when it has aged along with us for as long as we can remember.

Married less than year, their first baby was born. They named him Clinton Edward. They were two very young parents with one determined baby. Daddy got good at jiggling a crib with his foot in the middle of the night.

Mama walked a long, lonely and dark road of the most desperate of postpartum depression -- and WON.

Eighteen months later, Nelson Roy was born. They were young and full of energy, and they needed it for the two little fellows that kept them hopping. Daddy worked in a machine shop, but they dreamed of a place to call their own. Then Grandpa decided to move off the farm, and a young Mark Yoder jumped at the chance to buy the "home place" where he had lived all his life until his marriage. Two young people with two determined babies became farmers and partners together in a venture that would become HOME to all of us.

Before the transition was quite completed, and the day before their fourth wedding anniversary, their third child was born. That would be me, Mary Ann (who grew up to become Certain Man's Wife). Daddy was 23, Mama was 24. They were two young people with two determined boys and a beautiful, compliant baby daughter. (Actually, it was two young parents with three very determined babies!!! May God be praised, they were determined, too. And firm disciplinarians.)

A year later, to the day, on October 15, 1954, Hurricane Hazel went through, flattening almost every building on the place except the house and the barn. They surveyed the damage and gave thanks for God's goodness to them. Though their losses were great, the two things that mattered most were left standing. So many others in the community had fared far worse. There wasn't much money but there was plenty of love and determination and neither of them was afraid of hard work. They had dreams and they held on. And Daddy prayed.

Eighteen months after the hurricane, Mark Jr. was born. Clinton was five and a half, Nelson was four. I was two and a half. Daddy and Mama were partners in chores and outside work, but Mama kept the house, too. She cooked three meals a day, every day, and she loved flowers and babies. Pictures taken during this time show bouncy children, a still dark haired Daddy and a slender Mama. And yes, she was pretty. I didn't realize it then, because she was my mama. But my adolescent sons have been heard to say, "You know, Grandma -- She was a babe!!!"

They showed their love to us in different ways, but we knew we were loved, and we knew they loved each other. And we knew our Daddy prayed.

In 1958, they started to remodel their old farm house. My impressions of this time are garbled and not reliable, but there was a time when the six of us took to a trailer on the left side of the driveway and our house stood empty and gutted and ugly on the right. But again, they worked hard, pulled together and made their dreams come true, and in early 1959, we moved back in. And just in time, too, for in April, our little sister, Sarah Jane, was born in the new house -- at home, as we all were except for Clinton.

During the time that we lived in the trailer, and while the house was being remodeled, Daddy was having some serious back problems, Mama worked in the barn and the chicken house daily, filling in for Daddy with milking and feeding chickens and pigs. One of my memories from this time was an evening when the boys were asking Daddy to show his muscles. My Daddy, a skinny and sinewy man had arm muscles like a double-yoked egg, and my brothers reveled in their Daddy's strong arms. On that night, they prevailed upon Mama to show her muscles, too. She pulled up her sleeve and flexed her muscle and there was dead silence around the table as we realized that our Sweet Mama's muscle was bigger than Our Daddy's. I remember that she hastily pulled down her sleeve like she hoped that no one noticed.

One of the boys said, "Look at that! Mama's muscle is bigger than Daddy's. Show it again, Mama!"

But she would not. No amount of coaxing would induce her to show it again. It was during the time of Daddy's serious back issues, and I guess she felt that he shouldn't have to compete for his son's complete admiration and loyalty.

Those memories are vivid. But the things I remember most involve Family Worship. We would gather, usually after breakfast in our bright kitchen. Daddy would lead us in a hymn, and read from the Bible. We'd often be called upon to recite a memory verse and then we would kneel on the hard linoleum floor at our kitchen chairs.

Our Daddy has a reputation for praying long prayers, and he developed that talent by the practice he got all those years ago. He would pray around the world and back, for wayward friends and family members, for school teachers and our Christian Day School, for our ministers and for the church, for his brother, Dr. Paul T. Yoder's family, missionaries to Ethiopia, and for any of his other brothers and sisters that he may have felt needed remembering. He prayed for his Mama and Papa "in their declining years of life." He thanked God for "His Dear Companion" (our Sweet Mama) and thanked God for "this country place that we call home," and for the mercies shown to us as a family. He thanked God for Jesus and His shed blood on Calvary and asked that God would forgive us where we had failed and come short of his will. When it was dry, he prayed for rain. When it rained, he thanked God for sending the rain to water the earth. It seemed like he prayed for a very long time.

But how much better our world would be if more Daddies would gather their children together on hard kitchen floors and lovingly pray long prayers over them. And how wonderful it would be if those children, grown and raising families of their own, could hear the words in their heads and entreat God for the same, ageless things.

In 1962, Alma Jean was born, their sixth and last child. They were still young parents. Mama was 33, Daddy 32. We were all determined children, kept in line by those prayers, hugs, eyebrows and the ever present razor strop, but we never questioned if they loved us or each other. The commitments were strong, and Daddy was the king of the household.

Mama always let us know that our Daddy was somehow the best. He got the prettiest fried egg, he got the biggest piece of cake. I can remember her often saying, "Save the best for Daddy." It was one of the wisest things she could have done, and she did it consistently and well, building loyalty and respect in us, her children, for their Daddy.

And so, the years passed, marking the days of our happy childhoods. How little we knew of the burdens carried by parents. All that mattered were Mama's three meals a day, Daddy's hard work, smiling eyes, hugs, shoulder rides and whiskerings when we were little enough, and the sense of belonging. Our family wasn't perfect, especially in our adolescent eyes. How very little we knew.

Our home was always open. It truly was a rare time when no extra person was living with us in some way or another. Their love for each other gave space for other people and our lives were and are so much richer for it. They never bought into the notion that a home was just for the family, but rather, that a home was a tool, entrusted to a family to enlarge the borders of a greater kingdom. We all felt a part of that ministry. Sometimes not willingly, but never given a choice, and it stamped itself on our hearts.

It is hard to believe that all those years have passed since that October morning when Mark Yoder and Alene Wert pledged their lives and love to each other. The road hasn't been all sunshine -- and even when you're in your 70's there are still hurdles to cross, dreams to dream, children and grandchildren to encourage and love, conflicts to resolve.

But they've been faithful to God and to each other. They are still the focus of our extended family. And when our paths cross, as they sometimes do, we find that where Daddy and Mama are, is HOME.

My prayer for them is many more happy years. It can't be 54, I know, but for as long as it can be, I pray that they can be each other's best friend, that there would be peace in their hearts and in their home, and a commitment to their Heavenly Father and each other that never wavers, no matter what.

"Grow old along with me
The best is yet to be.
The last of life, for which the first was made.
Our times are in HIS hands, who saith,
'A whole I planned, youth shows but half.'
Trust God. See all, nor be afraid."
-Robert Browning

But it wasn't to be. On December 18, 2005, our Daddy went home to Heaven. It was a glorious homegoing, and we were able to be there to cheer him safely home. But we miss him incredibly much. The story of this journey will need to be in another book. Right now, it is still too fresh. - Mary Ann Yutzy 02-06-06

CMW Clashes with the Dryer Vent

Now it came to pass that the days in Delaware have been alive with Indian Summer. The children have gone barefoot, some flowers are blooming profusely (though there have been some killer frosts) and there has even been talk of starting up the old air conditioner again. Certain Man's Wife sweltered through half the night on Wednesday night before finally getting up and putting a fan into the window so that she could sleep. Certain Man views all of this with a benignly amused eye, while muttering things about mid-life trials. He endured the fan business by staying firmly under the covers.

Thursday morning is a morning for arising extra early. CMW begins laundry the night before by sorting everything out, and putting the first load in on time delay. In the morning, when she gets downstairs, the first load is ready for the dryer, and the whole morning goes so much more smoothly because she doesn't have to scramble about, trying to sort and load and get started before the morning race begins.

On this particular Thursday morning, the Indian Summer had turned into rain. CMW loves rainy mornings for a variety of reasons, but she especially loves rainy mornings on laundry days because she can put things into the dryer without feeling guilty about not using her clothes line. And this was one rainy laundry morning. She got downstairs and changed her washer around 5:15.

Several years ago, Certain Man bought a Maytag Neptune washer and dryer for her. The washer has a very large capacity, which is quite advantageous for the household of CM and CMW, but the cycle on the washer is considerably longer than that of her previous model. It is hard to calculate when it will be finished. However, among the features that she particularly likes on this pair is a loud bell signaling the end of the cycle. Without the bell, she would likely forget to change the washer in a timely fashion, but with it, she can safely go about her other chores without paying too much attention to the laundry room until the bell notifies her of the need for a change.

So she packed lunches, gave showers, made breakfast, and got people off to work and center and didn't pay any attention to the laundry room and the goings on there.

Along about 7:45 CMW suddenly realized that the first load in the dryer was still tumbling about with abandon. The washer was sitting silent, done with its cycle a very long time. Something was clearly amiss. This particular dryer is able to complete two cycles to one washer load if it is working properly. She checked the lint trap. It was nearly lint free. H-m-m-m.

Some years ago, Certain Man had built a deck on the side of the house towards Milford. This is a most wonderful addition, and it is probably CMW's favorite spot of all. However, the dryer vent came out of the side of the house under this particular deck. On cold, damp rainy days, there is usually a cloud of steam rising from under the deck when the dryer is running, so CMW betook herself to the side door to see what was the status of the steam.

There was no steam. She opened the door and listened. She could hear the hum of the dryer, but it was difficult to tell whether it was behind her in the laundry room, or if it was the sound that is transmitted through the dryer vent. It was very wet out there. Certain Man was inconveniently off to work. Eldest Son and Youngest Son were inconveniently off to work. CMW trotted down the deck steps and bent downward to peer under the deck at the dryer vent that looked very, very far away.

One time, a long time ago, in a different place, a house wren had built a nest in her dryer vent, causing great disturbance to the soul of Certain Man's Wife. She had seen some straw hanging out of the dryer vent, and was curious as to why her dryer wasn't working properly. Being more impulsive than insightful, she had marched right out there and stuffed her hand up the dryer vent. Merciful days!!! A very startled House Wren had been calmly sitting on her nest, and she was not very tolerant of this particular invasion. The first thing CMW felt was something soft and warm, and then there was a great whirring of wings, and a little brown bird catapulted past her hand, and out into the clear blue yonder. CMW yanked her hand back with such force that it crashed against the sharp tin on the side of the dryer vent causing great damage to the wrist and hand. It was a lesson that was not easily forgotten, and CMW had no intention of tangling with another irate living thing of any type that would be inclined to make its abode in her dryer vent.

So she studied upon the dryer vent from her vantage point at the edge of the deck and noted that there were no foreign objects protruding from it. There was no straw, no tails, nothing. Neither was there a slightest breath of air moving the dryer lint that was around the edges of the opening. CMW concluded that there must be a blockage somewhere within the dryer vent before it reached the outside. Now this was a pickle. The dryer is on the inside wall of the laundry room. Certain Man had run the vent down through the floor, under the laundry room floor, under the entryway floor, and to the outside, probably a good 20 feet. There are a great many turns and twists, but

102

Certain Man had been sure that it was not kinked in any way, so he was pretty much convinced of its efficiency.

CMW went back into the house. She had to think. Inside, the dryer was turning on and on and on. It was nearly time for Thursday Morning Bible Study, and the first load of laundry was not even dry. She had to think of something.

"I wonder," she said to herself, "if I would get a really long broom handle and duct tape another long stick to that, if I could reach that opening, and maybe poke around in there." So she laid her hand upon her Stanley kitchen broom and prowled about, looking for something that she could attach to her hapless broom handle. This search appeared to be futile. So she went into the basement to see if there was anything there, and behold, upon the wall was a telescoping handle to an old cobweb cleaning tool called a "Webster" that was missing everything but the handle. She fell upon it with glee, brought it up into the light, and determined that it had a great range, and the locking device to make it stay in position still worked. She almost thought that she would not need to mess with that duct tape after all, as the handle, when extended, looked long enough to reach to the back of the deck (if she could position herself carefully enough).

Oh, dear. Now that was another problem. If she was going to poke around in that dryer vent, she was almost going to have to lie prostrate on the ground. Certain Man had been digging around the deck, working on a water line the month before. Everything was wet from the rain. There was a great deal of mud. There was the little, unmentioned (heretofore) problem concerning the barn cats that often came to sit under the deck, beneath the dryer vent, who do not have proper bathroom etiquette. There was a distinct smell of male cat. This did not encourage CMW's digestive processes. And perhaps there were spiders under there, too. This did not increase her confidence.

CMW contemplated her options. Maybe she should just call Certain Man to come home to take care of this whole thing. He would actually crawl under that deck and do whatever needed to be done. If that didn't settle it, he would crawl under the house and check the dryer vent pipe and fix that (fearless and strong, that man). But that would take several hours.

She decided to look for a big piece of plastic to lay on the ground. Suddenly, she remembered that there were big, tough, 55-gallon drum liners in the garage. They would be perfect! She pulled one off the roll, and then, armed with her Stick of Great Length and her drum liner, she traipsed out again. She carefully spread the drum liner over the wet grass, over the mud, and gingerly knelt down upon it. Of course, it started to slip about, but she managed to lie down on her tummy to hold it in place, and she stretched the Stick of Great Length across the expanse towards the opposite wall. She had a brief, grateful thought that she was probably not visible from the road because it really was no position for a lady to be in.

Ah, sweet victory, her Stick of Great Length actually reached the dryer vent. She shoved it into the vent. No bird appeared. No rat. No snake. No hibernating groundhog. She poked it around a bit, and was gratified to notice some wisps of dust escaping from the vent. She poked a bit more determinedly. More lint and dust came forth. This was getting good. She really shoved the stick in there and wriggled it about. Suddenly, there was this great "whooshing" sound and a long gray fuzzy thing came out. It was a foot long, and it was nearly the size of the dryer vent. It plopped on the ground under the dryer vent, and the air from the dryer began to pour out in great quantities.

CMW had never seen anything quite like it. She poked it with her Stick of Great Length (from a safe distance away). It did not move. She gingerly slid her Stick under it and lifted it up. It hung off both sides of her stick like some great, gray, dead thing.

What was this???

With great caution and extreme care she lifted it with her Stick of Great Length and brought it forth and laid it on the ground beside her drum liner. It didn't appear quite so dangerous up close, so she tried to cut it in half with her Stick. It sort of separated, but not entirely. There did not seem to be any flesh or bones to this thing, whatever it was, and it did not stink. CMW reckoned that made it safe, so she picked it up and carried it into the house. She dissected it over the trash can.

What a bummer! There was nothing exciting at all. Just lots and lots of dryer lint wrapped firmly around and through itself, and mixed with the very long hair of the women of Certain Man's household. It LOOKED impressive. It caused a great deal of trouble. But it really wasn't anything interesting at all. Oh, well. At least CMW was uninjured, and her dryer was purring away efficiently. She cleaned up the inside part of the dryer vent and put away the mess. She was quite thankful that she had not called Certain Man home from work to deal with this scary animal. She could almost hear him hoot the way it was. (That hooting is the sort of thing that develops resourcefulness in the female gender.)

And that is the news from Shady Acres, where Certain Man is quite pleased that this was handled without too much crisis, where Certain Man's Wife is having trouble keeping up with that dryer today, and where all the children concern themselves with laundry only when there are no clean clothes.

CMW Goes to Parent-Teacher Conferences

Now it come to pass in the fall of the year, that Greenwood Mennonite School scheduled parent teacher conferences to mark the end of the first marking period.

And Certain Man's Wife said to Certain Man, "We need to decide about when we can go to parent teacher conferences for Youngest Son."

And Certain Man had extenuating circumstances and important appointments that made it impossible for him to go when his wife was able to go. And CMW had mandatory medicine class that prevented her from going when Certain Man could go. Furthermore, CM needed to stay home and take care of Old Gertrude and Blind Linda whilst CMW was in class. So after much debate and even some impatient words, it was decided that CMW would go alone.

Now the day of the conferences was not at all the way CMW had planned. She had strange things happening all day, so much so that she completely forgot about the conferences until Youngest Son came downstairs from his lair twenty minutes before they were to begin and said in his usual vague sort of way, "Mom, don't you have PTA tonight?"

"No," said CMW in her usual, puzzled sort of way, "I don't have PTA tonight, I have medicine class."

"No," said Youngest Son, "Don't you have something at the school, like, really soon?"

"I do?"

"Yeah, you know something with the teachers or---"

"Oh, my, goodness! Oh, Lem! Parent teacher conferences in twenty minutes!!! What ever will I do? Who will watch my ladies? Oh, no. I completely forgot! I'll just have to call and tell them I can't make it."

"You can't do that, Mom. You need to go."

So CMW picked up the phone and made a few urgent calls, and behold, Hortencia, her beloved, non-English speaking neighbor was able to ski right over so that CMW could leave. CMW was convinced that it was the provision of the Lord.

On the way to school, she tried to prepare her heart. She genuinely loves the people who teach Youngest Son, and she wanted to encourage them to be confident in the decisions they make even if he didn't particularly agree. She wanted them to feel affirmed and supported and respected. She prayed that God would use the fifteen minutes that she spent with each one to His glory and for the good of them and Youngest Son. And she felt cheerful and thankful for the wonderful opportunities before her.

She pulled into the parking lot with two minutes to spare, and she parked so that she had the shortest route to her first appointment. And she made it to the room exactly on time.

Mr. Kevin Yoder teaches music, and directs the chorus and ensemble that Youngest Son participates in. Youngest Son does not always respond correctly to these disciplines, and CMW often feels that he does not really treasure the opportunity that he has, nor does he comprehend how music may someday be not only a ministry tool for him, but also a much needed diversion from the intensities of life. So she sat in the music room with Mr. Yoder and the conversation was interesting and very agreeable. She likes Mr. Yoder and has the added blessing of being related to him in a distant sort of way. He and his brother, Lamar, have both had impact on Youngest Son's life in ways that have been for good. Kevin, with music and Lamar, as his basketball coach. Youngest Son respects both of them, and CMW has been thankful for them and their investments in Youngest Son's life and spiritual journey.

At the end of the 15 minute conference, Mr. Yoder was leaving his classroom to meet his wife so that they could attend their parent teacher conferences. Mr. Yoder walked with CMW down the hall to where she was to have her next conference. When they were nearly at the door, he put a gentle arm around her shoulder and gave her a few pats.

"By the way," he said with a reassuring grin, "You've been calling me Lamar all night, but I'm Kevin."

CMW was mortified to the nth degree. Of course he was KEVIN. She knew that. And though she does not particularly try to remember the names of strangers, she makes a point of remembering and using people's names who are participant in her life. She shuddered to think how many times she had used his name amiss that night.

"Oh, Kevin. I am so sorry. Of course you are Kevin -- " Her words stumbled about and she floundered rather helplessly (so helplessly that she doesn't really remember what she did say...)

He was clearly amused at her discomfiture. "It's alright," he said. "Don't worry about it."

"I really am sorry. Do you think I could be forgiven?"

His smile only deepened. "You already are. Don't worry about it." And he went on about his business, and CMW slithered, red-faced, into her next conference.

This conference was with a young woman teacher. CMW likes her very much, and she had chosen this teacher to visit because she was suspecting that Youngest Son may have been giving her a hard time sometimes. So CMW told her that if there was ever a need for correction or discipline, she should be confident of support from Certain Man and herself. She would have enjoyed this conference a whole lot more if she hadn't been experiencing such residual shame from her blooper just preceding it. She was honestly feeling that probably the whole world didn't particularly care if she was supportive or not, seeings how she was coming down with Alzheimer's at such an early age, and it wouldn't matter too much longer what she thought . . .

But she finished her conference with Mrs. Schrock and got directions to the last appointment of the afternoon. This appointment was the one that Youngest Son was particularly interested in her keeping. The teacher, whom he affectionately calls "Mr. Hoss," is young and single and good-looking and teaches his favorite class this year, "psychology." CMW has seen him on occasion but did not remember ever actually meeting him. Based on Youngest Son's appreciation for him, and the many recounts she has gotten from class, she felt like this conference would perhaps help to smooth over the rough edges of her soul and give her some cause to rejoice over her offspring. No real concerns over his class behavior or his giving the teacher a hard time were on her mind.

So she went into the classroom, introduced herself and the conference was everything she had hoped for. She felt like there was honest evaluation of Youngest Son's strengths and weaknesses, affirmation for his direction, and validation of her insights as a parent. She was impressed with Mr. Hoss, and she enjoyed the input and the exchange very much. But time was passing, and it was almost time for this final conference to be over. She was making some important, last observation while reaching down to pick up her purse from the floor beside her when everything fell apart. (Again!)

As she lowered her gaze to discover just where the purse handle had fallen, her eye was waylaid by the sight of the middle button on her blouse standing quite agape from its buttonhole. Oh, if only there could have been a loud diversion to provide her a way of escape. Time seemed to stand still as her mind assimilated her predicament. Amazingly, it seemed like there was a great many things processed in a split second.

("My most inopportune button is standing quite ajar," she thought. "If I see it, he sees it. I know it is open, he certainly knows it is open, so I might just as well button it up and be calm about it...")

What she actually said, very quietly, pretty much to herself was, "Mercy!" and she buttoned it up very quietly and went back to the sentence she was already in before the rude interruption. Except that she could hardly remember what it was that she had been saying, and she could hardly think to end the conference in a suitable fashion.

Somehow, eventually she was on her way home, and she glowered into the early evening darkness as she maneuvered the minivan towards Milford. She just could not believe how wrong everything had turned out when she was so well intentioned and cheerful when she went. She went over and over the events of the evening, trying to somehow make herself look just a little bit better, until suddenly, it hit her funny bone, and she laughed out loud in the stillness of the car.

"Just one more thing in the journey of life," she thought ruefully to herself. "And it really is all Lem's fault. I don't think I am ever going to another parent teacher conference as long as I live!!!"

And that is the news from Shady Acres, where Certain Man was again, unnecessarily amused, CMW is recovering, she thinks, and all the children are somewhat sympathetic in spite of their glee.

CM and a Very Snowy Evening

Now it came to pass at the end of January, that Certain Man was feeling quite restive concerning the weather of much snowfall and great cold that had come upon Delaware. And the state of his mind was such that he was unable to relax all the day of Saturday, so much so that Eldest Son commented, "He just never stops, does he, Mom? I can't see why he can't relax a little. Does he have to work ALL THE TIME?"

Of course, Certain Man's Wife had to use this opportunity to point out that Eldest Son and his siblings had benefitted their entire lives from their father's strong work ethic. (It could be mentioned that CMW was wondering just what was causing so much activity on a Saturday morning when he could have slept in. She finally chalked it up to the fact that the snow and ice made it more difficult to get ordinary chores done and that CM was trying to stay ahead of things.)

CMW did not spend a whole lot of time thinking about it as she was quite indisposed with a root canal that had gone very wrong and all the ensuing difficulties. So she just motored about her house under the influence of Tylenol 3 and Darvocet and penicillin and even some Motrin when the stronger stuff wore off. It was a rather fuzzy morning, but she was brought to straight reality when friends from Pennsylvania stopped by in the afternoon with their three children.

Sam and Belinda have been friends for a number of years and the thing that is sometimes disconcerting is that they are completely unpredictable when it comes to things like "How long will they be able to stay?" or "Have they made specific plans for supper?" or "Will they perhaps even need somewhere to sleep tonight?" Some of these questions hinge on other questions such as "Is their highly unpredictable extended family going to be there when they go there after they leave here?" or "If they *are* there, did they prepare supper for them?" or even "If they *are* there, and there *is* supper, will there be a big fight in the duration of their stay there which will cause them to need supper/place to regroup/sleep, etc., in spite of previous plans?" These thoughts gave CMW some concern as the afternoon progressed.

Certain Man had ceased from his labors to spend time talking to Sam, who has a history in plumbing, but is currently the manager of an egg producing farm in Pennsylvania. And they spoke intensely and long about the market and managing strategies and then progressed on to church issues. As the afternoon wore on, CMW realized that she had better plan some supper, so she began a shrimp chowder for which she happened to have all the ingredients. She also prevailed upon Youngest Daughter and Friend Lupé make some brownies from a box. Belinda came into the kitchen to lean against the counter and talk while CMW chopped and chopped, and the time spent was pleasant indeed.

And when everything was almost ready to serve, the decision was announced that they needed to go on to Sam's brother, who was expecting them, after all, yea, there was a sister in law who was a "little miffed," so they needed to "Hurry!" And "Hurry!" they did and made their immediate departure.

Certain Man decided that he needed to make a random check on his own chicken house and supper was set back on the stove to wait. Eldest Son and Youngest Son had things to do away from home and they had gone forth upon the face of the earth to pursue such things as friendships and entertainment suitable for a Saturday night. Middle Daughter was working, and Youngest Daughter was quite worn out from all the things that she had been doing with the three children of Sam and Belinda. CMW decided to get things finished up for the coming Sunday.

Then Certain Man returned to the house with the aggravating news that he was, again, OUT OF FEED in House Three of the chicken houses. There is nothing that troubles him under ordinary circumstances quite like this does, but when it happens on a Saturday, it is a dire strait to be in. He began calling his serviceman immediately. There was no answer. He tried the cell phone of his serviceman. No answer. He tried the feed mill. No answer. His aggravation turned into frustration. A delivery man had made a mistake somewhere, because there was plenty of feed in House One. There was "enough" in house Two. But House Three was "empty and banging." He fretted about for a while, waiting for a return call, but the phone was strangely silent and still.

It was very cold and slippery outside. He had an old rotator cuff injury to his right shoulder that had been scheduled for surgery in a month. The weather, compounded with the extra hard work was making it a "pain of importance." He had a very sore spot on his left ring finger that his family doctor had said was a "callus, complicated by dermatitis," the Public Health nurses (with whom he worked) thought was a "complicated wart" and the doctor who had scheduled rotator cuff surgery had looked at, pronounced it some kind of "Hemangioma" and silver nitrated it into a terrible mess, only to have it reappear, ugly and red and perfectly revolting. Certain Man did not wish to shovel feed from one house to the other with a sore right shoulder and a left hand so injured, especially with the cold and the slippery condition of the ground.

There were some great grumblings about servicemen, chicken companies, feed mills and truck drivers who worked for them. But a second attempt to reach all three failed, so, sighing deeply, he pulled on his insulated coveralls and departed for the chicken house to equalize some feed. There were offers to help from Youngest Daughter and Certain Man's Wife, but the impatient reply involved such things as it being a "one man job" and that it was going to take more time than anything else and that he needed to go to town to buy a scoop shovel before he did anything and that he didn't feel like buying two scoop shovels at $37.50 a piece for what was really a one-man job.

And so CMW busied herself around the kitchen, cleaned up the laundry room, scrubbed floors in preparation for the Sunday that was coming, and the hours slipped by. There was no return call from anyone. After some time, Beloved Son-in-Law and Eldest Daughter stopped by to play a game with Youngest Daughter. And CMW thought that she should take this time to check on Certain Man. It had seemed a long time since she had heard anything from him, and she began to be concerned that she might find him in some sort of dire circumstances. After all, he was not in the prime of life anymore. So she considered how she might best reach Chicken House Three, it being in the farthest position from the farmhouse. And being quite anxious about the state of slippery places and feeling woozy from all the pain medication, she decided to drive the family minivan to the chicken house to see what was going on.

So forthwith, she got into her van and cautiously maneuvered it down the lane that goes to the chicken houses, around and down past the front of House One, through the frozen puddles at the end of the house, and past the end of House Two, and on to where she could see Certain Man's tractor parked half in and half out of the big doors of House Three. The ground was very treacherous, but she slid out of the van, along the front side of House Three and slithered through a space that was not intended for her dress size into the warm, moist, aromatic inside of the chicken house. There was no scoop shovel in sight.

The mechanical advantage of a scoop shovel in this particular situation had come under the discerning eye of CM and had been found wanting. So, Certain Man had a ten gallon bucket that he was raking feed into and transporting it to the hoppers at the end of each feed line. He would fill first one and then the other, then the first one, and then the second one again. There were spaces of time in between as he waited for the auger to catch up, and then he would be back with his bucket to start all over again. He was not grumbling, but he was not very sociable. His shoulder was hurting badly, and he was tired. It looked like an interminable job. There were two feed lines that were over four hundred feet each, with a feed pan every two and a half feet or so, and the whole thing needed to be filled. Every now and then, he had to back the tractor up and go over to House One and refill his big, front loader with feed from there and return to House Three, where he repeated the process.

CMW felt very sorry for him, and stood helplessly by for a while, but then decided to go back to the house. She slipped and slid through the treacherous landscape, back to the minivan and evaluated whether she should back out the lane, or if she should turn around so that she could see where the van was going. The temperature had been below freezing for a number of days, and the ground was quite solidly frozen, so she decided to turn the van around in the area between the two chicken houses. Everything went well until she started to pull the van forward after her first back-up. Uh-oh. This was not good. She put the van back into reverse and went a little farther backward, then tried to go forward again. There was the ominous sound of tires turning without any progress.

There have been many times in similar circumstances where she was able to overcome such difficulties, but that would have been too easy on this particular night. So before she got in too deeply, she decided to check with her husband. So she clambered back out of the van, and over the slippery ground she floundered to the chicken house.

"Sweetheart, do I have 4-wheel drive on this mini-van?"

"No. WHY?"

"Because, I think. . . I'm stuck."

He did not shout. He did not sigh. He did not strike her or the minivan. He patiently came to see what had happened. When he saw the poor minivan, he still did not show any signs of anger, though he must have been shaking his head at her stupidity. These particular chicken houses are equipped with tunnel ventilation. Day and night, huge fans run to regulate ventilation and temperature. These fans are grouped together at the end of the house. They blow onto the ground, warming it so that it is deceptively soft and squishy. This area happened to be right where she had tried to turn around. The minivan sat in the water that was almost up to the middle of the hubcap on the one side, and ice floated around about it forlornly.

Certain Man assessed the situation and then said, "Get in and do what I tell you to do when I tell you to do it."

CMW meekly did as she was told. Certain Man gave instructions very specifically, and she followed them without arguing. He went from the front of the van to the back of the van, exerting his mighty strength. It was obvious progress was being made.

He said, "One more time ought to do it!" and went back and forth one more time. On the last time, he gave the van a mighty push, while she obediently gunned the motor forward. Ah, sweet victory at last. The van moved out of the water and mire and onto solid ground.

CMW was mightily relieved. She made sure the van was truly back on the driveway, and then she got out to thank Certain Man for all his kindnesses to her. He was walking back to the chicken house in a hurried sort of way.

"Sweetheart, wait—" She tried to catch up to him. "Thank you for helping me. I really do appreciate it." He did not stop walking. Then she noticed that there were droplets of water flying off the legs of his coveralls with every step he took.

"What happened, Daniel? Did I get you all wet while I was trying to get out?"

"Nope."

"Daniel, you are all wet."

"I know."

"What happened? You're soaking!"

"I slipped and fell into the mud puddle while I was pushing the van. That's all."

"Sweetheart, the wind chill factor is below zero. You can't stay out here like this."

"Watch me."

"You'll catch your death of cold. You need to come in and change and get dry clothes on."

He gave her a look that made the winter darkness even darker.

"I'm not coming in to change anything. I need to finish out here and then I will come in and change. And no sooner." And Certain Man kept on walking. Certain Man's Wife had seen a set like that to his broad shoulders before, and knew it was useless to argue. So she went helplessly back to her van, and went meekly back to the house.

Inside, she recounted all the misadventures to Eldest Daughter and Beloved Son-in-Law. BSIL said cheerfully, "I'll go out there and help him."

"He doesn't want any help," said CMW. "He is quite determined about that."

"Well, I can still go out there and be with him," said BSIL. "Maybe there is something I can do." He got bundled up and went out into the night. After a worrisome, lengthy absence, he returned saying that the job was finished, and that Certain Man was making some last minute checks to the chicken house and would be in shortly.

And sure enough, he soon came in. The bottom foot of his coveralls was frozen stiff, and he looked as cold as all get out, but he was surprisingly rather cheerful and smiling. He had conquered. His chickens had been fed. He was still the master of his fate. No one had made him change before he was ready. Now, he could trade his wet and smelly clothes for a hot shower, warm gray lounging pajamas and a cup of hot tea and it would be his idea. He was clearly pleased with himself and satisfied with his accomplishment.

And that is the news from Shady Acres where Certain Man has not gotten so much as a sniffle, where Certain Man's Wife is aware again that there are things about Certain Man that are beyond explanation, and where all the children truly have no concept of what an incredible man their Daddy is.

CMW and the Great Shoe Mix Up

It was the year of our Lord, 1982, and the summer was unbearably hot. Behold Certain Man's Wife was very great with child. And the encumberments of pregnancy made it very hard to pick her green beans, tend to her family and do the many things that young mothers need to do. But the days were happy days, and Certain Man and Eldest Daughter (who was five) and Middle Daughter (who was two – and the youngest daughter at that time) and CMW were somewhat poor but very content with their lives.

One of the funnest treats in all the world was going down to the Baskin & Robbins Ice Cream shop for an evening treat. 33 flavors of ice cream were pretty much the extent of excitement to those long hot days, and though it didn't happen very often, yet it was the one thing that seemed to make the hot summer go faster.

One night, shortly before the baby was due, Certain Man proposed a late evening excursion to the ice cream shop. There were out of state guests visiting, and they had been helping CMW with picking and canning the green beans. There was not a single dissenting vote. CMW had been padding around in garden shoes and everyday dress, so she slipped into a flowery kind of frock and traded her shoes of the garden variety for a pair of dressier pumps and they were soon on their way.

Now the Baskin & Robbins Ice Cream Parlor was a popular Mennonite hang out, and even though it was in the big bad city of Columbus, Ohio, it was not unusual to see people of "like precious faith" in the ice cream shop. On this particular evening, there was a large group of people there who were employees of Sunnyhaven, a Beachy-Amish establishment for the mentally handicapped. Certain Man's Wife was in good humor and she spoke with numbers of them. They were not especially friendly, and she wondered at their reserve, but she contented herself with speaking to the babies in their strollers and with minding her own children and ice cream and husband, and so the minutes flew by.

When it was time to go home, she noted that there was enough time to stop at the store before they went home. There were a few things that she wanted to pick up, so they proceeded to the local Harts Department store,

115

and she walked around there and procured the things that were deemed necessary.

Riding home in the big old blue van, she thought about the fact that she was excessively tired and was glad that the day was coming to an end. Behold, her feet seemed to hurt an inordinate amount, and the thought the La-Z-Boy was quite inviting. Probably, if she could only view those ankles, she would find them puffy and unsightly, what with the hot weather and the advanced pregnancy. And so, they came home to the little house on the hill.

It did not take her long to find the desired spot and she collapsed gratefully in its old, familiar comforts.

"Hey, Christy!" She called to Eldest Daughter as she pulled the lever to raise the footrest. "Would you please come and rub my fee--Oh, my goodness! Daniel! Look at my shoes!"

It really was unbelievable. In her haste to get something on her feet, she had slipped into the shoes that were right inside her closet, and had gotten one shoe of two different pairs. Now it would have been different if they had been similar, but this was not the case at all. Except that they were both black. All similarities ended there. One was shiny patent leather, the other was matte glove leather. One had a big shiny buckle as some shoes were liable to have in the early 80's, the other was a plain pump. And the worst thing of all was that one had a two inch stack heel, and the other had but a plain heel of probably 3/4" at the most.

No wonder the employees of Sunnyhaven were reserved. They were probably anxious to negate any suspicion of supposed connection.

No wonder the poor feet hurt so terribly, either. They had a full time job compensating for the unobservant brain that was so woefully inadequate. The thing that kept going around and around in CMW's mind was that she had never noticed the difference. That bothered her more than the obvious mistake.

Certain Man was very wise. He chose to not trifle himself with any word of reproach or ridicule. He did not even act like he was embarrassed with his clumsy, mismatched spouse. In fact, he acted like it was the most logical thing in the world for a pregnant lady who couldn't see her feet to walk about with mismatched shoes. Like I said, he was very wise.

And that is a perfectly true old tale from another place and another time in the lives of the folks that now live at Shady Acres.

CMW Chases the Bull

Now it came to pass on the very first day of September, in the year of our Lord, 2004, that Certain Man's wife was complacently enjoying a busy morning of preparing for her annual state inspection. On impulse, that very morning, she had hired a friend, Alma, to help clean the kitchen cabinets, while CMW was working at cleaning the bedroom that was to be inspected. It was a beautiful morning. There was a good breeze, the sky was blue, and all was well.

CMW had other reasons to rejoice.

For several weeks, one of the male bovines that Certain Man kept for meat had been showing signs of aggression, indeed, had charged Certain Man on a number of occasions, with great bellows and kicking up of the dirt. Now this Meany Pest of a bull was only 18 months old. Certain Man had not had him neutered because he had never had a problem with other bulls when he hadn't, and he liked it that an un-neutered bull would convert better to meat. Since he only keeps his meat animals for two years, it had never been a problem.

Until now.

This turn of events had been enough disconcerting to Certain Man that he had called the Honorable Allen Beachy and had him come and "band" the two young calves that he was raising for the spring of 2006. That done, he also called the butcher shop and arranged for them to come pick up Meany Pest. He hoped that they would come immediately. With the traffic of people and children through the property of Certain Man, he didn't want to take a risk. Unfortunately, slaughter time was a few weeks out, so close watch had been kept until this very morning when Tommy Eliason had come with his cattle trailer and hauled him off. CMW drew a great sigh of relief that was matched by her husband.

Now, at the same time that CM had procured Meany Pest, he had gotten another male calf which grew up alongside of MP. What Meany Pest had in aggression, Second Fellow, though also un-neutered, made up for in friendliness and complacency. When Tommy Eliason came to pick up MP, Second Fellow wanted to go, too, and tried to stick his head into the truck.

117

Certain Man and Tommy enjoyed a chuckle at the friendly fellow's expense. They had to chase him away.

When Certain Man came in from sending Meany Pest off, he said to CMW, "Hon, I locked the other three in the front pasture. Second Fellow is pretty upset, and I don't want him getting out."

Certain Man has always maintained fences in proper order, and it is a rare day when any of his animals get out. He learned the hard way that it is no fun to have creatures running around at night on busy roads. So he has a high tensile fence that has electric on the inside of it, nearly all the way around his pasture. He has a four foot high board fence that runs for a short distance between buildings, and he keeps all his fences in good repair. He has a large back pasture, well fenced, where he allows the animals to run around and graze, but it is behind the chicken houses, and out of deference to CMW, who cannot see back there from the house, he decided to confine them on the smaller, front pasture, where they could get into the barn if they wanted to.

The morning was so pleasant that the windows were open in the house, and all morning, Second Fellow was protesting loudly. Around eleven o'clock, he sounded louder and nearer, and Youngest Daughter of CM and CMW went to look what was going on.

"Oh, my goodness, MOM, there is a bull out. A BIG Bull. Oh, my, it is one of the big ones, Mom!!!"

Certain Man's Wife went out the back door to the deck, and sure enough, there was Second Fellow, prancing across the yard. Behold, her heart made a very fast trip to her shoes. He looked so determined and "bullish." She looked around for ammunition, and laid her hands upon a Stanley broom that was conveniently leaning against the deck. She hollered for Youngest Daughter to call her father, and took out across the yard as fast as her 50 year old body would allow her. In the past, getting animals back into their pens has been challenging but not impossible, and she had a great deal of optimism as to how quickly she would conquer again. Besides, this was good natured "Second Fellow" she was dealing with here.

But something had happened to Second Fellow. He had caught wind of a heifer in heat who belonged to a neighbor. He was determined to seek her out. By this time, Friend Alma had seen the predicament, and had come to join the fray. CMW sent Youngest Daughter out to the cow pen to open the gate. Youngest Daughter thoughtfully locked the two younger (now) steers in the barn, and opened the large gate wide to the front pasture. Friend Alma's young son stood on the deck and yelled.

Second Fellow saw two determined humans coming across the yard, and was suddenly urged to run in the direction of the road. He lowered his head and charged blindly toward the poorly armed females who were supposed to be directing him in the way that he should go. Whoomp! Went the broom, scarcely making contact, but diverting him slightly. Friend Alma and CMW ran to and fro, trying to herd obstinate Second Fellow towards the barn. Every time they achieved a few yards, down would go the head, and with a bellow, back the bull would charge. CMW noticed that he was not kicking up any dirt with his bellow, but it did not comfort her heart very much. It occurred to her that there were many guardian angels standing between the bull and the two inadequately armed females, for time and time again, he would head for them, only to turn aside in the nick of time. Unfortunately, it was pretty obvious who was winning the battle of the wills despite angelic protection.

After perhaps five or six time of attempting to head him off at the road, kindly neighbor, Eddie, noticed that there was considerable difficulty going on in the yard across the road. He and neighbor Steve left their task of putting siding on the house and came to help. One of them had a stick, and CMW had her faithful Stanley broom, but otherwise the crew was unarmed.

Said CMW, "I surely do wish Daniel would get here!"

Said Kindly Neighbor Eddie, "What would he do? Does he have a secret?"

"Not that I know of," said CMW heatedly, "but it would be HIS problem!"

About then, Kindly Neighbor Eddie's wife, Joan, appeared to lend her strong arm, and a shiny red convertible also stopped. Friend Bethany had seen the dilemma as she passed by and decided to help, too. CMW thought ruefully that RED was not especially the color that she had in mind for the present situation, but there was no doubt that help was needed, so she welcomed the extra body. By now there were fully seven people in hot pursuit of seemingly demented bull.

They managed to chase Second Fellow up the chicken house lane for a short distance, when he suddenly caught on to the idea that it was not the right direction. He turned and lowered his horns and headed back out the drive. Sticks and brooms and bodies had no effect upon him whatsoever, and the posse scattered before him in grave disarray. He headed out towards the road again, and then turned and trotted along the edge of the fenced woods where he was sure that his intended was hiding. He bellowed and stopped and sniffed and bellowed and trotted.

Of course, all the traffic on the busy road beside CM's farm were beginning to take note, and cars were going by slowly while gawking at the motley crew, and some were pulling off to see if there was something they could do. Chicken trucks and work vans, jalopies and minivans, town cars and meter readers got all jammed up on the road. CMW's face was as red as a turkey gobbler's, and not just from exertion. WHY DIDN'T CERTAIN MAN COME HOME???

Then the owner of the heifer, Neighbor Willey, came forth from his house down the road. He had probably heard rather than seen the hubbub, guessed what the problem was, and secured offending female far from the site of the battle. He picked up a sturdy stick and came to help, too. With his approach, Second Fellow decided to turn around and head back up the fence line towards Shady Acres. With great difficulty and many yells and wallops with the weapons, the Bull was directed towards the back pasture.

Certain Man had been called again, and he informed frantic Youngest Daughter that he was heading for home (in earnest with his state truck and his flashers going). CMW was pretty sure that they would be getting the bull in right before he got there, and that is exactly what happened. Just before he sped in the lane, Neighbors Eddie and Steve managed to drive him into the back pasture and hook up the electric fence.

Things started to calm down a little then. CMW was panting and tired, and the neighbors were saying friendly things about how "That's what neighbors are for..." and CM was going back to bring Second Fellow to the front pasture and secure him there. CMW was heading out towards the barn when she saw Second Fellow come around the edge of the barn at a gallop. At this inopportune time, she remembered that she did not know how he had escaped in the first place. It suddenly occurred to her that the two younger calves had been inside the fence the entire time he was out. It didn't make sense.

A great feeling of dread came over her as she saw him make a straight beeline for the four foot wooden fence. Was there a break in it somewhere? She watched in disbelief as Second Fellow trotted up to the fence and in one smooth motion was OVER it! If it hadn't been so terrible, it would have been beautiful. A perfect Olympic jump.

Believe me, there was some shrieking going on then! Certain Man jumped in his truck and headed out the chicken house lane, trying to head him off. If it had been his own pick up instead of his work truck, he said that he would have run into the critter, but since he needed to be careful with the state's property, he was unable to stop him. Once again, out on the road, traffic stopped, and neighbors running and helping. CMW was inclined to go inside and pretend that she wasn't home, but she ran and herded and walloped with her faithful Stanley broom until the entire group had successfully herded him to the entrance to the pasture. Certain Man had gotten out his blacksnake whip and was making good use of it.

Just before going through the gate, Second Fellow made a mighty dash for freedom. Certain Man snapped him soundly with the blacksnake whip, but lost his footing and fell into a very green, very stinky body of water that was left over from the latest rain. His efforts to divert the bull were effective, though, and while he picked himself out of the muck, the neighbors closed in and Second Fellow went back into the pasture.

CMW and Friend Alma and Neighbor Willey, and Neighbor Eddie and his Good Wife Joan, took up positions along the board fence. Good Wife Joan held the black snake whip, CM held the faithful Stanley broom and the guys stood there and looked MENACING. Youngest Daughter went into barn and called cheerfully to Second Fellow with promises of FEED. Certain Man gave her instructions from the pasture. Second Fellow was drawn by the cheery voice. He was tired from so much running. He ambled over and looked in the door. He went in a few feet. She continued to coax and call him from behind the feed bunker. Certain Man sidled over, out of sight, while she wove her deceptive web. Finally, Second Fellow was far enough in to shut the metal gate behind him. Oh, NO! It was hooked to the wall. Second Fellow acted like he was going to go out again. Youngest daughter took advantage of the situation to scramble into the pen and unhook the gate so it could swing free, then went back to her wheedling, cajoling call. Again, the pull was strong, and Second Fellow turned back towards the feed bunk.

Certain Man, muddy and stinky looked at the great mud hole between him and the gate and did not waver a single moment. Good work shoes and all, he plowed through the mud that was deeper than his shoes and grabbed the gate. Second Fellow made one final dash for freedom, but CM hollered mightily. When Second Fellow paused, CM clanged the gate shut, and this time the offending animal was fully trapped. Metal bars and chains and cement would need to be moved for him to escape this time.

"Whew!" said everyone.

"That was fun," said Good Wife Joan. "Quite a diversion from a boring afternoon."

Neighbor Eddie and Neighbor Willey did not say much. CMW noticed that they were looking positively cheerful, though.

"I'm glad I was here!" said Friend Alma. "I've had lots of experience chasing animals when I was a girl!"

"You aren't half as glad as I am," said CMW. "What would I have ever done without help?"

"That's what neighbors are for..." said Good Wife Joan.

"Well," said CMW, "I am quite certain of one thing. There is going to be a steak dinner one of these days and everyone who helped is going to be invited!"

That was well received, and the neighbors went back to their jobs and CMW went back into the house to cool off and rest her weary bones. CM, after making double sure of everything in the barn, came back into the house to change his clothes and shoes and to go back to work. He would have to call this time at home his lunch hour for the day, and CMW felt sorry for him. But the bull was in, he was cleaned up, and he could get into his air conditioned truck and leave. That didn't sound like too bad a deal to CMW. She needed to keep on getting ready for the coming inspections. But first, she needed to write a story.

So, that is the news from Shady Acres, where Certain Man is working on a new electric fence that will compliment a particular board fence, Certain Man's Wife's face still feels hot and her knees feel weak, and Youngest Daughter is the only one of the children who was witness to the events of this momentous day.

CMW goes to Graduation

Now it came to pass that Certain Man and Certain Man's Wife have had a year filled with many things to challenge their brains and to fill their hearts and to demand their emotions. And the last few weeks have been even more confusing as they have dealt with the illness of both of CMW parents, including rather troubling news concerning CMW's Daddy, the highly esteemed Mark Yoder, Sr.

Now it also came to pass that the siblings of CMW had discussed treatment plans, options and remote possibilities at great length and it was deemed important to come together at the parental home to lay out the options before Our Daddy and the Mother so they could think sober thoughts and make right decisions. All of this happened upon the day that was Tuesday, the 24th of May in the year of our Lord, 2005.

And this particular day also corresponded with the day that was the graduation from high school for Joe Slaubaugh, one of the 27 grandchildren of CMW's Daddy and Mama. In great travail did his family prepare for this momentous occasion as the house and lawn were carefully manicured and food planned for. Friends and Aunties wanted to help, and cakes were baked and vegetables made ready and lemonade in great abundance was planned for.

So the day was filled to the brim with many things for CMW, not the least of which was RAIN and an ailing Youngest Son and unexpected company and sewing for Eldest Daughter and committee work for a weekend Mission's Retreat and plans for the imminent departure of Certain Man with his work crew of young people to Missouri. In late afternoon, when there was still one cake to ice and nine gallons of lemonade to make, the phone rang and it was Certain Man. He needed someone to come and pick him up to take him to the repair shop so he could get his trusty pickup which had just gotten a new radiator. So CMW put aside her tasks at hand and flew forth with great cheerfulness to assist him, for it would give her a few minutes with the person she loves the most. She retrieved him from the State parking lot, and delivered him safely to the repair shop and was hurrying home when a thought struck her out of the blue like a lightning bolt.

"Today is Valencia's art show!!!" Oh, dear. Valencia is the second daughter of CMW's friend Jodi. Jodi has five daughters, and no husband (the girls' daddy died in prison a year ago by his own hand). Jodi tries hard to keep things together, but there is never enough money or emotional resources to go around. Sometimes the family will come to church, but often that is the day for Jodi to catch up after a week of working. Joanne is fiercely proud, independent to a fault sometimes, but the church has often helped her out with car repairs, insurance, phone bills and rent.

The children are needy, to say the least. But Valencia, who is affectionately called "Vinny" by people who love her, is smart and gifted and determined to make something of herself. She is 14, and she found an artist mentor who has provided her with art lessons, encourages her to think big, and arranged for this "one-man" art show at the Harrington Library last week. Valencia has been the student prayer partner of CMW for several of the past few years, and she is dear to her heart. When the pretty invitation had come several weeks ago, she had determined that nothing would stop her from attending this art show. But the busyness of the day had obliterated it from her memory, and now it was almost five o'clock. The show was from 4:30-6:30. Graduation started at 7:00. She calculated her options. She HAD to go to the art show.

So she telephoned home and said, "I just remembered Valencia's art show, and I really need to go. How can we organize things there so I can run over for a few minutes?"

And Middle Daughter, who was home and available, said, "Well, Mom, if you could finish making this frosting and frost this cake, I could take care of things here while you go."

The cake was a two layer chocolate that takes a bit more doing than usual, so that sounded like a reasonable request to CMW. She had started the frosting before leaving to pick up Certain Man, so she hurriedly finished that chore and grabbed the dress she was planning to wear for graduation. It was one of those dresses that always make you feel dressed up. It was black with red flowers on it in a tasteful sort of way, and had a black linen-type jacket that had red flowers embroidered on the lapel. The dress was a straight sort of thing that is popular these days with a string tie in back. So CMW took it from the hanger where Middle Daughter had hung it after she did the ironing, pulled it over her head, threw on the jacket and collected Youngest Daughter (who is Valencia's age and wanted to go, too) and flew out the door.

The art show was very nice. There were numerous people milling about, and the art, though the work of an immature artist, was still fascinating and tastefully presented. Youngest Daughter and CMW had something from the punch bowl, shared a cookie, made a small purchase, talked to Valencia and her mother and her mentor friend. They were there about 15 minutes or so, and then headed back home. It was almost six o'clock.

On the way home, CMW fished out her trusty cell phone again, and called Middle Daughter. "Deborie-girl, I need you to feed Gertrude and Linda for me. When I get home, we need to make the lemonade and get out of there if we are going to make it to Grad in time. Daddy is going to be home tonight getting ready for chickens, so Gert and Linda can stay home, but we need to get them fed and ready for bed before we leave."

So, Middle Daughter got supper on for Old Gertrude and Blind Linda and when CMW came in the door, they were happily eating. And CMW marshaled the troops and asked for help to make the lemonade, and all hands appeared in willing array. Youngest Son trimmed and quartered 27 big lemons, and dumped them, three at a time, into the blender. CMW put in the water, ran the blender, and poured the mixture through the strainer. Youngest daughter measured the sugar and sweetener into the ten gallon cooler. Middle Daughter ran errands, fetched the ice and other needed things, watched over the supper processes, gave meds, made coffee, etc. And in 15 minutes, nine gallons of lemonade was done. There were some perfunctory swipes to the counter, and the cakes and the lemonade were loaded in the back of the minivan, and it was off to Grad. On time, even. CMW was very impressed with her family.

When she got to Grad, she noticed that Eldest Daughter was sitting towards the back of the auditorium in one of the pretty frocks that had been sewed that day and the seat beside her was empty. So she slipped into the seat and propped her aching feet on the chair ahead of her. It felt wonderful to sit down. And the day had been rewarding, even though it had been so busy.

There was music and praying and welcomes and more music. The program was a Homeschool Graduation, and the involvement of the families and community was especially heartening. The six graduates had chosen Robert (CMW's family claims him as their own and call him "Bobby") Aycoth as the speaker. CMW was enjoying his address very much, and was feeling relaxed and cheerful. She looked down at her skirt as she sat there on the hard folding chair and smoothed it in that mindless motion that women everywhere use.

Suddenly something caught her attention. She smoothed it again. This was puzzling. She didn't remember that this skirt looked like this. Why was there half of a big, red flower right there in the middle of the skirt? She rubbed her fingers over the middle of the skirt, and behold, there was a seam down the middle of her skirt. Surreptitiously, she followed the seam up the middle of that straight dress all the way to the neckline. Oh, no, there, right in the middle of her neckline on the inside was a tag the size of Sussex County. That straight dress was on backwards with the sting tie belt around the front of the dress which was in the back.

CMW nudged Eldest Daughter with her elbow. "Hey, Chris!"

125

"WHAT?" whispered Eldest Daughter in her characteristic fierce whisper.

"Look!" CMW turned her neckline down just far enough for Eldest Daughter to catch a glimpse of the tag.

"What in the world??? Mama, you have your dress on BACKWARDS!!!"

Grown women getting the giggles in the back row at a graduation ceremony may not be particularly appropriate, but it couldn't be helped. After Bobby had finished his encouraging talk, CMW took the chance to slip out to the ladies room and change things around so that the front faced forward and the string belt tied around the back of the dress which was, properly, of course, in back. She thought dismally about parading around at the art show among some of the "elite" of Harrington, wondered if anyone had noticed, and decided that couldn't be helped, either. This was one of those disasters that seem to come naturally into CMW's world. She isn't calling it an "act of God" but she is quite aware that He intends to keep her humble.

And that is the news from Shady Acres, where Certain Man is on his way to Missouri with a van load of volunteers to help with a work project, and Certain Man's Wife is hoping for a less eventful week.

CMW goes to Niece Holly's Party

Now it came to pass that on this day, Friday, that Certain Man's Wife was possessed of the equanimity that comes of a day that had no outside demands upon it except that she needed to make 10 gallons of lemonade for the grad party of Niece Holly and attend said event. So she baked bread and finished the laundry and talked to her sons and inspected Eldest Son's hair length to determine if he had, in fact gotten it trimmed or was merely trying to tease her, and talked on the phone, and visited with Friend Lynn Lee over an egg salad sandwich at lunch.

Certain Man was still gone with his work crew to Missouri. Though CMW missed him, the week had flown by much faster than she had anticipated. As the afternoon passed, the rain that had kept the Eldest Son and Youngest Son home from work got heavier, and the old farmhouse was an especially comforting place to be. CMW does dearly love a rainy day, and this was one of the best. Late in the afternoon, she fetched the ten gallon cooler and got it washed and ready for Operation Lemonade. Since Youngest Daughter was at a birthday party for Friend Laura that was lasting until the evening party, CMW was pretty much on her own.

She started in what she felt was pretty good time, and was making short work of everything when her capable helper, Jenny, arrived to take care of Old Gertrude and Blind Linda for the evening. She had in tow four beautiful little kids that CMW very much enjoys, so she had to talk to them and find out what was happening in their lives. It was quarter after five by the kitchen clock when she realized that her watch was running fifteen minutes behind, and that the time had come to hurry a little. The bread was still on the cooling racks, so as she was finishing everything up and leaving, she asked Helper Jenny if she could please stack them into a clean kitchen size trash bag to keep them from drying out. Helper Jenny said she would take care of it. Strong Eldest Son, (whose hair cut didn't affect him at all the way Samson's did) picked up the eighty pound cooler filled with lemonade and loaded it into the back of the van for CMW.

And it came to pass that Certain Man's Wife went forth to the grad party of niece Holly with those ten gallons of lemonade, and everything was very fine. And the atmosphere was wonderful, and Youngest Brother, Mark,

127

Jr. outdid himself with grilling many hamburgers, and the food and the variety of beverages was impressive and tastefully arranged and the array of pies was delectable, indeed. And the people came and came and came. The reception/food line waxed long, and CMW began to be thankful that she had to be there early, thus avoiding the long, long wait.

Certain Man's Wife sat at a table and had good conversation with friends and was thinking how nice everything was when Niece Holly tapped her on the shoulder and handed her a cell phone (CMW had left hers at home) saying, "I believe you have a catastrophe of sorts at home." This was not on the planner's page for the day!

"Hello?"

"Uh, Mom," crackled Youngest Son's voice, "I think umf flummer hire dsk contruction worker fligger flmph."

"What? I can't hear you. Wait a minute. I need to get away from all this noise. . . What did you say?"

"I said, 'I think you are going to need to hire someone to replace the ceiling in the study!'"

"Why?"

"Because there is a whole lot of water coming down through it."

"Lem! What happened? Everything was fine when I left."

"Well, you know that the drain in the kid's bathroom sink has been clogged up for nearly three weeks--"

"No, I did NOT know. Why didn't you say something?"

"Well, it wasn't all the way clogged up, just really, really slow. I mean, the water would go down after a while, but it was slow like."

"And--?"

"Well, someone went up there today (Idon'tknowifitwasmeorRachbutitwasprob'lyme) and left the water running into the sink and it flooded everything up there, filled up all the drawers in the vanity that has our toothbrushes and stuff in them, and came down through the ceiling into the study and filled up the light that was in there up against the ceiling, and then a bunch of it got all over the floor. I took down the light fixture, and I cleaned everything up, but there is still some water running out of the light and I think that ceiling is ruined."

"Oh, Lem!"

"Yeah, well, I took all the drawers out of the vanity upstairs in the bathroom and I mopped up all the water, and I set the drawers around so they could dry out and I think everything is pretty much okay but I thought that you should know."

"What did Jenny do?"

"Well, she pretty much helped me, and we used up some clean towels so you are prob'ly gonna have to wash them, and there is a bucket in the middle of the floor under the light, but we pretty much took care of everything else. But it was a pretty big mess. And I'm outta' here to come to the party."

"Okay, Son." (Sigh)

"Bye, Mom, I love you!" (That fixes a whole lot of stuff!)

"Love you, too, Son!"

CMW looked at her unfinished plate of food, and was not hungry any more. What was really going on at home, and how was Helper Jenny handling everything? She had better go home. So she quietly disposed of her plate and headed out. She had been at the party for over an hour, anyhow, so it was probably the best thing to do.

She came into the kitchen, and it had lost some of its cozy charm. The adjoining study had great layers of big blue towels around a huge dishpan. Water was merrily plopping into it and splashing out around. Helper Jenny was loading the dishwasher. CMW noticed that her bread was no longer on the counter. She glanced around the kitchen and her heart sank as she saw a kitchen size trash bag sitting on a kitchen chair with her tender loaves of bread plopped into it like dirty laundry. Too late, she realized that she hadn't taken time to explain to Jenny that she laid the bag on the cupboard and carefully arranged them in the bag in a single layer so as not to squash them.

CMW lifted the bag up to the cupboard and tried to sound optimistic and casual. "You know, I might as well get these cut and into their individual bags..." They tumbled out onto the cupboard in various shapes and sizes. Thankfully, only two at the very bottom were irreparably damaged.

Helper Jenny said cheerfully, "I tried to stack them in there really carefully, like each one directly on the other so that they wouldn't get too squashed."

"They'll be fine," said CMW, "I didn't tell you how I usually do this." She reminded herself that there are some things you cannot know unless someone tells you. She also reminded herself that this delightful helper had gotten more than she bargained for this particular night. She hadn't been hired to clean up water messes or tend to homemade bread that she knew nothing about. So CMW sliced a loaf and sent it home with Helper Jenny to share with her family, and she methodically sliced the rest of the bread and bagged it up and got it ready for the freezer.

Suddenly she missed Certain Man with a sharp, lonely emptiness. Cutting the bread and bagging it up was a job they almost always did together. And water from the ceiling was definitely his department. The week had been long enough. She wished that there was some way to shorten the 20-hour trip home. Lennox, Missouri seemed a half a world away.

But then the phone rang, and it was Certain Man. He and his trusty crew had just gotten on their way home. CMW filled his ears with her tales of woe and his cheery laughter lightened her heart. After all, Youngest Son HAD cleaned up most of the mess. And the bread wasn't totally ruined, just squashed a bit. Tomorrow, Lord Willing, Certain Man would be home and the extra responsibilities would rest back on his shoulders. CMW got herself a tall glass of water, and finished loading the dishwasher. It wouldn't hurt to have the kitchen clean when he got home.

And that is all.

That is all the news from Shady Acres this time.

CMW Gives Blood

Now it came to pass on the 28th of September, in the Year of our Lord, 2005, that Certain Man's Wife had an appointment to give blood. There had been many causes that had depleted the nation's reserve blood supply and earnest and urgent pleas had gone out to anyone registered as a "Life Saver" to come and do their duty by their conscience and their country. Certain Man had gone to the Blood Bank several days earlier and made a donation of his healthy, A-positive blood. When he returned home, he noted with great satisfaction that it was at least 66 pints that he had given over the course of his lifetime. CMW was properly impressed. Though a regular donor, she will never reach such lofty heights. However, her B-positive blood was also in great demand, so she was glad to make a donation.

This particular day was unusually fair. Autumn was turning the long, hot summer into gloriously brilliant days. Everywhere there was evidence of Harvest, as farmers were getting their corn picked, mums were making their showy appearances, and some of the perennials were beginning to go into decline. CMW loves this time of year. There are apples and grapes and butternut squash to fill the air with wonderful smells. There are Holidays coming that will bring together people she loves, and her heart constantly turned to the counting of blessings when she thought of last year's holidays and all the unknowns that were glaring down upon them. The year has been full of the mercies of the Lord.

So it was with great joy that she went to breakfast with her Mother, daughter, sisters and sisters-in-law. It was easy to linger and laugh and enjoy the fellowship together. Brother Nelson and his wife Rose were in the community for a week, and to have Rose along was a grand treat indeed. Talk around the table was of the forthcoming wedding of Sister Alma's son, Jerrel, Jr., to the delightful Sarah Troyer. CM and CMW were planning to attend, as were all the offspringin's that still made their abode at home. After the long breakfast, CMW invited Sister-in-law Rose to go along on a shopping adventure. She wanted to go to T.S. Smith and Sons in Bridgeville to get some fresh cider and some apple donuts for the small group meeting scheduled at Shady Acres that evening. From there, she wanted to jaunt about to see if there might be a new frock that would be suitable for the wedding. Rose was glad to accompany her. Then CMW remembered her 1:30 appointment at the blood bank. No matter. There was time to do most of it if they hurried.

So the cider was bought. Wonderful stuff. The donuts were bought. They looked delicious. Then it was on to Milford, and to the shopping grounds. Around 1:00, CMW and Rose decided that it would work best for Rose to go back to her sister's house. Rose's sister, Gloria, is married to CMW's honorable cousin, Joe Bontrager. Joe and Gloria recently moved to Delaware to help care for Joe's aging parents, Uncle Eli and Aunt Ruth. Brother Nelson was there, helping Joe with some cement work, so Rose thought that she would go and see if she could find something to occupy the afternoon.

It was only a hop and a skip from Uncle Eli's house to the Lutheran Church where the Bloodmobile was parked. As CMW parked the van, and gathered her identification and purse, she realized again that this was an incredibly delightful day. She had a fleeting thought about whether everything would pass the scrutiny of the phlebotomist, but mostly she was just bouncing along the sidewalk thinking happy thoughts. The Bloodmobile is a big, big bus. It appears to have been commandeered from the Greyhound Bus Company, and repainted to certain specification. This big old bus was parked parallel to the sidewalk with no windows. When you traverse the sidewalk, you somewhat hemmed in on both sides with the church on one side and the bus on the other. Little did CMW know that she was in the Valley of the Shadow of Death. (Well, maybe not death, but treacherous places).

Suddenly, without warning, the toe of her sandal caught on a crack in the sidewalk. It wasn't necessarily a big crack, but it threw her off balance just a mite. She realized that she was starting to fall, so she took a few hurried steps to regain her balance, but there was nothing to stop her now hurtling progress forward. She felt her feet trying vainly to outrun the imminent disaster, but all to no avail.

Suddenly, she was face down on the sidewalk, with many strange sensations assailing her quite damaged dignity. Both hands were beside her head on the pavement. She felt that her glasses were still on her face, but there was the sensation of concrete pressed against them. What do you know? They were not broken!

Then she felt the spreading warmth of blood. Great amounts of blood were pouring forth from somewhere. She raised herself up to her knees and explored the damage. There was a very mangled lip, and her nose felt like it had been dealt a mighty blow. She applied pressure to her mouth in an effort to stop the gushing, but realized that she was going to have to get some help. She got up, slung her purse over one shoulder and held the pressure of her flat hand against her mouth and nose. And walked into the donor reception area. She was mortified and aggravated and injured.

"I fell!" she announced to the receptionist, while the waiting donors stared. The receptionist looked up.

"Oh, my goodness!" She leaped up from her chair. "Someone come help. Someone get some towels. Oh, dear. Can someone please help me here?"

People came out of the woodwork. The person in charge came in and handed CMW a two inch thick stack of paper towels. "Here, put this over your mouth and hold it firm."

"Where can we put her? She needs to lie down." (CMW didn't think so, but she really didn't just want to stand out there in the waiting room like a circus sideshow. There seemed to be a lot of people standing around and gawking.)

"What happened?"

"I caught my sandal in a crack in the sidewalk."

"Did you pass out?"

"No."

"Are you light-headed or dizzy or woozy now?"

"No, not at all. I'm just aggravated!" (Could someone tell CMW what the difference is between "light-headed," "dizzy," and "woozy?")

"Here, come on back here, we will put you on this cot." CMW was gently guided back into a room that contained a canvas cot. She lay down and kept applying pressure. People seemed to be milling about in that state of concern and near panic. There was lots of blood.

"Does it hurt a lot?" queried a Bloodmobile nurse

"Actually, not that much."

The Bloodmobile nurse was very kind. He checked everything carefully and then said, "We need to get you to the hospital. That cut is going to need stitches."

"Are you sure?"

"Yep, I'm pretty sure."

CMW sighed a deep, discouraged sigh. "We have a wedding this weekend in Ohio." she said in a small, sad voice.

"Oh, you poor dear," said the attending female person. That was when CMW knew that things really must not be very pretty.

"Could someone please call my husband?"

Things were happening at a great speed, and CMW lay on the cot and wished for his comforting presence. She didn't feel like making decisions. She didn't feel like going to the emergency room, she didn't feel like holding ice on her now throbbing mouth. She especially didn't feel like having this delightful day spoiled by her clumsy inattention.

"Do you want us to call the ambulance, or is it okay if someone from here drives you?" was the next question.

Then someone stepped forward and said, "I could drive her over in her car, then it would be there when she needed it, and someone can come over and pick me up." They brought forth a wheelchair (cumbersome and unnecessary) and insisted that she ride in it to the car. As they wheeled her down the same old sidewalk, there was a big wet spot where someone had washed up the blood that CMW had donated that day. (It seems that blood on the sidewalk leading the donor center was not seen as an incentive.)

Just before pulling out, someone said, "Your husband is in Greenwood, and he will meet you in the Emergency Room." On the way to the hospital, CMW's cell phone rang. It was Eldest Daughter.

"Mom!" Her voice was cheerful and buoyant. "Where are you? Are you giving blood?"

"No, Chris, I'm not. Actually, I'm on my way to the emergency room." This was spoken through a stack of paper towels and an ice pack.

"Mama! What happened? Oh, Mama, What did you do?" Brief advisement was given, and then, "Mom, I'm coming. I will be there as soon as I can!"

And so the few blocks to the hospital were covered, and CMW found herself telling her story again and again, and then waiting and waiting and waiting. Certain Man arrived, and commiserated and spoke loving words, but had to leave to return his state vehicle and claim his pickup from the parking lot. He promised to return as soon as possible. Eldest Daughter was faithfully there until Second Daughter came in from school.

"I don't think I'm going to go to that wedding," said CMW to Eldest Daughter. "Everyone will look at me, and I don't feel like having it."

"Don't worry, Mama," Said Eldest Daughter. "Just put a bag over your head, and cut out two holes for your eyes, and you'll be just fine."

An hour later, when she had pretty much convinced herself that there was no need for stitches, that she should just betake herself and her damaged lip and bulbous nose out of there and go home, they called her name.

A pleasant nurse gently evaluated and murmured comfort. "Do you really think it will need to be stitched?" asked CMW plaintively.

"We'll leave that up to the P.A.," she said, "but it looks to me like it would be better if it had a few stitches."

CMW lay there and worried. Her face was really hurting, and the lip was throbbing. The thought of sticking a needle in there to numb it caused her to wince. She didn't have much longer to wait (or worry). An efficient, kind-faced young woman put in her appearance and came to a quick decision.

"We need to put a few stitches in that." she said firmly.

"Are you really sure you need to?" asked CMW again.

"Well, we don't usually stitch the mucosa, but this is on the upper side of it, and it is in the place where it will get bumped and stretched, and I think it will heal a whole lot quicker if we just put a few stitches in there. But I won't do it if you say not to."

CMW pondered a bit, and finally decided to go with the professional opinion. She squinched her eyes shut so she wouldn't see any needles and prayed for courage. Second Daughter got called in as an assistant when the attending nurse got called away, and between her and the confident Physician's Assistant, the job was soon done. Much easier and much quicker than CMW had dared to hope. It was astonishingly simple and had very little extra pain.

Certain Man put in his appearance just when everything was finished up and took her carefully home. CMW thought home had never looked so good. She settled into Certain Man's La-Z-Boy with a sigh of relief. It was time for a nap.

So, today she has been taking it easy, trying to be careful. Her lip sticks out like a Botox job gone bad, and there are bruises in strange places, but the overwhelming emotion is one of Thankfulness.

THANKFULNESS??? Yes!

~If the lip hadn't been where it was, there would probably be two missing front teeth. A lip is easier to fix than two front teeth. Thank God not a single tooth was chipped or broken.

~If the ski-slope nose of CMW's hadn't acted like the stop on a skate, the glasses could have been broken, the forehead could have slammed into the ground, and that would have been a whole different ball game. As it is, CMW's nose is very sore, and there is a bruise around the top of it where it got jammed back, but there isn't a single mark above it anywhere.

~If CMW had landed even a slight bit differently, there could have been broken wrists or busted knees. None of these happened. Just a most unattractive face job with brush burns and bruises and those unhandy stitches that stick up and make CMW feel like she needs to bite them off. And that seems insignificant when CMW considers the people who needed the blood she didn't donate. There is ample reason to give thanks.

And that is the news from Shady Acres, where CM has been overly solicitous in the care of his injured wife, where CMW is re-thinking that "bag over the head" business, and where all the children have been properly sympathetic towards their mother's plight.

CM, CMW and the Quilt

Now it came to pass that Certain Man and Certain Man's Wife have been married for nearly 33 years. And in that time, there have been relatively few squabbles over small things like blankets and who got their fair share. There has been peaceable agreement over such things as room temperature, how many blankets and even the firmness and size of the mattress and pillows.

Several years ago (nearly ten, to be exact) a Hispanic friend who worked in a local stitching factory gave CMW a large flowery bedspread that has been the covering of choice and that, coupled with a sheet in the summer and a very large fuzzy blanket in the winter, has been all that was needed for warmth most of these years.

However, within the last year there have been several things that have marred the peace at the Church of the Inner Spring, St. Mattress Cathedral. Mental Pause with its heat flashes and irritability and sleep disturbances has made some minor inroads into the established patterns. Aching joints and changing schedules and adult children have also made for some differences in sleep habits.

And then something else came along that further upset the balance. The QUILT.

CMW is not a quilter. In fact, in her cedar chest there resides a very old quilt top that was given to her for a wedding gift by an old friend, Mary Belle Hostetler, that has never been quilted. There have been times when she thought to make a quilting and make use of the top, but Mary Belle was quite elderly when the top was pieced and the workmanship is not her best. Plus, it has nostalgic value to CMW, and just to think of it brings her joy.

There was time when CM and CMW were given a beautiful friendship quilt by the church they were leaving when they moved from Ohio to Delaware, but it was loved and used into great disrepair, and finally put on the shelf. Other than that, not one solitary homemade quilt has ever been in CMW's possession.

The interest in quilts and the desirability of quilts has not been lost on CMW. Her friends and relatives not only made beautiful quilts, but it seemed like they all owned several that could be brought out and examined and exclaimed over when the subject came up. She was not consumed by a longing for any specific pattern, but thought it might be nice to own just one. So when she was visiting her friend, Bea, a few years ago, and Friend Bea's Mother had numerous quilt tops that she was working on, it was arranged to purchase a very nice looking non-difficult-pattern sort of quilt and Friend Bea's Mother agreed to quilt it for CMW. Nearly two years ago, this project was finished, and the quilt duly sent, received and admired. Then it resided in the closet for about a year until CMW had the urge to put it on her bed one day. It looked very nice there, indeed. It actually was perfect in color and size for the summer months, and when winter finally came, the weather was so mild that an occasional blanket thrown over all was enough to keep CM and CMW in comfort.

Then Certain Man took it upon himself to lose a few pounds. This always is accompanied by a shift in body temperature for him. He feels like he is freezing a lot of the time. So, CMW found a vellux blanket that was adequate to cover the bed, but did not stick out below the quilt. This did not lend itself well to one of the parties wrapping it all around themselves in an attempt to keep warm, but usually it did not matter too much as the other party was usually affected by the aforementioned "mental pause" and had no interest in wrapping up in a thick vellux blanket.

However, in the mornings, there was evidence of struggle with quilt and blanket on one side of the bed and sheet gathered morosely on the other. When CMW made the bed in the morning, she pondered about whether two people with such disarray of blankets and sheets could have slept well. She had a vague, disquieted feeling that maybe neither party was getting enough rest.

Then CMW developed an abscess on a molar that she had been trying to get her dentist to do something about for several months. No longer could it be a "wait and see" proposition. This thing was hurting with a vengeance, causing much nocturnal pain and wakefulness, and making CMW tearful over many things.

And it came to pass that one of the things that was troubling her very much was that there were great snatchings going on over the blankets at night. And it was being done under the great cover (excuse the pun) of sleep, and she was as guilty as the second party of being disruptive. Certain Man would turn over in his sleep and hitch the quilt and blanket around his strong shoulder and it would conveniently leave Certain Man's Wife and snuggle onto his back while she lay out in the cold, clutching the sheet.

If she had been sleeping in her usual deep way, she would never have even noticed, but most of the time, she was half way between sleep and misery and thinking that she was almost asleep when the covers would whoosh off of her. This apparent lack of concern for her comfort would only make her more miserable. So she got to holding onto the edge of the blanket and quilt with a firm grasp and in her half-sleep, would hang on for dear life when the covers started to move. That would actually pull her over sideways when her bed partner would decide it was time to turn over. CMW did not BLAME him, as it is no fun to turn over and have cold air blasting down your back, but these narrow blankets were obviously causing a problem between two usually agreeable bed partners. It was making them tired and irritable. When you added in the tooth and medication, the freezing man and blanket grabbing woman were both being aggravated beyond what was necessary.

So, one particular morning, Certain Man's Wife looked at her bleary image in the mirror and pondered the options. Suddenly, it looked very simple. Where were the big old fuzzy blanket and the big flowery bedspread? Right there in the closet. It was time for a change. In a great burst of inspiration, she took the offending blanket and quilt off and replaced it with the familiar generous coverings of last winter. It looked so familiar that Certain Man, in from the chicken house and dressing for the office never even noticed. Certain Man's Wife looked forward to a good night's rest and behold, peace returned to the Church of the Inner Spring.

And that is the news from Shady Acres, where most solutions are not quite this simple or effective.

CMW goes for Cow Feed

Now it came to pass that Certain Man's Wife spent a day in early April abroad upon the face of the earth. (Well, not too far abroad, as she did not leave the State, but she was, nonetheless, not at home.) It was the birthday of Middle Sister and she was so inconvenienced as to have a doctor's appointment in Dover that day, so CMW and Youngest Sister decided that they would accompany her and do some other things as well (i.e. lunch and some minimal shopping).

And the day went well, indeed, though they didn't really get much shopping done and lunch, out of time constraints, was picked up at Byler's Store and eaten in the confines of the van. However, the three sisters enjoy greatly just being together, so there was some time "wasted" just sitting in the van outside of various establishments, just talking. And after the Doctor's appointment was over, they decided to head on home. Middle Sister was only about ten days post surgery, and her Solicitous Sisters did not want to overtire her.

CMW came home around 3:15 and found that none of the work that she had left behind that morning had walked off. And so she looked at things with a rather dismal eye, and made some half hearted attempts at getting something done, but made little headway, indeed, nothing seemed very interesting to her. So she did some computer work, and then Youngest Son Called from Phoenix, and she happened to notice the time. Oh, NO!!! It was almost 4:30.

It so happened that Certain Man had planned to try to pick up feed for his cows on the way home from work, but CMW had said, "I should have plenty of time to go and pick up feed for you after I get home from Dover. We do not plan to make it a long day, and I will just run out to Wall's Farm and Garden and pick up your feed. Then you won't have to worry about it."

"Well, you also need to pick up some cat food for the barn cats, too."

"Gotcha! I'll get it."

But now it was almost 4:30 and she had forgotten all about it. She passed the phone that had Youngest Son on it to one of his eager siblings and picked up the cell phone.

"Walls Farm and Garden--How may I help you?"

"What time do you close?"

"Five o'clock."

"Do you know if Mr. Yutzy called an order in there today for six bags of sweet stock and a bag of PMI Cat food?"

"No, he didn't."

"Okay, I need to pick up six bags of sweet stock and one bag of cat food, and I will be there in a few minutes."

CMW picked up her purse, got her jacket, and tried hard to close her ears to the conversation going on between Youngest Son and Middle Daughter. The hardest thing in the world is to miss out on conversation with the offspringin's, but if she was going to get to Walls Farm and Garden on time, she needed to hurry. So she wrenched herself away, and headed on out.

As she pulled up to the loading dock, an elderly gentleman, Ned, appeared with a push cart loaded with six bags of something or other. He is a good friend of Certain Man's and when CMW rolled down her window and asked if that was six bags of sweet stock, he grinned broadly.

"Got it right here," he said proudly. His good humor is contagious and CMW felt the stresses of the day melt away in the face of his efficiency and cheerfulness. "Just pull your van up a little further and I'll load her fer ye. He prol'ly wants a bag of cat food, too, don't he? I'll load her right up."

"Can I go in and pay while you load it? Would that be okay?"

"Sure, go right ahead."

So CMW trotted off around the corner to the front door. When she was almost to the corner, Ned said, "Why didn't you just go through here?" He motioned to the stairs going up to the loading dock and through the darkened feed room to the back door of the office.

CMW didn't say so, but she doesn't really care for that feed room. It is dusty and dark and it feels like she is trespassing on territory that she would be better off away from. So, she just said, "Oh, well, I'm almost there now, so I'll just go this way."

It was a beautiful day. The sun was shining and there were people milling about the greenhouse in front of the main office. CMW came up the steps to the office, thinking about the beautiful day and planting flowers and how people were enjoying gardening. She pushed open the heavy glass door that goes into the little office/showroom with her checkbook and pen in one hand and her big old purse slung over her shoulder. And yep! She did it again. Caught that toe of her sandal in the little piece of metal at the bottom of the door and down she went! Mercifully, she was actually able to clear the door closing behind her, so she was sprawled in a heap on the rug just inside the glass door. Nothing had cracked, nothing appeared to be broken, but she was in a most undignified position, and some of her joints had been forced into positions they had long been unaccustomed to.

"Ouch!" She said as she tried to straighten her arms and legs out of their contortions into a position to facilitate rising from her embarrassment. There were no shoppers in the showroom, and only one lady, out of sight behind the desk. If CMW had been home, she may have stayed on that floor and pitied herself awhile, but there were, just outside that glass door behind her, a bevy of shoppers who had probably witnessed the unrehearsed show, and CMW not only wanted them to not come running to help, she could not even bear to look to see if they had seen. So she gathered herself and her belongings off of the floor and made her way hurriedly out of the door area.

"Are you alright?" queried the lady behind the desk (a little belatedly, thought CMW).

"Yep, I'm fine," said CMW with more levity than she felt. "I just caught my sandal on something, but I don't seem to be injured in anyway." She walked across the small showroom floor, paid her current bill and a previous bill at the tall counter, then collected herself for the walk back out. She decided to go through the feed room. That way, she wouldn't have to face the people who may have seen her fall. As she made her way out through the feed room, she came face to face with smiling Ned.

"You know, Norman, I should have listened to you. I went around the other way, caught my sandal in the door and fell flat on my face."

"Oh, no! Are you okay?" Concern darkened his usual smile.

"I'm fine, I truly am, but I AM insulted!"

"Well, now, you take care," he said, "And try to control my buddy."

With his words echoing in her mind, CMW got into her van and started home. *"Try to control his buddy???"*

First of all, Certain Man has never been very apt to submit to any efforts to control him, and though CMW will admit to trying on occasion, it has almost always had disastrous results.

Besides that, how in the world would anyone think that a woman who cannot even keep herself in an upright position in public places could begin to control a man like Daniel Yutzy? Seems like she has enough to do without taking on that project.

And that is the news from Shady Acres, where Certain Man was happy that he had feed for his steers, Certain Man's Wife is surprisingly unscathed from her tumble, and she even got home in time to rescue the phone from Middle Daughter and had a good chat with Youngest Son. And that was sweet.

CMW Braves the Storm

Now it came to pass that the fair state of Delaware has endured a very dry spring. And Certain Man's Wife has prayed earnestly for the Lord to send rain upon the land, for she remembers the days of her father's prayers when the land was dry. She remembers that often the Lord would heed his prayers and send the rain in a timely fashion. So, over the past weeks, it has been a frequent request of CMW. In fact, there was a time that she hung laundry out on a starry night by the light of the moon and said, "Lord, you know how much we need rain, and I would be willing to take this laundry in tomorrow morning and have to dry it inside if you would just send rain tonight." That prayer was not effective. Perhaps the Heavenly Father perceived a lack of faith.

But this past weekend was the NASCAR Race at Dover Downs. And, seriously, it usually rains on race weekend. This is unfortunate, really, because it is also the weekend of the Greenwood Mennonite School Festival, and it seems to get rained on more than it doesn't – either in the setting up or the actual day or the taking down thereof.

So, sure enough, the forecast was for rain. heavy rain, in fact, and it was supposed to come on Thursday evening, Friday afternoon and even scattered showers on Saturday. The honorable weather forecaster even took pains to say that there could be heavy downpours on Friday evening, causing the postponement of some graduations and some graduation parties.

Now Middle Daughter had agreed to manage the book booth at the festival, and for the past several weeks, there had been telephone calls, and visitors and organizational things to deal with in preparation for the big day. There had even been cars, sneaking surreptitiously into the driveway and boxes of books delivered quietly with the donors speeding away without disclosing their identities. And Middle Daughter worked feverishly to categorize and box all of the books into some sort of order. At the back of her mind was always the threat of rain and what she was going to do if there was a bad storm. The tents provided for the different booths at the festival were not exactly noted for their protection from a stormy blast.

And when everything was tallied up on Friday afternoon, there were 50 some boxes of books all together, and she needed to get everything into one spot at the festival grounds for setting up "her " booth. So she called upon the general labor force available to her, namely Eldest Daughter and Beloved Son-in-Law, Youngest Daughter, Certain Man, and the brothers of BSIL, Joel and Caleb.

In the meantime, Certain Man's Wife was cleaning her house in preparation for the coming Lord's Day when CM and CMW's household was the designated Host Family for the day. Then sometime in the afternoon, Eldest Daughter called and asked if CMW would like to go help wash vegetables at Friend Ethel's house when Middle Daughter was finished with their services at the book booth. CMW thought that would be a good diversion. She wanted to see her friend, and she hoped for a break in the tiring work. So they set 6:30 as a time to meet.

When Eldest Daughter and BSIL stopped in on their way to help carry books, CMW was on the floor with a screw driver, trying to fix a dressing table bin that wasn't behaving to her satisfaction. Beloved Son-in-Law came into the laundry room, and looked a bit disconcertingly at her unusually prone situation.

"Uh, Mom," he said worriedly. "Are you alright?"

"Yep, I'm fine. I'm just taking these screws out so I can take this bin off, so I can get whatever fell behind it that is keeping it from shutting right."

"Oh. Well. Uh. Did Dad say anything to you about this soccer movie that we wanted to take Youngest Daughter to?"

"I think I did hear something about it. Why?"

"Well, I checked around and I checked around and I thought that it wouldn't be anywhere close where we could go and see it, but I found out that it is going to be in Chestertown, and there is going to be a 9:30 showing, and I thought maybe we could go over there and see it if you thought it would be okay. I know it is an hour over there, and it will be really late when we get home, but I am afraid that it will be our only chance to go see it since it isn't doing very well and I am afraid they will cancel the showings."

Now Beloved Son-in-Law and Youngest Daughter share a passion for soccer that is unmatched within the family circles. And CMW does not find such things appealing at all, but knows that this is something that is important for some reason to these two. So from her disadvantaged position on the floor, she said that she would see what Certain Man thought and she would let them know something. So off the troops went to the festival grounds to set up.

And the rain poured down, and things were somewhat "iffy" for a while, but eventually, the books got gathered into one spot, the vegetables got washed and CMW and Eldest Daughter returned home so that Youngest Daughter and Eldest Daughter and Beloved Son-in-Law could sally forth to Chestertown. (Which they did.) Thankfully, the rain had abated somewhat, and it was looking more favorable for the next day's activities.

146

Certain Man's Wife was taking a quiet break at home when suddenly, the heavens opened and the rain poured down with unbelievable volume. The lightening was flashing and the thunder was crashing, and it was a magnificent storm. Haste was made to unplug the electronics to protect them from power surges, and CMW was thinking how thankful she was for the safety of her house, while worrying about the safety of Certain Man who was in the chicken house, when the phone rang. Middle Daughter picked it up from the safety of her La-Z-boy rocker. It was Eldest Daughter, on her way to Chestertown.

"Is it raining there?" She asked anxiously.

"Uh, Yeah!!" Said Middle Daughter. "Like buckets and buckets."

"Well, could someone go down to my house and shut the windows and turn off the exhaust fan? I left windows open and the fan on."

"Christina, it is raining terribly hard! Couldn't someone from Jess's family go shut your windows?" (They live across from them on the same road.)

"I know, but Jesse's family doesn't have a car at this present moment and Mom and Dad could drive their van right into the garage and not need to get out in the rain."

This information was duly passed on to CMW who mostly only heard the "I left the windows open " part of the message.

"Just tell her that I will go on up and take care of it," she said to Middle Daughter. "And tell her that I am going right away." And she immediately proceeded to do just that. She flew out to the minivan and backed out of the garage. The van was immediately struck by the full fury of the storm. It was some of the worst rain that CMW has ever driven in. She planned her strategy as she made her way the mile and a half to Eldest Daughter's house. Some months ago, she had programmed the garage door opener for Eldest Daughter's house into the buttons on the ceiling of her mini-van. She had done this over Eldest Daughter's initial objection, but had convinced her that it would come in handy for all concerned. She couldn't help but think that this was one of those times. She also couldn't help but wonder if being "right " was all that wonderful at this particular time.

All the way to Eldest Daughter's house, the wind blew sheets and sheets of water across the road. There were places where the road was flooded and she had to go very, very slowly. She heard the belt start to squeal the way it always does when it gets wet and then remembered that she had brought neither cell phone nor umbrella with her. What if she got stranded in one of these oceans of water? Oh, well, she might just as well forge ahead since she was almost there.

The driveway loomed ahead of her, and she pulled gratefully into the small shelter made by the overhanging garage roof. She reached up and pushed the button. Nothing happened. The door didn't even lurch. She pushed it again. Nothing. She pushed and held it. And then she pulled up close enough to the door that her van was almost nosing into it. Nothing happened. So she backed up and came in at a different angle. It didn't budge. And then, suddenly, all the lights went out. The power to the house was off.

Certain Man's Wife sat in the dry warmth of her van and looked at the rain pouring off the roof and onto the hood of her car. She thought about going home again and just forgetting the whole mess. She looked down at her sandals and cotton dress and dreaded the thought of getting out of the car and trying the small garage door, but knew that she had no choice. So she mustered up her courage and made a dash for it. The rain dripped down her neck as she darted to the door. It was locked.

She was almost sure that she could get in if she went around back, but that looked like it was a half a mile away. Then she remembered the driving rain and the open windows, so she gathered her courage about her once more and made a run for it. Around the front of the garage, to the side of the garage she slipped and splashed. The ground was squishy and the water came up over her sandals. As she came around the back of the garage, there was sudden, bright lightening.

"If I get struck by lightning out here," she thought grimly, "someone is going to be sorry!" She made the final plunge to the door of the screened in porch just as the thunder broke around her head and she came breathlessly out of the wind and rain into the shelter of the porch.

"Ah, yes!" The sliding glass door was slightly ajar. She could get into the house.

But now there was another problem. The electric was off. It was dark outside. And it was pitch black in there. (To quote Laurel from a "Laurel and Hardy " movie, "It was so pitch, you couldn't see your hand behind your face!") Certain Man's wife tried to feel her way around to find a candle or a match or a flashlight. There was absolutely nothing to be found. She felt like a blind woman along the edge of the counter, over to the microwave. Pat, pat, pat. What was this? Oh, a pencil. And this was this and that was that, but not a solitary helpful thing. Finally, CMW decided that she would need to look hard every time the lightning struck and pounce on whatever she needed when she had a brief illumination. But all of the things that were illuminated did not help her a bit to shed light in the dark.

So she felt around and closed the kitchen window, and then started back the hall. One of the things that was concerning her most was the exhaust fan. She felt like she had to make sure that it was turned off if all the windows were going to be closed. If the electric came back on, and the windows were closed, she was afraid it would burn up the fan motor. But the control was so obscure that she couldn't figure it out.

Maybe there would be something on the bathroom sink to help her. She patted her way into the hall bathroom, and felt around on the sink in there. There were soap dispensers and pretty baskets holding supplies for guests, but no candles and no matches. She felt around on the cupboard shelves. Nothing there either. She went into the study; there was the computer. She frisked it and the CD's around it. Nothing. She shut the windows which were slightly damp, and went on to the Master bedroom. There wasn't a single romantic candle there or matches, either, so she shuffled her way blindly into the Master bedroom bath. There was toothpaste and combs and such in there, and there was a cup. She patted the back of the toilet and opened the cupboard above it. There was nothing with which to light her way.

And then, it happened. Her foot inadvertently kicked the digital scale on the floor of the bathroom and it lit up like a Christmas tree. She looked at its neon green light but it quickly disappeared. She tapped it again, and it came on cheerily. Wait a minute. If she could just keep it on, maybe it would be a help. She picked it up and gave it a squeeze. It stayed on for a while and she held it up to the cupboard and surveyed the contents. There were no candles, matches or flashlights there. Then the light went out. She squeezed it again, but it didn't light up.

"Oh, great! Probably the battery is out." She squeezed it some more, and it wouldn't come on. So she put it back down on the floor. It promptly lit up again.

"Okay. If I need to set you down in between times, I'll just have to do it." So down the hall she went. Set the scale down, on came the light. Pick it up, squeeze it, move down the hall. She finally got to the controls for fan and illuminated it enough to see to turn it off. By then, she was just anxious to get on out of this dark, dark cave and home to the safety of her own house where a generator would be lighting the dark. So she set that scales down in the hall bathroom and made a quick exit though the dark dining room, kitchen, laundry room and into the garage where her van lights were providing a bit of comforting glow.

She went out of the small garage door, locking it behind her and made a quick dash to her van. The rain had abated a little, and her drive home was uneventful other than wet. But she had conquered the windows and the fan, and the rest of the problem would be Eldest Daughter's to cope with when she got home.

And that is the news from Shady Acres where CMW came home to find that Certain Man had also braved the storm to close the doors on the chicken house. Behold, he had fared even worse than she had. His dripping wet coveralls hung dismally in the downstairs shower stall.

The escapades of the afternoon made the warm and sheltering comforts of the big old farmhouse on Shawnee Road welcome indeed.

CMW and the Snake

Certain Man's Wife and snakes are best separated by a long distance. She does not like them. In fact, she cannot even think of them as "useful" in her most optimistic moments. There is a good reason for this. Whenever the subject of snakes comes up, it so happens that she is reminded of one of her lesser "shining" moments of parenting.

Back in the late seventies, Certain Man and Certain Man's Wife were foster parents to three boys. Ziggy was ten, Benji was four and David was two. (All unrelated. Ziggy was white, Benji was bi-racial and David was black.) They also had two little girls of their own -- Eldest Daughter was four and Middle Daughter was a very wee girlie. That made the number of youngins five, and quite honestly, for the most part, things went pretty smoothly.

"For the most part," I said!

The middle foster child, Benji, had been abused and had life pretty tough. The only thing was, the longer he was in the home of CM and CMW, the more sympathy CMW had for his poor mother. She would never have been abusive to him, knowing what he had been through, but there were days when CMW thought dismally that, if she had been his mother, and not had the resources for life and help that were available to her, she might have pulled his hair out in patches, too.

He was a beautiful child, but he was so naughty. And he lied and lied and lied and lied. The one thing that was helpful was that whenever he lied, he would pull his mouth around his teeth into this wide-eyed, surprised kind of look, and that was pretty much a clue for CMW to not believe whatever wild tale was forthcoming. (Tell-Tale Face – known hereafter as "TTF")

On one particular morning, CMW was busy with household things, cleaning and such, and Benji and Eldest Daughter were playing outside. They pretty much knew their boundaries, so CMW wasn't surprised to see them running around the front side of the house and having themselves a grand old time. Suddenly, Benji was in the house, with Eldest Daughter trotting on behind.

"Mom! We saw a snake out there!" puffed Benji. (TTF)

"You what?"

"We saw a snake outside. It really was a snake." (TTF)

"Benji, are you sure?"

"Yep, we both saw it, didn't we, Christy?"

Eldest Daughter was markedly lacking in proper frantic actions, but she nodded assent. "Yeah, we saw a snake out there."

"Yep, we really did, Mom. It was really, really big! It was this long!!!" And he made a motion about as far as his hands could go (followed by his tell-tale face).

"Listen, Benji. I don't even want to hear it. There was no snake out there."

"Yes, there was! There really was a snake!" (TTF)

Eldest Daughter nodded her head beside him.

"Where was it, Christina?"

"I don't know, Mama."

"Benji, where was this snake?"

"Well, it was outside somewhere, I'm not sure, but we saw it, and it really was a snake!" (TTF)

CMW was feeling pretty impatient with him by now. She had lived in Ohio for almost ten years, and really doesn't think she had ever seen a snake in any of her yards during that time.

"Benji, you need to tell the truth. Why do you always lie to me? Christy are you SURE you guys saw a snake?"

By this time Eldest Daughter was beginning to recant. Since then she has protested that CMW always thought that she wasn't telling the truth so that sometimes she would lie just to get done with the inquisition. CMW resents that accusation. She does not think she did this, but out of fairness to Eldest Daughter, this bit of history needs to be included because Eldest Daughter was definitely distancing herself from Benji about now and coming around to pretty much saying that she wasn't sure.

"I'm not sure, Mama. Maybe we didn't see a snake."

"Yes, we did. We saw a snake! It was a great BIG snake!"

CMW decided that she had just about had enough.

"Benji. That's enough. You go back to your room and sit on your bed until you can tell the truth."

"Mom −!"

"Benji!" said CMW, sternly. "That's enough! Now go!"

He trudged back the hall to his room, and Eldest Daughter began playing on the living room floor. CMW tried to think what she had been doing, and found it hard to collect her thoughts. She noticed what time it was and thought that probably the mail had gone, and so decided to make a quick trip to the mail box.

"Christy, I am going to run get the mail," she told Eldest Daughter. "I'll be right back."

"Okay, Mama. I'll be alright."

CMW opened the front door and stepped out into the sunshine. It was a cool morning, but the sun was shining on the front stoop and the cement blocks beside the front door. She took a step over the ledge – And almost put her foot down on a SNAKE!

It was sunning itself in the morning sun that was streaming down in front of the little gray house. She looked down and was so surprised she could have gone sprawling. (Knowing her recent history, it is surprising she didn't!) She looked down at that critter and wished with all her might that she wasn't seeing what she was seeing. (Why did God put that snake right there???)

CMW poked her head back into the house. "Benji. Come here!"

He came out, probably wondering what accusations would be hurled at him now.

"Benji. Is this the snake you saw?"

"Yes, that's it. Yes, Mom, that's it. That's IT!!!"

CMW looked at that little garter snake and thought many self-justifying thoughts. It wasn't great big. It was very, very small. But in her heart, she knew that she hadn't been fair to one little boy, either. So she duly apologized and set him free from his confinement and went to get the mail. She did not disturb that snake. It had caused enough trouble for one day. If it wanted to sit on the front stoop and sun himself, that was alright by her. She had better things to do than chase a harmless garter snake. And she was getting on with them right away!

CMW Stays Home

Now it came to pass that the second Wednesday of September in the year of our Lord, 2007, was a beautiful day indeed. And Certain Man's Wife was delighted at the opportunity to open windows and air out the house and get some things done.

She was especially looking forward to this particular day, because she was invited to a luncheon with some special friends on the lawn of a Xanga friend, Curtsellie. Indeed, she was greatly anticipating an encouraging afternoon.

It hasn't been an exactly fun week for CMW. Somehow, though she doesn't remember when or how, she bumped her head. She thinks it happened on Wednesday past when she went to Dover, and managed to tangle with the car door, but the details are very fuzzy in her brain. What she does know is that when she combs her hair, there is a very tender spot there. However, what really got her attention was a very stiff, very painful kink in her neck. This pain radiates out her right arm and makes many daily chores difficult; like combing her hair, and giving showers to Blind Linda, and hanging up laundry.

Last Friday, when it first became apparent that there was a problem, she called her good Chiropractor, Dr. R, and was dismayed to hear that there were no openings at all for that day. So she took a Monday morning appointment and prayed that the weekend would be okay. Saturday was rather uncomfortable, and Sunday morning, she sat in her beloved La-Z-boy with an ice pack and try not to cry.

Certain Man, from the other La-Z-boy looked on with concern. "Hon, do you really think you should even go to church?"

"I need to go. I have the casserole for the Leadership Team meeting. Besides, I'm afraid I will miss something important."

"Sometimes you just have to miss."

"I know, but it seems like every time I do, I am so sorry. Like last weekend at Retreat. Sunday morning, I was feeling more than a little depleted, and I left the service to make sure the lunch was in the oven, then just went over to my cabin and sat there for a little, and missed the best part of the whole weekend! I came in on the tail end of things, and that was sweet, but I've been mad ever since that I wasn't there for the whole thing!"

Certain Man just shook his head, and said no more. He knew she wasn't staying home. Some ice and some Advil and a prayer did their part, and she managed to get through the day quite well. Better than she expected, actually.

Then Monday morning dawned and she headed out to the Chiropractor bright and early. This was important, because Our Girl Audrey needed blood work, and in the afternoon, CMW was scheduled to have a molar pulled. Dr. R is young and exuberant and encouraging. He is daddy to six young children, and CMW likes to hear him talk about his life and his theories and his family. He was quick and efficient as he adjusted the hurting neck.

"Not only did you do a number on that neck," he said, "you also rotated some ribs. I think I had better see you back again this week." So an appointment was made for Wednesday morning early enough that CMW could make it to the luncheon, and then she headed out to pick up Our Girl Audrey for blood work, and eventually, ended up at the dentist's office with great dread and trepidation.

This dentist was CMW's Daddy's dentist through the last years of his life. He was incredibly kind and accommodating during the last few difficult months when, in addition to the chemo and the lymphoma, Our Daddy got a bad toothache. CMW trusts him as much as she would almost any dentist, but that isn't necessarily saying anything profound. He is professional and good, but he still was pulling her molar, and there just is no fun way to do that. The procedure went well, and there was very little alarming noise on the part of the patient or the tools needed to do the extraction. It's just that there is something so devastating about having a tooth extracted. But eventually, after sectioning it and pulling it, one root at a time, it was all done, and CMW was on her way.

So the past few days have been of the kind that made CMW want to just climb into bed and stay there. Of course, that wasn't to be. Our Girl Audrey had an appointment in Millsboro yesterday, and CMW's Sweet Mama was leaving on a trip, so it seemed like there were lots of things to demand attention.

Today. Ah, today! CMW was looking forward to this day!

This was the day that Youngest Daughter had a dentist appointment at 8:30. She does not have her car right now because Eldest Son is using her car while his is in the body shop. (That is another story that I am not at liberty to tell.) CMW had a Chiropractor appointment at 9:30 in Milford. Lunch at Curtsellie's was starting at 11:00. CMW was supposed to take a dish of food to share. Then Blind Linda's bus was late, and Our Girl Audrey was almost in reverse when it came to getting dressed. CMW sent out a frantic SOS for

Middle Daughter who was just getting off work at eight, to please come and put Linda on the bus so that she could take Youngest Daughter to the Dentist appointment. Middle Daughter was cheerfully obliging.

There was general melee when Beeba's Bug, the DART Bus and the Family Van were all occupying the driveway at the same time, but eventually, CMW and Youngest Daughter got on their way. Ten minutes late, and minus CMW's checkbook and billfold. After dropping Youngest Daughter off, CMW flew back home to cook some eggs for the egg salad sandwiches she was taking to the luncheon. She loaded the dishwasher, and got Our Girl Audrey on her bus, listened to Middle Daughter's account of her night, and collected her billfold and checkbook. By now, it was obvious that someone besides CMW would need to pick up Youngest Daughter and take her to school. So Middle Daughter willingly agreed to do that, and CMW was off for her appointment at the Chiropractor.

The appointment went well, and when the staff heard that she had a luncheon to attend, they were able to speed things up a little, though not enough to insure that CMW would be able to make it by 11. This concerned CMW, but a conversation with Middle Sister made her feel like being late would be better than not going, and she was looking forward to it so much, that she decided that she would persevere and go!

So, she went home and made her egg salad and put it on her homemade bread that she had remembered to set out from the freezer, and cut the sandwiches in little squares and arranged them on a Corningware tray and covered them over with plastic wrap. She turned out the lights in her house, and she gathered her stuff together. Come to think about it, she needed her camera. And maybe the batteries weren't fresh. So she added a pack of batteries to the things she was carrying and mentally ticked off her list. Camera. Batteries. Phone. Egg salad sandwiches. Glass bottle of ice tea to drink on the way. Everything was just fine.

So she headed out the door to her van, arms full, but happy to not be any later than she was. She came around the end of the van on her way to the driver's door when her left foot went off the edge of the concrete, and just that quick, she was on the floor of the garage. Her camera and phone bounced across the concrete, her tray of sandwiches slid unceremoniously out of reach. The glass bottle of tea landed "Ker-shlam!" but didn't break. The left foot was doubled in half with the little toe turned under and the right knee was in a most uncomfortable position. CMW knew that there was no one that was going to come flying over and ask stupid questions, so she took her time in unraveling herself to a straight position. She lay on the hard floor and thought dismal thoughts of discouragement.

But she wanted to go to the luncheon. She wasn't broken. She wasn't bleeding. She was not even brush burned as far as she could tell. And she really wanted to go. So she picked herself up from the garage floor. She gathered her scattered possessions. She put things into the car, and started it and backed it out of the garage.

Once outside the garage, she began to think. Her foot was hurting. Her knee was hurting. Her shoulder and neck were still hurting. And the jaw, where the molar had come out was hurting. She looked at her poor, almost squished sandwiches and started to cry.

And she called Eldest Daughter and she didn't answer her phone. So she cried some more and left a message that she wasn't coming. And she called Middle Sister to see if she had left for the luncheon yet, and cried some more and told her that she wasn't coming.

Then she put her sandwiches in the refrigerator and took her things into the house and cried some more. There were things that she needed to do, so she changed the washer and folded some laundry and swept the entry. Nothing she put on her foot felt good, but she took some strong pain medicine and rubbed everything down with Blue Emu Cream and decided that it was time to stop crying.

It was time to get perspective. There were no busted lips, no concussions, no need to call for help. Sometimes we don't know what we have been spared by what we miss. And this is one of those times when CMW believes that she may never know the reason, but senses that she should be content in what is. Not everything in life is hers to know, though she often wishes it were.

And that is the news from Shady Acres, where there have been great expressions of sympathy and caring. Eldest Daughter came home from the luncheon with a card that brightened the day considerably, and CMW is awaiting the morrow to see if she will be able to walk.

(Note: Late in the night, the foot was hurting even more than it was earlier in the day. CMW climbed out of bed, drove herself to the ER, and discovered that she had broken a bone in her foot, close to the joint that went to her little toe. There was great discussion concerning a genetic deformity in that left foot, but eventually they encased her entire leg in a cast and allowed her go home. Great was the inconvenience.)

CMW and One Un-Glorious Day

Late last night, Certain Man's Stepmother called to say that her brother, Lawrence Beachy, had just passed away. Lawrence's twin, Laura, had made her Heavenly Journey just one month and one day earlier (August 25th). That passing was a long, drawn-out process. This one was sudden and unexpected.

This morning, amid phone calls and plans and such, Certain Man's Wife has been surprised again by tears. She knows that these tears are selfish. They have a whole lot less to do with Uncle Lawrence than they do with CMW.

And then the morning proceeded to go so very wrong.

The phone calls did set her behind, but not terribly much. She should have had plenty of time to get around, or so she thought. So she packed lunches and got her ladies up, and gave Blind Linda her shower. The troublesome foot was hurting a bit. Well, actually a LOT. She had some narcotics that she was allowed to take, but really didn't want to take first thing in the morning before she got a few things done.

As CMW brought Blind Linda out from dressing her to sit at the breakfast table at about 8:07, she caught sight of the DART bus, pulling into the driveway, and with a sinking feeling, CMW knew Blind Linda would not be going to Easter Seals on the bus this particular morning. You see, Blind Linda has a "be ready" time of 8 AM, but the bus has been coming around 8:30. Not always predictably, but not ever at 8:07. So CMW went out and told them that they would need to just go on without Blind Linda. (This is called a "no show" and is not good for the transportation record. Sigh)

CMW went back into the house and called DART Paratransit and explained the situation. She did think that maybe she should take her in. It is a "Special Olympics" day at Easter Seals and there are lots of exciting things going on. However, Blind Linda is never quite happy with such things, so it was tempting to think that maybe she should just stay home today. It would be fine with CMW. She didn't have anywhere she needed to go.

Our Girl Audrey was busy with her morning stuff, and Youngest Daughter ran out the door to school. She was not long on time, and CMW saw that she dumped the last of her hot chocolate down the sink as she headed out the door. "I'm late!" she explained, "And I don't want to drip hot chocolate on me while I am driving."

Youngest Daughter was feeling bluesy anyhow about some things going on at school, and CMW's heart went out to her. She had spoken encouraging words to her the night before, and hoped that she would be able to put some things into practice, but almost 17 is a difficult age for kids with confidence issues and career/college choices and friendship challenges, and Youngest Daughter had wept much over several concerning things.

About ten minutes after she left, she called home on her cell phone. "Mom--." She was crying. CMW's mother-mind dived into its rapid fire, "Oh, no, what has happened - Kicked in the stomach - Can't breathe" mode.

"Rachel-- What's wrong?"

"Mom. I ran out of gas. I'm out here just past Dover Mill Works." More tears.

Isn't it strange how Moms can drop into relief, then happy, then relief, then irritated mode without even thinking?"Rachel! Didn't you know you were low in gas?"

"Well, yes, I was gonna get it today. But I hadn't gotten my check cashed yet. I just thought I could make it."

Over and over in CMW's head were the words of Gomer Pyle on an old Andy Griffeth's show. "A car needs four things. Gas, oil, water 'n air. Water 'n air are free. Gas and oil are a differ'nt matter entire!" (CMW has a reputation for thinking of unhelpful things at random times!)

"Rachel, you could have backed out to Dad's farm tank and put enough in for today -- "

She was in no mood to hear any "could've, should've, ought to have's." So CMW promised to get some gas and be there as soon as she could. But in the meantime, Eldest Daughter and the little guys had come. Our Girl Audrey's bus was due. Eldest Daughter needed to get the Oldest Little Guy to preschool. And Blind Linda was still sitting at the breakfast table. CMW sighed deeply and clumped out on her cast and walking boot to look for the gas can. Nothing in the Old garage.

"Certain Man has certainly been cleaning up in this place," She noted. "This really looks nice." On with the search. There was nothing in the old barn. In the woodshed, she found a two gallon can with no lid or spout. Nothing in the manure shed or the lean-to barn. So CMW trudged back to the house and called Certain Man.

"She should have known to just back out there to the farm tank and put enough in to make it through today," he said with the same degree of helpfulness as Youngest Daughter's Momma.

"I know, but don't we have anything here to take gas to her?"

"There's a five gallon can in the old garage--."

160

"I already looked there. I couldn't find a thing. I found the two gallon without a lid or spout – "

"No, there is the five gallon one in the old garage by the light."

By now CMW was heading back out to look again.

"Daniel, I don't see a thing."

"There's one there on the floor by the light switch. I just saw it there. I'm sure there is one there."

"Oh. By the light switch. I was looking under the light. Um. Yeah. Here it is!" Certain Man talked his poor befuddled wife through getting a few gallons into the red, plastic gas can, and she clumped back to the house.

Once in there, it was time to call Our Girl Audrey's bus driver and tell him not to stop for her. Eldest Daughter graciously offered to drive her to her center when she took Oldest Little Guy to preschool. And time for morning meds for Blind Linda who would need to ride along on the gas delivery trip. About the time Certain Man's Wife was walking out the door, the phone rang again. Eldest Daughter picked it up.

"Yes, she's coming!" CMW heard her say. "She had to get the gas can, and fill it with gas and work out all the stuff for Blind Linda and Our Girl Audrey, but she is coming!"

"Tell her I am walking out the door right now!" CMW hollered over her shoulder as she did precisely that. (It had been twenty minutes since Youngest Daughter had called. CMW was sure it must have been embarrassing to sit beside one of Delaware's most traveled secondary roads.)

CMW got to where Youngest Daughter's little green Mazda was parked beside the road, and pulled in behind it. She got the big red gas can and set it on the ground behind the car.

"Rachel. This car is pretty close to the road, don't you think?"

"I thought so, too, but I couldn't get it to go any farther."

"Why don't you get in and put it into neutral and guide it and I will push it off a little farther. I don't want someone coming down the road and taking one or both of us out."

Embarrassing for days! CMW had to feel sorry once again for her teenager. It was obvious to every single car going by that she had run out of gas because of that big red gas can sitting on the ground. And now, here was her decidedly plump Momma with her foot in a cast pushing her off the shoulder and partially into the grass. CMW was quite sure that she was praying, "Please, God, don't let anyone come along who knows me!" The task got accomplished fairly readily, and then it was time to try to get some gas into the tank.

Of course, that wouldn't be easy. The gas can spout was one of the new kind that needed to be forcefully pushed back to open the end to allow gas to flow out. The car's receptacle was one that had a spring loaded cover on it that needed pushed back to allow gas to flow in-- which is all well and good under normal circumstances. The problem was that the spout was just a tad bit bigger than the opening and every time CMW upended the can and tried to put gas in there, there was this volcano of gas that just ran right out on the ground. Youngest Daughter was becoming more and more nauseated by the minute, and CMW kept almost falling while she ran around trying to figure everything out. Finally, she retrieved a sturdy plastic knife from her trusty mini-van (even it won't run without gas, though) and instructed Youngest Daughter to push back the flapper to the gas tank while she attempted once again to pour in whatever she possibly could get in there. Finally. A small measure of success!

Then. "Uh, Mom--" said Youngest Daughter uncertainly. "Um. I think -- that knife broke off into the gas tank." She held up half of the red plastic knife. "This can't be good."

While CMW was pondering this, a truck pulled up behind the pair and a clean-cut gentleman got out. Maybe some help! He walked up towards the two woebegone females, holding a sheet of paper.

"Hello, Ladies. I need some eyes!" CMW must have looked puzzled. After all, he had just been driving down the road. He had better be able to see! He went on to explain. "I need you to read something for me. You see, I left my reading glasses at home, and I need to know what this paper says, and I can't see a thing!" He spread the paper over the trunk of Youngest Daughter's car.

A sudden thought hit Certain Man's Wife. "You know what?" she said excitedly. "I have a pair of reading glasses in my car at this very minute. Someone left them there and they do not belong to me, and I have considered giving them away. You can have them if you want them. I think they belong to my brother and he only has about a hundred pair-- Here, Rachel, hold this can steady and I will go and get them." So she clumped back to the minivan and retrieved the brown male-looking reading glasses from the side pocket where they had been residing for several months. She took them back to the Man by the Side of the Road, cleaning them on her skirt as she walked.

He took them delightedly, put them on his face, looked at his paper and burst into a grin. "They're perfect!" he pronounced happily. And gave CMW that fist-bump sort of thing people do when they have just had a victory of sorts. "That's a wonderful thing!"

"That's a God-thing!' Certain Man's Wife told him. (He didn't acknowledge that statement, but it doesn't change the fact.). And he returned to his vehicle.

"Mom, that man said that it won't matter a bit if that plastic knife is in there. I asked him while you were back there getting the glasses."

"Well, let's see if we can see the plastic when we are done, and if we can get it, we will!" So they held the can steady until there didn't seem to be any more going into the opening, and then took it down and looked in the opening. The piece of plastic knife was right there. Stuck in the little flapper. Youngest Daughter took a scissors that CMW had conveniently in the car and used it as a tweezer sort of thing and got the pieces out.

"Okay, let's see if we can get this car started," said CMW to her weary offspringin'. Youngest Daughter got into her car and started the car on the first try. "That's good. I will write you a note, and you can get yourself to school."

"Mom," said Youngest Daughter tearily. "I feel sick. I am so tired and I have gas on me. The smell is making me feel like throwing up. Please, can't I come back home, clean up and get my note? I don't feel like going to school at all, but I need to go for Geometry and Chorus. Please, can't I go back home for a little bit?"

CMW looked at her precious woman-child and had mercy upon her. They got both vehicles turned around and started back home. CMW called the school and explained the circumstances. And she found not only understanding, but mercy at the other end of the line. Then she called Easter Seals and discussed the day with them, and decided that she was going to keep Blind Linda home all day, too. She came home and found the day vastly improved with the decisions behind her and the quiet day ahead.

And the day was very quiet until almost 4 pm, when she heard a wailing noise at her door. It was Youngest Daughter, and she was making very distressed noises .

"Oh, Mom! I can't stand it! Something terrible happened to me!"

How could this be happening again??? Certain Man's Wife sprang up from her chair where she was trying to rest her foot.

"What's wrong, Rachel? What happened?"

"Oh, Mom. I was on my way to the chicken house and I stepped on a snake! It was brown and yucky looking and I felt it slither its tail through my toes." She shuddered. "Come out and see it, Mom. It felt terrible!"

So CMW clumped out to the generator shed and there was this very brown and healthy looking snake slithering through the grass. CMW did attempt to catch it in a bucket so she could show it to Certain Man, and Youngest Daughter gave brave chase, but it slithered into the brush pile and was gone. Youngest Daughter shuddered again, and made noises concerning the fright and surprise, but went to the chicken houses to complete her evening chores and CMW returned to the house to hope once again for some peace and quiet and the chance to put her foot up.

And that is the news from Shady Acres where the foot doesn't actually feel too bad tonight and CMW is going off to a women's meeting at Eldest Daughter's house.

CMW Bakes Bread

Saturday Morning, 5:30 AM.

The rain was dripping off the eaves, and Certain Man's Wife, snuggled under the covers to catch a few extra winks of sleep. There would be no wood cutting for the few brave men of Laws Mennonite Church, so Certain Man wouldn't be down the road for most of the day, working himself half to death. In fact, this was the day that Certain Man and Certain Man's Wife were to go out hunting for the great Wedding Suit that would be suitable for the "father of the groom" for not only one son's wedding, but actually, two!

"I refuse to buy separate suits for weddings that will be only eight weeks apart!" he stated, rather emphatically. And so, since Youngest Son and Girl With a Beautiful Heart suggested that he wear a black suit for their wedding, and Eldest Son and his Ohio Heart Throb didn't really care what he wore as long as he was dressed, the decision was made to go looking for a black suit that would serve a dual purpose. (Now if only Certain Man's Wife could do the same with "mother of the groom" dresses. Ha, Ha!)

Certain Man had proclaimed that he really didn't have time to go shopping. His chickens were going out early Monday morning, there were things to do in the chicken house, and there was a dinner and a play at Youngest Daughter's school at 5:30 in the evening that Youngest Daughter was a part of. It was imperative that they attend. Certain Man decided that, if they got off early, they should be back early, and that would leave plenty of time to do everything at home that he wanted to do. So the time was set to leave soon after nine o'clock Saturday morning. CMW thought briefly that the Mall wouldn't even open until ten, but reasoned that CM is quite often not ready when he thinks he will be, so thought that it would be fine.

As she lay sleepily listening to the rain and thinking about the day ahead, it suddenly dawned on her fur brain that she was almost out of bread. And tomorrow, the families of their small group were coming for lunch, (this particular small group is the designated host for the first Sunday of every month) and the food had been taken care of except the bread. Usually there is plenty of bread at the house of Certain Man and Certain Man's Wife

165

because CMW bakes ten loaves at a time whenever the supply gets low. CMW had planned that she would just provide the bread needed for this meal.

This actually is not the job that it might appear to be. Certain Man put a second cookstove in a little alcove in CMW's laundry room, and it is usual for her to be able to bake those ten loaves from the beginning mixing to the finished baking in about three hours.

Of course, CMW calculated the time between her head on the pillow and 9:00 AM (well, actually, 9:30 or 10:00) and realized that there was enough time to bake bread before she left for the shopping mall. That way, she wouldn't get into any complications after she got home, and there would be bread for lunch the next day. So before she (or Certain Man) could change her mind, she leaped out of bed and started rummaging for day clothes.

"Where are you going?" questioned Great Sleeping Bear. I mean, Certain Man.

"If I get busy right now, I can bake bread before we head out for Dover. I think I will be glad later tonight that it is done." He made some mild objections, but didn't actually tell her she couldn't, so she descended down to the kitchen to commence to start.

Three cups of dry milk powder went into her big Pyrex mixing bowl, then she filled it until it was ready to overflow with hot water. making ten cups of reconstituted milk. That went in to her gigantic metal bowl. Three more cups of warm water went into the same Pyrex mixing bowl, and she added a half cup of active dry yeast. She measured two cups of sugar, poured a small amount over the yeast and stirred that mixture, then added the rest of the sugar to the hot milk. Then she added 1/3 cup of salt to the milk and sugar, and went to get 2 cups of Crisco to melt in the microwave. After the yeast has risen, and she pours it into the milk, salt and sugar mixture, she adds a five pound bag of flour before adding any of the melted shortening. This has something to do with the yeast binding to the flour before the shortening is added that makes for a better texture in the finished product.

This is where everything went wrong. There was no plain white Crisco in the entire house. CMW looked. And looked. And looked! Here and there, up and down, under and over. And then did it all again. She was sure there was some white Crisco shortening somewhere in the house, but it was nowhere to be seen. She finally found a can of Butter flavored Crisco that she looked at dubiously. She just didn't think it would be okay, but after the third time through the kitchen, she talked herself into using that butter flavored Crisco, even though she was afraid that it wasn't a good idea.

Thus begins the saga of another, "I can't believe I really did that!" But it is in retrospect. Nothing would have prepared CMW for the real problem.

As most yeast bakers know, there is nothing like baking bread on a rainy day. The atmospheric pressure does something special with the dough, and the bread is often much better than CMW really deserves. And Saturday looked like it would be no exception. The bread went together beautifully. She added the melted yellow Crisco to the original mixture, and worked most of another 5 lb. bag of flour into it. The dough whistled while CMW kneaded it (a sure sign of a good batch of dough) and it felt and looked like some of the better bread that CMW has made in her time. It rose beautifully and was perfect in so many ways.

It was a little more yellow than usual, and CMW thought that there just might be a little different smell. But it looked so nice, she brushed off her anxieties. She's been often told that she is like her Lauver ancestors when it comes to cooking. Something is just never quite right, somehow.

Certain Man's wife set the ten beautiful loaves to cool and got ready in plenty of time to go to Dover, and left everything in the care of others. It was a perfect day for suit shopping, as JCPenney had 50% off their suits on a six hour sale and CM and CMW were there at the exact right time. A nice suit was procured in anticipation of the upcoming weddings, and CMW came home early, and looked at her good bread. It made her feel really good to think she had discovered that, in a pinch, bread made with butter flavored Crisco was just as good as bread made with regular flavored Crisco.

That was what CMW thought until she tasted it. Oh, no! You could taste that butter flavored Crisco, and believe you me, it didn't make the bread taste buttery. It had a very strange taste to it. CMW held her peace. Maybe no one would notice it.

The first loaf got sliced and half eaten before it was cool. Certain Man, the official bread slicer, cut the rest, put eight in the freezer for later use, and left the loaf and a half out for Small Group lunch the next day.

The Small Group families came, and everyone that took bread ate it, and nary a complaint was made, but CMW just couldn't quite put her finger on what there was about it that was just so wrong. So she took a loaf to the gathering at her Sweet Mama's house on Sunday night. Again, though it was discussed at great length in company of all those good cooks, the smell and the flavor were something elusive. Familiar – but elusive.

"Hey, Mom," said Youngest Daughter on Monday (having been absent from the other discussions), "this bread has a funny taste, somehow. It actually smells like homemade doughnuts!"

Maybe that was it. CMW came over to take a sniff, and sure enough, it did smell like a homemade doughnut. And it did not set right with her. She still had seven loaves that she needed to get rid of somehow.

So she has faithfully packed Eldest Son's lunch all week with it. He doesn't like it much, but since he is on a diet, he says that pretty much anything tastes good to him once he gets used to it.

CMW cannot "get used to it." It actually turns her stomach when she smells it.

Middle Daughter optimistically says that it is okay as peanut butter and jelly sandwiches.

Certain Man says to just get rid of it.

Eldest Daughter says to take it in to a local "recovery house."

"They won't know the difference, " she says cheerfully. "And besides, it will be gone by the time they figure it out, so it won't matter."

CMW thinks of those loaves of bread in her freezer and wishes they would disappear. She doesn't want to give them away because it might damage her reputation. (!) Uh-huh. She especially doesn't want to give it away to people who "won't know the difference." That is against the way she has been taught. It seems a little like giving used tea bags to the missionaries. But neither does she want to give it to someone who *would* know the difference. They would probably wish they hadn't received it. And even though it is nice that she isn't tempted to eat that bread, it doesn't seem fair for it to expect her family to eat it.

So. Is there any advice for this dilemma?

What would you do if you were Certain Man's Wife?

CMW and the Saga of the Errant Cat

It's been anything but a quiet weekend at Shady Acres.

Certain Man has been in a fit of getting things done around here. On Saturday morning, he propped a ladder up against a rather precarious limb to trim several other limbs from the Thornless Honey Locust Tree that were getting too long. While he had the ladder out, he propped it up against the side of the house to fix the topmost gable end of the house where a tree had bumped against the soffit and pulled up the roof and damaged the siding.

He scares Certain Man's Wife spitless when he does these things. CMW is very uncomfortable with a man on a ladder perched anywhere that is higher than her head. She was in the middle of doing the usual Saturday "catch-up" laundry and baking bread, so she didn't stand out there and hold the ladder or holler. She didn't figure there was too much that she could do, anyhow, with a ladder that is 30 feet long and a full grown man on the other end. I guess she sorta' thought that if it was gonna' go, it was gonna' go and she didn't want to be there to see it happen.

He came down, then, eventually, with his mission accomplished and asked CMW if she had any more of the "Mr. Clean Erasers®" that have been found to be very effective in washing off siding. Certain Man's Wife happened to have a whole box of them from Sam's Club, and he proceeded to inform her that since he had the big ladder up on the deck anyhow, he was going to wash the upper part of the house where the moss and green deposits had built up. CMW got him a bucket of warm water and the dozen or so Mr. Clean Erasers®, he got himself a hook to hang that bucket upon and he set out to clean the house. Certain Man's Wife went back to her bread.

In the middle of CMW's periodic checking on Certain Man's progress, the family cat, Tatters, who has been a part of the family for almost nine years, made a mad dash for the slightly opened door and disappeared under the deck. This did not trouble CMW inordinately since she sometimes does get out, and seriously heads back inside at almost her first chance.

After a time, Middle Daughter and Youngest Daughter returned from the Festival at Central Christian School and the Hospital Fair at the Hospital where Middle Daughter works and set about to help their beleaguered parents. Middle Daughter got up on the ledge of the roof and helped to wash the siding and Youngest Daughter helped CMW in the house. No mention was made of the missing cat.

In the afternoon, Certain Man's family headed out for the wedding of Eldest Son's friend, Matt and his girl Dorothy. It was a lovely wedding. The bride was beautiful, the groom's eyes were so full of love and happiness, the sermon was well done, the vows were traditional and sweet, there was not an unduly long wait between the wedding and the reception, and the food was excellent.

Certain Man's Wife's Sweet Mama sat with Our Girl Audrey and Blind Linda whilst the family was gone, and when they returned, the almost first words were, "Have you seen the cat?"

Sweet Mama said, "No, I haven't seen her at all. She has been nowhere around."

This was when Youngest Daughter realized that Tatters was missing. "She's gone for good," she stated emphatically. "I know that she is. She will never come back!" This was followed by a great treatise on people who didn't watch properly, didn't care whether the cat was out or not, and a great trembling of the lip.

Certain Man's Wife didn't share this view. "She has always come back. Don't worry, Rachel. She gets out a lot, whether you know it or not, and she always comes back"

"But she comes back right away. If she's been gone all day, she will not come back. She's probably dead somewhere."

Then the whole family got involved in the looking. They looked in the basement, in all the bedrooms, in the side "dungeon" space. No Tatters. Middle Daughter, who is, by far, the most involved with this capricious animal, went up and down the road, calling and looking. She got down and looked under the deck. She went out and looked in the dog pen. (We have an Australian Red Heeler, and he has killed many a cat that has ventured into his domain.)

No tattered remains of Tatters.

Middle Daughter and Certain Man went out to the barn where there are myriads of cats that have been dumped off here over the years. There is a barn cat that looks like our Tatters, but when it ran away as fast as it could go, they knew it wasn't her.

Certain Man's Wife's heart got increasingly heavy. Usually, when Tatters has been gone for some time, CMW can go to the sliding glass doors and call her, and she will dive for the open doorway and slither past like a banshee is after her. Though there were numerous callings made at all the doors, there was no sign of Tatters. Midway through the evening, there was this thunderous descent from the upstairs by Middle Daughter. She bolted through the family room and through the kitchen, past Certain Man's Wife.

"Deborah! Whatever is --"

170

"Sheppie is barking and I heard a cat scream!" She threw over her shoulder as she pounded through the laundry room and out the back door. This set off a whole new round of looking for the cat; searching through the dog pen, getting down to look inside the dog house to see if the body of the unfortunate beast had been drug into the dark confines of the canine abode. NOTHING!!!

And so the evening passed with no sign of the missing cat. Just before going to bed, Certain Man's Wife stood again at the darkness of the sliding glass doors and called for the furry little beast that has lightened many a heavy heart over the last nine years. "Lord, there are so many things out there that are heavy and sad. People are dying without a Savior and there is earthquake and war and famine and cyclone. A lost cat is pretty inconsequential in light of all the terrible things going on. But could you watch over our Tatters tonight? And if it is your will, could you bring her back to us? But if she is hurt or suffering, could you just allow her to go quickly? And would you comfort the hearts of Youngest and Middle Daughters?"

Morning came, bringing with it drizzle and cold. "If anything will bring her back," said Middle Daughter hopefully, "it is the rain. She HATES being out in the cold and rain." But there was no sign of the missing cat.

"I just want some closure," said Middle Daughter for the fourth time. "We need to call the neighbors and see if they have seen her. Maybe one of the barn tomcats chased her away. She doesn't have any claws so it would be difficult for her to defend herself."

"Do cats fight to the death?" wondered CMW aloud.

"Not usually," said Middle Daughter, "but usually if there is a fight, one of them will run away. And if Tatters ran away, the tom could be keeping her from coming back. She might have just gone to a friendly house and stayed."

When Certain Man came in from the morning chores, CMW looked at him questioningly. He shook his head. "Nope, I didn't see anything of her," he said softly to CMW.

"Do you think she will come back?" queried CMW.

"Nope. I think she is gone for good."

"That's what I'm afraid of, too." Said CMW sadly. "I think if she could come back, she would have by now. I suspect that she is dead somewhere, or at least severely injured." CMW began to think about a cuddly little kitty or a cat that would be more friendly and less independent.

"NO!" Said Youngest Daughter. "Tatters was the kind of cat I like. She wasn't so "needy" as some cats are."

"NO!" Said Our Girl Audrey. "I don't want another cat. I think it's better not to have a pet in the house."

"Alrighty then!" thought Certain Man's Wife. She wasn't going to ask Certain Man. Back when Tatters had first appeared on the doorstep, he had been thoroughly against her staying.

"If you keep that worthless bunch of fur," he was heard to say on more than one occasion, "you will have to call it 'Daddy' 'cause both of us can't live in the same house."

The pleas of his children, and their offer to help pay for some of the cat "needs" finally won him over, however, and he and Tatters entered into a guardedly peaceful co-existence, though "affection" would not be descriptive of their relationship. In fact, CMW heard the words "worthless bunch of fur" and "ugly fleabag" thrown about with random indignation with more regularity than would bespeak congeniality.

Sunday morning was filled with the usual last minute church preparations, getting lunch into the oven, checking family schedules and such, and then it was off to church -- but not without CMW looking intently one more time around the perimeter of the garage and flower gardens to see if maybe there was the familiar furry friend.

And so Sunday passed. CMW took a nap while Certain Man prepared the sermon for the Communion Service in the evening. And she dreamed mixed up dreams of cats that looked like Tatters in the dumpster with wild claws and teeth, and of injured cats in the grass. And since she overslept there was a mad rush to get everything done before leaving for evening church. She did call at the basement steps and the sliding glass one or two times, but was chided by family members. "Mom, she's gone. You might just as well accept it . . .

There is nothing quite like communion at Laws Mennonite Church. It is warm and personal and encouraging and strengthening. There is always a number who hang around late and talk and fellowship long after the meeting is over. Middle Daughter and Youngest Daughter went home fairly soon, but since Certain Man has a creed (The 11th commandment: "Thou shalt not leave the church parking lot until there are only two cars remaining, one of which is thine own.") it was over an hour before Certain Man and his wife had finished talking to good friends, cleaned up the communion remnants, and headed home.

As they pulled into the driveway, CMW commented about the number of cars parked around the circle and on the grass. "It looks like the boys have some company," she observed. Youngest Son's Girl had come home from college, and several of their friends had come to rejoice with them.

CM and CMW unloaded the van, and came into the house to be greeted with the words, "The cat is back!"

"What?"

"How?"

"Is she alright???"

Here Middle Daughter took up the story. It seems that Youngest Son came into the back door to find her waiting patiently on the floor inside the entryway to get into the laundry room. And of course there was no explanation for her whereabouts for the past 36 hours. Youngest Son was mad because all the emotional energy had been wasted when she was "just in the basement." But Certain Man and his wife think she may have found a way to get from the crawl space to the outside, or that she may have eaten something when she was out and didn't feel good for a while and just slept it off. She seems a little subdued, maybe less energetic, but we cannot find any cuts or scratches or such. Whatever happened, and where ever she has been, she has been welcomed with a great deal of affection and relief. I am so glad that she isn't somewhere injured or dying with no one to watch over her.

And then it occurs to me that there are plenty of humans out there tonight in that very circumstance -- dying. With no one to watch over them or care whether they live or die.

Do I seek them with the same heavy heart that I had when I was looking for my errant cat?

Do you?

Does anyone care?

Ponderings as Youngest Son Marries

It is no secret that the Youngest Son of Certain Man and Certain Man's Wife (Lemuel) has kept them on their toes and on their knees. Many have been the anxious moments that accompanied his childhood and Addled Essence. (I know, I know. It's "*ADOLESCENCE.*" But I'm his momma. I know whereof I speak!)

Throughout the years of elementary school and middle school, he was bravely and usually faithfully homeschooled at the kitchen table of Shady Acres Homeschool Academy, but when he was 16, it became apparent that he was no longer satisfied therewith and had no intentions of being homeschooled another year.   So it was that he was duly enrolled in Greenwood Mennonite School in the fall of his junior year.

It is also no secret that the Youngest Son of Certain Man and Certain Man's Wife has always had an eye on the opposite sex.   Indeed, his appreciation for their beauty went back to his baby sister. He had wanted a brother, but when God saw fit to bless him with a sister, it wasn't long until his admiration of her beauty had softened his little heart into pure devotion.

One day he was patting her head affectionately and he looked up and said apologetically, "I thought I wanted a baby brother. I just didn't know a baby sister would be so pretty!" And that was pretty much the way it was throughout all his years. Somewhere in the world, nearly every day of his conscious life, there was someone whose beauty he thought was rare and magnificent. And this was cause for even more concern on the part of Certain Man and Certain Man's wife.

Somehow, he actually made it through almost to graduation without falling prey to the wiles of any of his classmates. But, there came a day in May when he came to his Momma and said, "There's this girl in my class. Jess Lee. Anyhow, her parents are out of town, and her brother is gone to his girlfriend's house, so she is all alone for Sunday lunch. Would it be okay if she came and ate lunch with us? I hate for her to be all alone."

We didn't know very much about Jessica Lee. She was on her way to being the Salutatorian of Youngest Son's graduating class, so we knew she was intelligent.   She was beautiful.   But we had no idea what kind of personality she had, or if she would be comfortable with the noisy Yutzy Sunday lunch. But the way to find that out was to have her come.

"I guess I don't care, Lem," I said. "What does she like to eat?"

"Well, she's sorta' a health foods freak, but she'll eat what we have. She *is* big on vegetables, though."

"Just tell her to come, Son. It will be okay."

And so, it was settled. This Momma kept her radar out in the days before the Sunday to see if there was any chance that something more than just friendship was on the horizon. She even asked Youngest Son.

"Nah, Mom. She's just a friend. It's nothing. I just feel sorry for her having to be alone."

The Sunday came, and with it, Jessica Lee. My memory of that day and what we ate and what was said is very fuzzy except for one thing. I KNEW there was an unusual connection between these two young people. After lunch, Youngest Son was running around the yard, trying to keep starlings and blackbirds off the bird feeders, and this girlie was trotting around behind him, laughing and talking and admonishing him in the ways of rightness. There was this free and easy exchange between them that was a delight to see.

I was standing at the double windows in our family room, and there is this picture that will be forever in my mind. A guy and a gal against the green of the spring grass. His hair is askew, and he is laughing. She is beautiful and she is protesting something, and she is also laughing. It was pure and sweet and good.

I turned to Certain Man and said. "I'm not so sure. Lem says that there is nothing between them, but there *is* something there. I would not be surprised at all if something came of this." He came and looked over my shoulder and smiled his wise smile.

"Could be," he said in his non-committal way. "I guess we'll see."

And so it was. We *did* see. We learned to know and love this Girl With a Beautiful Heart, and she was good for Youngest Son in so many ways. And he decided that he wanted her for more than just a friend. And so the days and months and even years passed. Then there came a day when he asked if he could talk to us.

"I just want you to know that if you are against having Jessica for a daughter in law, you had better speak fast, because I have every intention of marrying her . . ."

Looking across at those clear eyes, so intense and so full of light and love, we knew that he had found his soulmate, and that "something between them" was strong and beautiful and good. And his Daddy and His Momma were glad.

You go son. Go with our blessing.

CMW and the Family Does Corn (Again!)

It always happens, that is, if the rains come in a timely fashion, that the daughters of Mark Yoder, Sr. get just a little bit obsessed with getting their sweet corn done. Last year there was not enough to go around. One of us got none. The other two got far less than they had hoped.

Now, granted, the families are shrinking (at an alarming rate in all three households, to be honest!) but to put a proper Sunday lunch together, a Yoder gal needs home-frozen yellow sweet corn. So this year, there has been careful attention paid to where it could be procured, and, sure enough, this week was the week for it.

Now Certain Man's Wife likes to do some up for the very married, newly married and nearly married in her family. And Middle Sister likes to have a goodly supply for her family, and the two "nearly marrieds" in her family, so CMW, in a mode of thinking ahead, remembered that there was a time when 6,000 ears were done by the family and she settled upon a figure of 3,000 ears for the family. But when the price was a bit steeper than she anticipated and Youngest Brother's patch held some promise of later corn, she changed the amount to 2,000. Middle Sister added her 750 ears to that, and they decided that, bright and early on Monday morning, they would set to it.

Certain Man took his truck and trailer to the property of the esteemed Corn Grower and left it there overnight so that the corn could be picked directly into the said convenience, and there wouldn't be as much hauling and transferring in the morning. Certain Man also took a vacation day from work so that he could be home to help. CMW felt in her heart that this would prove to be the most important blessing of the day, and she was RIGHT!

The corn arrived and the hands that were available set about to husk. And husk. And husk. Certain Man's Wife looked at the pile when it arrived and thought it would not take too much time to do that corn. But the hands worked steady for hours and hours before it was finally finished. The gals got busy around the "cow" and washed and silked the husked ears in a continuous fashion (also for hours and hours).

The help was phenomenal. Sweet Mama was there. Middle Sister came and brought her three youngest offspringin's. Youngest Sister was there from the start to the finish. All five of Certain Man's children and the two spouses helped at various times during the day. Youngest Son's Mother-in-Law came for a while and two young friends showed up and helped for a great many hours. And so the day went on and on.

Sweet Mama baked a chocolate sheet cake and also brought some Oreos. Middle Sister brought garden tea, Youngest Daughter brought meatballs in a barbecue sauce, Certain Man's wife had egg salad and chicken salad and a casserole of chicken and dressing and gravy. Once the cookers got fired up, there was hot corn with butter and salt to grab in between all the many jobs and the day wore on.

Along about two or three o'clock, a sense of something not being quite right began to tug at Certain Man's Wife's subconscious thought. Things were just not getting done like they should. Where was all this corn coming from? She kept mulling it over and over in her head.

"I know that we did 6,000 ears one year," she contemplated. "Where is all this coming from? We aren't going to be done here for hours and hours. I just don't understand it." There were a few comments about how the corn was multiplying rapidly, but people were good natured about it, and the hands kept on moving.

"How many ears did you say we got?" was a frequent question, and Certain Man's Wife tried to reassure people with logic. "We ordered 2,750 with Aunt Sarah's. Kauffman's sent us an extra 75 ears, so we should have around 2,825 or so. One year we did 6,000, so we should be able to wrap this up pretty well."

In a reflective moment, CMW began to go over the year of 6,000 ears, and a slow, sickening realization began to creep into her very soul. Oh, dear! There was a year that 6,000 ears of corn were processed, but that was in one week, not one day. Oh, dear! What should she say? How should she comfort all these hard workers?

"You know what, guys?" she said in the most contrite voice that she could muster. "I've been thinking about those 6,000 ears of corn. And I am ashamed to say this, but that was the total for a week, not a day!"

"I wondered!" said Youngest Sister. "I was sure we never did this much corn, and we don't have the help that we did back then."

"It did seem like alot," said Sweet Mama, who stayed until the last ear was silked. "This seemed like a terrible lot of corn to me." And various and sundry others added their opinions. But it was too late to do anything about it. The corn was picked, the corn was husked, it had to be processed. And so, the faithful labored on. Automatically filling the cookers, cooling, draining, cutting it off the cob, packaging it, getting it to the freezer. Over and over again.

And it came to pass, that Beloved Son-in-Law and Eldest Son pulled the last two loads out of the cookers to the sound of great cheers around 10 pm and the weary cutter-off-ers got the last ears finished and Certain Man carried the last bags to the freezer, and the major job was done. Some scurried off to their abodes, some stayed and helped to clean up, but finally, the wash baskets were clean, the muck buckets washed and upside down on the lawn, the tables washed off, the corn cobs taken to the pasture, and the cookers disconnected and put away and the floor sprayed down and the towels and hot pads hung on the wash line. Some very, very tired, but some very, very pleased people were finally done.

Each of the four Newly/Nearly Married couples had 25 "pints" of corn. Eldest Daughter had 50. Middle Sister had 80 "almost quarts" and Certain Man's Wife had 100 of the same. Next week we will do some for Youngest Sister, Lord willing, probably some for Sweet Mama, and if there is extra in Youngest Brother's patch after his wife and children do what they need, we will add to the coffers of whoever wants to have more.

It is so nice to have corn in the freezer again. Now and again, Certain Man will make muttering noises about how CMW should just buy frozen corn from the store and "doctor" it up. He thinks she could make it taste almost as good. But then he goes out of his way to help in any way possible for her and her sisters to freeze whatever amount they feel is necessary, and when it is finally done, oh, how sweet it is!

And that is the News from Shady Acres. Certain Man is suffering greatly today from an old shoulder injury that was aggravated by all his hard work yesterday. Certain Man's Wife is not getting much done in the way of homemaking duties, and the children have proven once again that days like yesterday wouldn't get done without their stellar help.

CMW Helps in the Chicken House

CMW posted a Xanga post with pictures about her collection of pilgrims on a September afternoon, and then went out to talk to Certain Man about the state of things in the chicken house. In the middle of his Sunday sermon that morning, he had stopped and said, "You are going to have to excuse me -- Deborah, the chicken house alarm is going off, could you or Gary or someone go and check it for me please?" And so Rachel, who is the chicken house gal, went home to check on things. For those of you who were in Delaware on September 14, 2008, you may remember that it was an oppressively hot, humid day. Certain Man had big chickens, and as careful as he was to manage things properly, Shady Acres Farm still suffered a heat loss. 500 of the biggest, nicest birds. Chicken growers know that heat always gets the biggest ones. Sick at heart, CMW asked him what he was going to do about picking up the dead.

"Oh," he said, matter-of-factly, "I've been throwing them to the doors all day. it is just a matter of picking them up."

"I'm going to come help," CMW said.

"No, you stay in the house. It's too hard for you." He smiled at her reassuringly and headed on out.

The humidity was still high, the temp was still over 80, but he thought that since night was falling he might just as well get busy. CMW took care of some in the house things, fielded a call from Youngest Son in Ohio (Who was out of electricity for almost 30 hours) and finally got out of her still Sunday dress and pulled on an old dress from the closet. She found an old kerchief to put around her Sunday clean hair, and found an old pair of chicken house sandals.

Where was all the help? Beloved Son-in-Law is the one person who so often helps at a time like this, but he was out with an old friend. Youngest Daughter was memorizing for Quiz team, Middle Daughter had disappeared into the upper story. And Eldest Son and His Beloved were at their home. Eldest Daughter does not do Chicken House Stuff. She had come to spend the evening with home folk while Beloved Son-in-Law was out with his friend.

"I'm going out to help Daddy pick up dead chickens," CMW said to Eldest Daughter as she sat with her laptop in her Daddy's La-Z-Boy recliner.

"Nice do-rag!" she commented briefly, looking at CMW's perky kerchief over the edge of her computer.

"Yes, well --" Said CMW, and went out into the dusky light. The magnificent sunset stopped her for a minute, but then she saw Certain Man out by the chicken house with his reliable little tractor and loader and knew she had best get on her way. She came around the tractor to see a great pile of chickens inside the chicken house on the floor in front of the main door. Certain Man was methodically throwing them, one by one, onto the loader.

"How's it coming, Sweetheart?" asked CMW cheerfully.

"Well, it's not going too bad," said her husband. (She never quite knows just how things truly are by his responses. Sometimes she thinks that something cataclysmic has happened because of what he says, and then she finds out that it wasn't really quite as earth-stopping as it sounded. And then there are times when things are really, really awful, and he is unusually cheerful about it all.)

"Are you almost done?"

"Well, I'm done with house one, and have the worst half of house two done, and I have house three yet to go. House three will be the worst."

"What can I do? How can I best help?"

"Suppose you drive the tractor!" he says with a gleam in his eye.

"I don't know how to drive the tractor!" said CMW indignantly. In her mind's eye, she can see the posts to the compost bins come tumbling down while she tries to dump the bucket load of chickens into what seems like an inordinately small space.

"Sure you can. I'll teach you!"

"Why don't you drive the tractor and I'll pick up chickens."

"You should go in and get boots," he said sternly, looking down at the chicken house sandals. "These chickens have sharp claws. You're liable to get hurt."

"I don't have any chicken house boots," CMW said cheerfully. "Let me try and see how it goes, and if I need to go get shoes, I'll do it."

And so they set to work. He loaded the chickens that were thrown to the door, and then came and helped her to pick up in the house. Then, when there was a big pile by a door, he would go and load them up and take them to the compost bins. One of the best blessings of this particular marriage has been that the two of them can work together really well (once they settle who is doing what!) and the time passed with good camaraderie and cooperation. They finished house two and went on to house three.

House Three *was* worse than house two, but Certain Man had gone before, and many of the chickens were picked up and thrown to the doors. There were still a number to pick up, but while he loaded and hauled the ones that were already gathered, CMW was able to finish covering the house and finally, they were down to the last door. CMW stood on the inside, while he stood on the outside with both of them loading the last load. That was when CMW noticed that he was only using his left hand to pitch them on except on very rare occasions. Then his right arm would only bring them up to somewhere between his knee and waist, and with a wrench somewhere in her middle, CMW knew that his troublesome shoulder was giving him alot of pain.

"Sweetheart, is that shoulder really hurting?"

"Yeah, well, it is the way it is. It's been bothering me ever since this morning at church . . . It'll be alright."

They finished up, and he took the last load to the compost bins. CMW went in to get a shower and wash her hair and get ready for bed. It was already pretty late. She was amazed again at how dirty a person can get, and how wonderful it feels to be clean. CMW watched the dirt swirl down the drain and thought about pilgrims and clean houses and celebrating Harvest and keeping family traditions and being thankful. And she thought about how her life holds so many incongruities and contradictions. She can be in the middle of one beautiful thing and enjoying it to the fullest, and in such a short time be at an entirely different place with anything but beautiful and esthetic surroundings, and yet it is all life. Even in (maybe especially in) the dirt and the smells of death.

Yesterday in that smelly, hot chicken house, CMW saw again how Certain Man's courage and love give life and meaning to her and to their children. How his example of keeping on when it's hard and when it hurts and when it seems like you have to do it mostly by yourself is something that is beyond price.

And so, while CMW is glad for the finer reminders to be thankful in this Season of Grateful Praise, tonight she gives thanks for a reminder that was found among the losses strewn in the heat at a chicken farm in Delaware.

CMW and the Old Piano

Certain Man's Wife said goodbye to an old friend on Saturday.

When she was about eleven years old, her auntie offered her the old piano that had been at their house for years and years. CMW wanted to learn to play piano. Her desire was to get as good as her cousin, Bonnie, who could play for crowds while they sang, and it looked so wonderful. CMW was probably just looking for the attention, more than anything else, but when her Aunt Freda said that she could have their old one, CMW was elated.

It rode from Wilmington to Greenwood on the back of a truck. Not an easy or gentle ride. It was big and black and ugly, but it played, and the tuner said that it was a "diamond in the rough" and that was enough for CMW. Especially after her Sweet Mama and Oldest Brother spent a day with paint remover and uncovered a beautiful piece of furniture under all that black paint.

CMW tried hard to learn to play it. She took lessons from old, wizened Southern Gentleman and was pretty much a sore trial to his orderly soul. She early learned to play by ear almost anything that she knew well. The melody line was usually accurate but the harmony wasn't played by the notes, but more like the chords. Oh, and she never figured out many complicated chords. CMW found her twelve bass accordion an accommodating friend as well, and spent many hours squalling away on that or plinking her own versions of familiar songs on the piano. Eventually, she spared her elderly piano teacher some anxiety by quitting the lessons. And so, the years passed.

Then she met and married Certain Man and moved to Ohio. The heavy old piano stayed at the old home place, and been relegated to a closed in porch. Through the heat of many a summer and the cold of many a winter, it was pretty much just a space occupier. But then Youngest Sister and her husband bought the home place and by that time, Certain Man and Certain Man's Wife were back in Delaware.

"Mary Ann," said Youngest Sister one day (probably in 1985), "If you want that old piano, you had better get it. If you don't want it, I'm getting rid of it. It can go to the dump for all I care."

CMW was alarmed. Not her piano! "No, don't do that," pleaded CMW. "I want it."

"Well, if you want it, you had better get it. I want it out of here!"

And so CMW went to her patient and loving husband and prevailed upon him to line up some help to move the heavy old piano from Youngest Sister's house to their home on Andrewsville Road. It was just a short trip – maybe two miles. Again they brought it on the back of a pickup truck, and heaved and groaned and shoved and pulled until they had it almost into the big green all purpose room.

And then it happened. As Certain Man and his trusty helpers were trying to slide the piano down a plank from the truck to the house, it ran off the plank and landed squarely on Certain Man's toe. CMW did not witness this, but she certainly witnessed the aftermath.

This piano weighed 560 pounds. Crashing it down on a toe is not advisable, either in consideration of the toe or the disposition of the one to whom the toe is attached. Certain Man writhed in pain and made great unhappy noises. If he hadn't been in the company of watchful beings, the piano may have suffered bodily injury as well.

CMW has often said that Certain Man had a grudge against that piano from that moment on. This is a subject which comes up frequently in the discussions about the piano. But the piano was in the house by the time the toe was injured, so it stayed. And when Certain Man's family moved from Andrewsville Road in 1989, Certain Man looked at it darkly, hinted that this might be a good time to get rid of it, but he and his reliable helpers eventually loaded it up on the back of a really big truck and took it 15 miles to Milford, where it was unloaded into the living room at Shady Acres. It has been here ever since.

The family has a great many happy memories surrounding the old piano. They used it for many a year for the inspirational and energetic singing that their small group loved to do together. Friend Karen has made the old piano do things that made some pretty pitiful sounding people sound (actually) pretty good. The families from Certain Man's office have come every Christmas for almost seven years and one of the things that rag-tag group always does is sing the songs of Christmas with the glorious music that Karen was able to produce out of the century old instrument.

In the last few years, the tuner has been warning CMW that the days were numbered. He would sigh and try to once again get it into some resemblance of tune to see it at least through the holidays. Last week, he came out to the kitchen where CMW was making a pot of soup and told her that it was just useless.

"If you gave me $10,000.00 and told me to fix it," he said sadly, "I couldn't do it. There is just nothing left. The hammers are moth eaten and the screws won't stay tight. I'm so sorry, but I cannot conscientiously charge you to tune this piano when I know it isn't any use. What it needs is an international prayer chain for its healing, but I'm afraid that even that isn't going to do much good."

CMW reasoned with him, reminded him of its wonderful tone, its gorgeous woodwork, and the memories that are all tied up in the old piano. He was very understanding, and he offered to try to get it through the holidays again, but he said that it really wasn't a good investment of time and money.

"What should we do with it?" CMW asked him. She thought that maybe there was a place just looking for old pianos like this. She loved it so much that she could hardly bear to think of it not being worth something.

"I can tell you the place," he said firmly. "It's down at Hardscrabble (an actual place in Delaware where our most famous landfill is located). It's called the DUMP. It's the best place for it. Yes, it's a beautiful piece of furniture, but it is useless as a piano. And old pianos are a dime a dozen. There are so many of them around, and there just is no use for them."

CMW likes her old piano tuner. He is a little like her piano. Old and worn out, but precious because of a rich history, and because someone loves him. And he is a person. Not a thing, and as a person with a great deal of earnest emotion, he told CMW these things in the presence of the Man with the injured toe. And it didn't take Certain Man very long to decide that if the piano was really not worth repairing, that the best time to get rid of it was NOW.

So, once again, he rallied his troops around him, and called up the swarthy forces that involve Beloved Son-in-Law, Eldest Son, and friend Joel, and they showed up on Saturday around noon and they took that old piano out of here. For good. Before they all descended upon the house, CMW went in and sat at the old piano one more time. She looked at its intricate woodwork, and played a few of her familiar old songs. She thought about the need that it filled in her life, and the memories that are so full of warmth and hope and laughter and music. And CMW cried some silly tears.

They dismantled part of it to try to make it a little easier to load, and CMW rescued the intricately carved front piece/hymnal holder. Middle Daughter has a strong artistic imagination, and CMW was certain that she could think of something that would be an interesting use for that almost perfect piece of antique wood.

She couldn't bear to watch as they slid it out of the living room and onto the waiting pickup. Yes. It rode out on the back of yet another pickup.

"Aw, Mom," said Eldest Son tenderly. "You really feel bad, don't you?" He hugged her against his strong chest and patted her shoulder. "You'll be okay, Mom. But I know it is hard." That made her cry some more.

CMW felt like she was betraying a friend, and it tugged at her heart more than she ever dreamed that it would. She kept telling herself it was all so silly. After all, it was just a piano. All over this world, there are far greater losses than an old piano that isn't worth fixing. And that causes CMW to think about what is really important to her. What are the things that cause her to bend the proverbial knee of her carnal heart? And why can't she recognize those behaviors and things that make her want more when so many people in this world have so little?

CMW doesn't think it is wrong to enjoy things that make memories, bring us pleasure, allow us to share, etc. But this old piano has made her do a lot of thinking about holding things dear to our hearts that aren't eternal. What we've been given can become so important to us when in fact, it is a tool, entrusted to us for the sake of the Kingdom. And it is right to use things to make memories, draw people in, share with them the good news of Salvation. But things should be a means to an end, not the stuff we hang our hearts on.

"You can get another one," say the soothsayers.

"No, I can't," is CMW's standard answer to that. "There isn't any other piano that is worth the money when it doesn't have the history, the memories that this one did." Maybe she needs to rethink that. It's a little hard to tell. That old piano isn't somewhere feeling rejected. It isn't troubled by the way Certain Man felt about it or the decision to get rid of it. It bothers CMW, but it doesn't bother the piano. It won't shed a single tear if Certain Man and his wife decide to replace it. And the things they always used it for are still a part of their lives, of their plans for the future.

And so, this is the conclusion to which CMW has come: "I guess there is a *place* for another piano at our house. I just don't know if there is *space*."

CMW, The Traffic Cop and a Winter Day

Now it came to pass that January 13th, the year of our Lord, 2009, was a most scrambling and bustling and busy day for Certain Man's Wife. There were many things to be accomplished and much was joyfully anticipated, but the day was fraught with unexpected events, as well.

It all started well enough. There was a young friend, Celia, who had begotten a beautiful, healthy, fat baby son, and Friend Tammy, with her usual benevolence, had discussed with CMW about a baby shower. Of course, there is nothing more pleasant than a baby shower, and it was with delight that CMW planned to attend. In talking with Tammy, CMW discovered that it would be nice to have some help with meals, so she told Friend Tammy that she would be glad to bring a casserole or something for the family for supper. All of these things were discussed on the Saturday before the Tuesday when the shower was to occur.

As the plans were being finalized, actually the afternoon before the shower, she said to Friend Tammy, "By the way, is there anything you need yet for the refreshments? I'd be glad to he - - " She actually stopped, mid-sentence, because she suddenly remembered that she had, in fact, already promised to help with the refreshments. Something specific. Chicken Salad Sandwiches. On homemade bread.

"Oh, that's right," she said, trying to sound confident. "I *am* bringing something, am I not?"

"That's right," said Friend Tammy, brightly. "I am counting on you for the chicken salad sandwiches. Does it still suit?"

"Yes, it does. I had actually forgotten about it, so I am glad you reminded me. I have some chicken in the fridge that I can cook up, there's bread in the freezer, and it won't take long to make the chicken salad. I will bring it."

And CMW flew off the phone, got her two chickens into the pot and got them started cooking rather speedily. There were various activities that evening, and CMW even spent a happy time at the home of Eldest Son and his Sweet Wife. When she came home, there was some laundry to finish and kitchen to straighten and the chicken to take off the bones. Certain Man, still feeling lousy after having two wisdom teeth taken out, went to bed early. And

CMW, with no one to bother her, sped through the rest of the laundry and then looked at the two chickens waiting to be deboned.

"Oh, well," she thought wearily. "What gets done tonight won't have to be done tomorrow morning." So the midnight hour found her carefully deboning the chicken and getting it into the fridge. There would be time in the morning to mix up the casserole and make the chicken salad and sandwiches.

It was a short night, but CMW felt pretty good, in spite of it all when she got up on Tuesday morning. And she flew around, getting Our Girl Audrey and Blind Linda ready for Center and out the door. Eldest Daughter showed up with the two little boys she babysits for who had come for hot chocolate at "Aunt Mary's house," and she cheerfully pitched in and helped. She wasn't planning on attending the shower, but as the time passed, she decided that it was something that she could, after all, accomplish, so she made arrangements to go along, taking Carson and Nevin with her. CMW's Sweet Mama was also going, and she showed up at the house about a half hour early, and lent her ready hand to making sandwiches, helping with the casserole and it was with a great flurry that everything got done and loaded into the trusty minivan for transport.

And so they all set forth. Eldest Daughter and her two sweet little fellows in the one car, and CMW and her Sweet Mama, following. And the way to Sandy Bend Road is very long, and very twisted and hard to remember sometimes. The little caravan did much conversing with each other over the cell phones, and one of the vehicles missed a turn, but eventually they arrived at the place where they were to hide the cars. There was a bitter wind blowing, and there was a large yellow dog that frightened the two little boys, but eventually, everyone got themselves across the frozen garden and into the warm house and there waited for Celia and her little family to return from a doctor's appointment.

Eventually, Celia and her happy, bib-overalled husband, their precocious three year old, and their precious 4-day old, put in their appearance. Celia was properly surprised and there was a sweet, sweet little baby shower for her and her baby, with many thoughtful and useful gifts and a nice array of refreshments and wonderful punch. CMW and her Sweet Mama didn't tarry around too long, as they didn't want to overly tire the new mother, and they had hoped to make a trip into Sam's Club for some much needed supplies since they were almost to Dover anyhow.

So off to Sam's Club they went. It was so painfully cold that they sat in the warmth of the car for a while, building up the courage to sally forth. Eventually, they hustled in, rounded up their groceries and paper products and such, checked out, went back out into the bitter cold, loaded the car and headed for home. The heater was bravely putting out heat, and CMW was feeling pretty pleased with the way things had gone. That morning, she had requested Youngest Daughter to be home for Our Girl Audrey's bus, because she was pretty certain that they would not be home for Audrey's 2:45 arrival from Center. This suited Youngest Daughter's schedule just fine, and she was quite willing to do it. However, as CMW made her way down through the traffic of Dover, she realized that she should easily be home before Audrey needed to get off the bus. As soon as she was out on the freeway, she decided to call Youngest Daughter and tell her that she needn't worry about being available for the bus.

And while she was talking on her cell phone, she was blithely going down the road (it wasn't against the law in Delaware at that time) and approaching a construction area near the airbase. So wrapped up was she in the conversation that she never noticed any speed limit signs, though she knew she was approaching the place where the speed limit was lowered. She suddenly became aware of a Dover city police car, parked in plain view, directly across from the gravel pit that is along this well traveled highway. She thought momentarily that maybe she was going too fast, but looked down and did not necessarily think so. Certain Man repeatedly tells her that there is a "cushion" and it seemed to her that she was within the "cushion."

Now let it be known that Certain Man's Wife is not a fast driver, as a rule. She has been driving almost 39 years and in that entire time, she has gotten one (1!!!) speeding ticket. This is not to say that she hasn't deserved them, but she usually tries to keep her speed down, as she does not like to pay fines, and she doesn't like points on her license, with the accompanying high insurance bills. But there is another compelling reason. She really doesn't think it is a good testimony for Christians to be breaking the law. It seems especially incongruous for a Mennonite woman (who is dressed like a traditional Mennonite) to be sitting beside the road in the company of the traffic cop.

(She has even secretly applauded her sister-in-law who has been known to reach over and forcibly remove her husband's black hat from his head when he is barreling down the road at an excessive speed.) So, it really isn't her intent to get herself into situations where she warrants the attention of the enforcer of the speed limit.

However, it became obvious that the (negative) attention of this particular traffic cop had been obtained, and as she passed him, he pulled out behind her with an expert, fluid motion. There was nowhere for him to pull her off because of traffic barriers that began just as she passed him, so he followed her for quite a distance before turning on his lights. The entire way, CMW was making helpless comments to her Sweet Mama.

"Oh, no! I believe he is after me!"

"You weren't really going that fast, were you?" Asked the ever supportive Sweet Mama.

"Well, I didn't think I was into the lower speed zone yet, but maybe I was . . . He hasn't turned on his lights yet . . .maybe he is just going down here to turn around or something . . .I probably was going too fast . . . course I couldn't pull off here, anyhow. . .I hope he isn't going to pull me off. . .oh, dear! He is! There go the lights!"

"Oh, Mary Ann! He isn't!"

"Well, it certainly looks like he is!"

Certain Man's Wife obediently pulled off the road and stopped. She flipped the power switch that put down her window and waited. Suddenly, someone knocked on the window of the passenger's side. Surprised, CMW looked up to see that the policeman was on the passenger side of the car. There have been some unfortunate accidents lately on Delaware roads involving people along the road helping people, and apparently, he wasn't going to take any chances. Certain Man's Wife flipped the button to lower the window where he was standing.

"Ma'am, I'm Trooper B from City of Dover police force. You were speeding in a construction area. I clocked you going 61 in a 45 mile zone. I need your license, registration and insurance cards, please."

CMW fumbled in her purse and retrieved her license, she opened the glove compartment and found the necessary papers. "I'm sorry, sir. I didn't realize that I was into the reduced speed zone yet."

"It was clearly marked a mile north of where I clocked you."

This was hard for CMW to believe, but she decided that she would say no more. The policeman took her license, and insurance cards. "You don't need to give me your registration," he said, "I don't need it." (Apparently he had already verified that) "I will be back. This won't take long." His breath made white clouds in the cold, cold air. His manner was professional, and he wasn't surly. He headed back to his car. CMW wondered grimly why those big blue and red lights had to be so bright and noticeable. Cars were going by in great numbers. She was mortified beyond words.

"You should probably put up your window" said Sweet Mama, sympathetically.

CMW had neglected to close it when the policeman had appeared at the opposite side. Funny, she hadn't even noticed how cold she was. She put the window up, and waited pensively for the return of the policeman. Suddenly she thought, "I really ought to pray about this."

And so, she bowed her head and silently entreated the Lord for a small miracle. "Lord Jesus, I know that I deserve to have been caught. I really wasn't paying attention, and I know that I've been getting careless. Would you please grant me favor in the eyes of this policeman? Could you cause him to have mercy on me? I know that I don't deserve it, and I have no excuse, so all I can pray for is mercy."

And then they waited. And waited. And waited. Sweet Mama was quietly sympathetic. CMW kept an eye on the activity in the car behind her, and there didn't seem to be much.

"He said it wouldn't be long," she said to Sweet Mama, hopefully, "but it does seem to be taking a long time." Aha! Suddenly the door of the police car opened and the officer came up to the passenger side window of the minivan.

"Mrs. Yutzy," he said kindly, "I've done some checking and it seems that you haven't had a traffic ticket for a very long time. I think your last one was 1998 or '88."

"I've only ever had one in my whole life," said CMW quietly.

"Well, I'm going to do some things here to help you out. For one thing, I'm going to completely ignore the fact that you were in a construction zone. Fines are double in a construction zone, so we are going to not even mention that. Secondly, you were 16 miles over, but I'm going to write you down for the very lowest amount that I can -- 5 miles over the speed limit. And since you haven't had a ticket in such a long time, you can go into court, and receive Probation Before Judgment which means that you pay your fine, but if you don't get any more citations in the next six months, the whole thing comes off and there are no points, no record of the incident at all."

"That's very kind of you, sir. I really am sorry. I do try to be careful, and I appreciate your efforts on my behalf."

"You're quite welcome," he said cheerfully. He went on to give CMW a few more instructions concerning the contacting of the court, reminded her to be careful and bid her adieu.

CMW's Sweet Mama closed the window while CMW perused the ticket. It looked harmless enough, but CMW was quite saddened by it. Soberly, she pulled the minivan out into the line of traffic and headed for Milford.

"I'm so sorry that happened to you," said Sweet Mama as they started down the road.

"Yes, well –" said CMW, "I'm kinda' sorry myself!"

"You didn't deserve that!" said Sweet Mama heatedly. "You worked so hard this morning, and took all that food. It doesn't seem fair!"

CMW looked at this beautiful lady that she calls "Mama" and felt that familiar rush of love for her. She can always be counted on to take CMW's part in a fracas. She is intensely loyal, fiercely protective and always wants what's best for her children. "Ah, Mama," she said, and had to laugh. "I did deserve it! When you think about it, I was given a great mercy today. I really did deserve that ticket. I was going too fast. And he could have thrown the book at me. The fine for being five miles over the speed limit is $60.00. If you think in terms of $60.00 for each five mile increment, and realize that I was actually into the fourth increment, I could have had a basic fine of $240.00

and if he hadn't taken off the construction zone business, my fine could have been close to $500.00. Plus, I shudder to think how many points that would have been. But to be given Probation Before Judgment on top of everything else – all I can say is that I have been given a GREAT MERCY today."

"You're right," said Sweet Mama, ruefully. "But I sure wish he had decided not to give a ticket at all. That's the way I would have liked it."

"Yes, well. Me, too." Sighed CMW.

And the trusty old minivan brought them safely home, through another speed trap and on to the inviting shelter of the big old farmhouse at Shady Acres. How comforting and wonderful it was to be home to the fire and the welcoming warmth and light.

CMW has had herself quite an interesting few days since then. It's funny how fast everyone else out there is driving. It would be easy to glare and mutter at the disappearing tail lights as people go roaring around her, but a saying of her Grandma's keeps her heart in check.

"Others may. You cannot." She would say when her children wanted to do something that she felt was not in their best interest. CMW doesn't know what God is saying to all those other people out there who are speeding and getting away with it. But it does seem that His words to her heart are just that: "Others may. You cannot!"

And that is the news from Shady Acres, where Certain Man's gentle love and good humor were not rocked in the least bit by this ripple on the sea of life, where Certain Man's Wife's eye on the speedometer is a bit more steady, and where all the children are unduly amused by their Momma's misfortune.

CMW Copes with the Big Snow

Certain Man's Wife has long been a fan of a Big Snow. Although being instructed often in the inconvenience of it, and even having some firsthand experience with how difficult it makes things for the man in her life, she still LIKES it. Even after having an awful lot of it, and having been housebound nearly continuously for a week, and having her ladies home 24/7, and having Certain Man fussing around, she still LIKES IT!!! Even with the snow covered paths and difficulty getting to the bird feeders, and the snow tracked in and extra laundry and extra cooking, and even having to carry bags of pellets to the stove in the absence of Certain Man, she still LIKES IT!!! And even now, after confessing to such and expecting the avalanche of objections that are sure to follow, and knowing that Certain Man will quite possibly be wroth with her, and will heap upon her ears the reasonable objections and arguments, She does, and probably WILL CONTINUE TO -- LIKE SNOW.

The week has been incredibly special to CMW. Her beloved Certain Man has only had to work two of the days, and having him around home is a real boost to the atmosphere around Shady Acres. He is so adept and has so many ingenious ideas about how to fix things when they go wrong. He has a rapport with the neighbors that cause them to call CMW and gush on and on about how helpful he is with his tractor and loader and blade, extolling his virtues and intelligence and neighborliness. Beings that most of our neighbors are either elderly or have serious health problems, they find him a ready help for all sorts of things. I am so proud of him, even though he doesn't share my great love for a Big Snow. Besides, it is no secret that opposites attract—and besides being MALE, he really is quite my opposite in many things.

So, we've been muddling through, he and I, and have actually been pretty good friends through most of it. We've worked together to get the birds fed, he has done more than his share of shoveling and such. The one thing he has been vocal about involved me going out in the snow.

If I've heard it once, I've heard it a dozen times. "Hon, what do you think you're doing?"

"I'm just making a little path here so I can get to my bird feeder."

"You are going to slip and fall, and I'm going to have to fix the new knee again and the other one, too. I don't think you should be out here."

"But Mr. Yutzy, I like to be out here. My knee doesn't hurt, and I'm being careful."

"You are going to hit a slippery spot and down you'll go, and you are going to really be in trouble."

"I know that I need to be careful, and I'm not doing a lot of stuff. Just shoveling a little and feeding my birds. Besides, I think my boots must have pretty good grip, because I hardly ever have even a little slip."

He would shake his head and sometimes grin at what he thought was my stubbornness, but he didn't forbid me to shovel a little here and there. So I cleaned off a path on the deck, and I cleared a path to my squirrel feeder, and I tromped through the snow with some cob corn for another feeder that I thought I could reach pretty well. I re-cleared some areas after the second storm and he pretended to be cross with me, but his eyes were smiley. So I didn't think I was in too much trouble. Besides. I WAS being careful.

Today was the day that I was to go back to my orthopedic surgeon. I was supposed to see his assistant, but earlier this week they called me and said that they had changed things, and I was supposed to see Dr. Choy because he wanted to evaluate whether I was truly ready to have the second knee replaced. He was going to check on my broken toe, do an evaluation, and then, if he decided that it was okay to go ahead with my surgery, I was going to do the pre-op paperwork.

This morning, before Certain Man left for work I said, "I really wish you were going along with me today. I wish you were driving and if Dr. Choy decides that I am not ready for the surgery, you could talk him into it." He thought that I would be just fine by myself, and he was almost certain that he was going to be the only Plumbing Inspector in on this snowy day, so he went forth to his job and I got ready to go to Lewes. I decided to wear my boots with the good grip.

The drive to Dr. Choy's office usually takes only 30 minutes, but this morning, it took me almost 20 just to get out of Milford. The streets I chose to get to Route 1 South were ones that I thought would be clear, but alas, were not. I had left extra time, and Route 1 was pretty good, but was still mightily relieved when I pulled into the parking lot with five minutes to spare. There was a great traffic jam in the parking lot. There was an ambulance in front of the entrance, and four cars waiting to get past. So instead of trying to go in front of the office to park, I swung around the other side where I saw a parking place. I pulled in, and collected my purse and phone.

The area around where I parked was relatively clear, and I thought how blessed I was to be able to walk without pain. There was no need to use my handicapped parking permit. Besides, I had those boots on with a really good grip. I locked the car and came around the end of the car towards the entrance to the parking lot where I would make a turn and walk down the parking lot in the other direction. The macadam was slushy in places, and there was lots of melting. I stopped as a car went through the slush in front of me, and made long tracks in the slush. I was on a mission! I walked purposefully through the slush, my boots holding their tight grip, my knee working beautifully, no pain, just easy, free movements.

Well, maybe too free. Suddenly, my feet went out from under me. There was no watching this fall in slow motion the way I have sometimes been able to. One moment, I was on my feet. The next, I was flat on the blacktop on my left hip, in the slush, with my purse beyond reach and some of its contents spilling out. The first thing I evaluated, of course was my new knee. It seemed to be in wondrously good shape – still no pain, no twisting. No significant pain anywhere else, no blood, so I decided to try to get up. I am still not sure how I did that. I must have gotten on my knees and pushed myself up with my hands, but I don't really remember.

There was a terrified little man who came over and stood there helplessly wondering if he could help. I remember telling him that I was fine, and that I thought I could get myself up, even as I was doing it, and he was worriedly trying to get things back into my purse. Somehow, I was suddenly in an upright position and all in one piece. I collected my purse and thanked the kind gentleman, who was looking relieved. Then I headed across the parking lot towards the office entrance, not nearly as free and easy. Indeed, it was with great picking of the place to put my foot down. Slush was dripping off my skirt and the sleeve of my coat with every step, and I felt the cold wetness soaking through my clothes to my skin.

When I was about twenty feet away from the entrance, I was suddenly stopped short by the sound of great shouting going on behind the emergency vehicle that was beginning to move from its place where it had been unloading a patient (and making the great upheaval with the parking lot).

"STOP!!!" screamed someone from behind the vehicle. "STOP!!! Don't back up any more!!! STOP!!!" The young female driver brought the large ambulance to a lumbering stop.

"Someone is right behind you!" scolded someone from the office staff who had come out to help with the patient. "You almost ran over this couple." she said loudly, indignantly. Visibly shaken, two elderly people came out from behind the vehicle. Snow had been piled up over the sidewalk, and they were headed to the door on the shortest possible route, never realizing that the ambulance was getting ready to move.

The driver was more than a little disgruntled, too. "I didn't know they were back there!" I heard her say defensively to no one in particular. "There was no way I could have known they were back there! Everything is in such a mess!"

My little spill on the driveway certainly paled in comparison to being backed over by an ambulance, but I was still very embarrassed, very dirty from landing in the grimy slush, cold and wet. When I signed in, I told the receptionist that I had taken a tumble in the parking lot. I needed some paper towels to clean up the area where my coat had left water all over the counter, and I did want to clean myself up as well.

A nurse came out with a hand full of paper towels for me, and said solicitously, "We need to file an incident report and someone needs to look you over to make sure you're okay."

"I'm fine," I insisted. "Really. Nothing seems to be hurting overly much at all."

She eyed me dubiously. "We still need to check it out."

I went into the restroom to dry off, and that is where I discovered that both knees were soaking wet. (That was when I decided that I must have gotten up on my knees when I was trying to get up. That is still a miracle to me.) They didn't hurt, they weren't bruised or skinned, and my nylons weren't even torn. I took stock of the rest of my body. My right hip was starting feel like it was going to have a bruise, my right shoulder was beginning to ache a little, and my hands were bright red. I thought that was pretty small consequence for a woman of my (ahem) social standing who had such an ungraceful fall.

But you would have thought that I was broken and bleeding. The office staff was galvanized into action. This fall certainly expedited things as far as getting me in and evaluated. The waiting room was full, but the next patient they called was "Mrs. Yutzy". They had their service rep come in and do an accident report, complete with little drawings. I had to sign a paper saying that what she said on the report was true. I insisted that everything was fine. I was fine. My knee was fine. My wrists were not broken. My hip was okay. I mean, I landed on my most padded part, and had a heavy coat on to boot. So they finally decided that they would let the doctor do a brief evaluation when he got in, and went on with the program.

My broken toe was x-rayed and found to be healing, and then Dr. Choy made his appearance. He checked hip, hands, both knees and found nothing amiss. "You'll be really sore tomorrow," he said cheerfully. He grinned with delight over the range of motion of the new knee, and pronounced the progress there "outstanding." I told him that I had been shoveling snow over the past few days and that my husband was so afraid that it wasn't good for me.

"It's very good for you," he said, laughing. "It is excellent exercise. Falling isn't the best idea, but shoveling is just fine. Getting out in the fresh air makes you feel better."

Then he checked the knee that hadn't been replaced, and put it through a short range of motion. It didn't take him long to agree that it should be done as soon as possible. He answered a few questions that I had, and suddenly, the paper work was finished, and I was going through the waiting room. The elderly couple was sitting there, still talking about their frightening experience.

"Yeah, she almost ran over us! We were right behind the ambulance and all the sudden it started coming back. If that lady hadn't hollered, she would have run right over us. We were right behind it. It was scary!" Listening to their account made my heart lurch with thanksgiving as I was reminded again that things could have been so much worse.

And then, I was on my way home. All in less than an hour after I had pulled into the parking lot. That has to be some sort of record for that office.

There is one thing, though, that I'm a little bit puzzled by. That business about being "really sore tomorrow" must not have been any sort of guarantee. At least something appears to have set in already, making me wish for some sort of diversion.

However, Youngest Daughter is on her way home from college for a week, and Youngest Son and His Wife just called and said they are coming home for the weekend, too. If plans carry, Middle Daughter will be back home on Monday night. How much more of a diversion could a gal want?

Methinks it will serve me well.

CMW Hears a Noise

Now it came to pass that Certain Man's Wife has been recovering from her second knee replacement with somewhat less aplomb than her first one. There haven't been any real glitches in the process, in fact, range of motion is considerably better than the previous knee's ability at the same stage of recovery. However, the pain has been raucous.

CMW has spent considerable amount of emotional energy trying to stay optimistic, trying to be brave, trying to OVERCOME. With the admission of the pain, CMW risks being the recipient of pity -- which she hates with a passion. But one Saturday morning, there was a great deal of *self*-pitying going on in her chair in the corner. It wasn't just the pain, although that was a contributing factor. It was a whole conglomerate of things. Stuff people don't really need to know, CMW figures, but still important enough to her to cry about.

It didn't take too many minutes of writing all her feelings down to discover that she really did have things pretty good, and so she decided to get on with her day. It was a lovely day outside, and the next day was Easter. Certain Man and Middle Daughter were very busy with many things outside and so CMW stirred about and made a salad for the next day, and worked on plans for Easter family Dinner. Middle Daughter spent some time in the basement, getting a few things organized and airing the place out.

That evening, just as Middle Daughter was getting ready to go out the door, she said, "Oh, Mom!!! I forgot! I opened one of the windows in the basement, and forgot to shut it. Maybe Dad should go down there and close it."

"Uh, Beebs. Does the window have a screen on it?"

"No, it's one that doesn't have a screen, but it was the one I could get to."

"Something could crawl in there, Deb, and really make a mess. A cat, or a squirrel or even a skunk!!!"

"Yeah, so probably Dad should shut it before it gets dark."

"I should say so!!!" said the longsuffering CMW, thinking to herself that if she could just get down the steps, there would be no reason to involve Certain Man, whose knee has a torn ligament behind the knee cap and has been giving him a lot of trouble. (He has his own appointment with the good Dr. Choy, but not for a couple of months yet.) She tucked the information into the back of her mind with a mental note to tell him the minute he got in.

Of course, she forgot.

She stayed pretty busy in spite of the pain, and later that evening, after it was dark, she decided that she needed to do her daily physical therapy. So, while Certain Man was checking some scores on the computer, she set up her folding chair and began the slow stationary bike pedaling regimen that gets thing loosened up for further torture. She was (maybe) half way through the 12 minutes when she heard a muffled thump in the basement. Sorta' like something falling off the shelf. It was an isolated noise, but it really got her attention. All of a sudden she remembered the open basement window, and realized that she hadn't told Certain Man about it.

"Sweetheart--" she called hopefully from her therapy chair in the family room. She thought she heard an acknowledgment from the depths of the study. "I just remembered something. Before Deborah left this afternoon, she said that she had opened the one window in the basement and didn't have time to go back down there and close it. I wonder if you should check it. It was the one without a screen."

There was no noise from the study. If Certain Man heard, he didn't answer. CMW pedaled on. Suddenly, she heard it again. It sounded like something alive. "Daniel-- Sweetheart, did you hear me?" she asked. He came out of the study looking like a man who had been interrupted when he had been checking out his favorite team's scores for the day.

"What? What did you say?"

"Deborah opened a window in the basement that doesn't have a screen on it and she forgot to close it. And I keep hearing noises down there. I wonder if something got into the basement."

"Its okay," he said with that unflappable calm that men are capable of when they really don't want to check things out. "It would be hard for anything to get in there." And he disappeared into another room. Right about then, CMW heard the noise again. She made a quick check to be sure that the family cat wasn't somehow in the basement, and saw her lounging under a table in the family room.

"Honey, I heard the noise again. It sounds like a cat is down there knocking stuff down, or jumping or something. I wish you would check it out."

He wasn't very enthusiastic, but he did betake himself to the basement and checked everything out. He was back shortly to report. "There is nothing there. I shut the window, but there is nothing down there, running around."

CMW left her therapy then for a quick check from the windows around the perimeter of the sun room and CM joined her to make sure there wasn't some wild animal of some sort throwing itself against the outside of the house. Certain Man didn't actually hear anything, but he must have decided that if CMW was so sure she had heard something, he wasn't going to get any rest until he at least gave some attention to the story.

When neither of them could find anything, he went back to the computer, and CMW returned to her physical therapy. Scarcely was she back on her chair until she heard it again. It seemed louder, but just when she was sure that she would have to call CM, it stopped. A short time later, she heard it again. It sounded like it was coming from the air conditioning vent that was on the floor about six feet away from her chair. So she pulled her chair over there, and waited. Yes, sir, it happened again. Definitely in the air vent. It sounded like an animal of some sort was down in the air vent, struggling to get out. It was brief, but very definite. CMW pulled the grate off and peered into the darkness of the vent. And waited. Sure enough, it happened again. Struggle, struggle, struggle. Then silence.

Certain Man's Wife debated her options. She continued to do her physical therapy while listening to the poor trapped animal. It seemed like the struggle was less with each episode, and the episodes kept getting further and further apart. She finally went into the study to talk to her poor beleaguered spouse.

"Sweetheart, I keep hearing this noise. I know you are tired of hearing about it, but it seems like it is in the air conditioning vent. It sounds like an animal is caught in there and is trying to get out. And it sounds like it is getting weaker and weaker. Would you come out here and sit in a chair beside the air vent and just listen?"

He is a good man, and he knew that his wife was obviously upset about whatever it was that was dying in the air vent, so he came out and parked his folding chair by the air vent and waited.

Sure enough, there was a sudden scratching noise that came from the vent. Certain Man's indifference disappeared in a snap.

"What in the world?!?!?" he asked of no one in particular.

"Did you hear it?" asked his excited frau, "Did you hear it?"

"Yes, I heard it," he said, "But I can't figure it out. I don't see how anything would have gotten into the air conditioning vent. There shouldn't be any way for that to happen."

His wife had no trouble at all imagining how something had gotten into the duct work. First of all, there are so many lengths of ductwork that run under the house, through the attic, through the basement and wall. She could see any of a number of animals finding a place to squeeze in. "Well Daniel, maybe it is a bird that came down the chimney or maybe a squirrel found a place where it was apart, or maybe a rat chewed a hole through somehow."

He looked at her askance. "I've not seen any rats around here for a long, long time. Have you?"

"Well, no, but it could have come in from somewhere --" She could tell that he wasn't very enthusiastic about checking this out, but she also knew that he wouldn't rest until he knew what was going on. He looked thoughtful, and got some gloves and headed for the door.

"What are you going to do?" asked his ever helpful wife.

"Well," he said with a great glint of determination in his eye, "the one thing that is convenient is that I can get to that air vent. The duct work runs right across the basement ceiling, so I can certainly get to it. I'm going to go down there and see what I can find."

"Oh, honey, it could have rabies. Be careful!!!"

"I will. I just can't figure out what could have gotten in there." He disappeared down the steps to the basement and CMW stayed in the family room, still working at her physical therapy. Suddenly, there was a great scrambling noise at the air conditioning vent. So much so, that the family cat went flying over to investigate with her tail as big as a toilet bowl brush. She sniffed and stood watchful guard over the hole in the floor. This did not do much for CMW's peace of mind. What could be in there that interested the cat so much? She hobbled over and looked down again to see if some beady eyes were peering up at her. She put her hand down there and waggled it around. Nothing. So she hobbled back to her chair.

About five minutes later, she was aware that Certain Man was back upstairs. And he was clearly amused. "What was it?" she asked. (She didn't want it to be anything that would bite him, but she HATES it when he laughs at her.)

"Oh," he said teasingly, "It was really scary!!!"

"Daniel, what was it???"

"Well," he said kindly, "I got down there and checked and couldn't find anything in the duct work, and I was just ready to give up when I heard it again, and I looked up there and here the pipe from the sump pump is against the duct and every time it turns on and off, the pipe shudders, and it jiggles the duct and that is what you heard. Sometimes the pipe has a stronger shudder than at others so it sounds louder. Also, the episodes get further and further apart as the basement gets more and more pumped out. And there you have it. Mystery solved!!!"

"Oh," said Certain Man's Wife in a very, very small voice. "I see." And she went back to finish her physical therapy without calling Certain Man even one more time about a single thing.

And that is the news from Shady Acres, where CMW hears that animal in the air conditioning duct every time she does therapy and it doesn't worry her at all. Not even a little tiny bit.

CMW and Middle Daughter have Nocturnal Feline-icky Adventures

Now it came to pass that Shady Acres has enjoyed quite a lengthy respite from the onslaughts of a feline nature for some months. There have been the usual barn cats, of course, but nary a furry body has bothered the house and its surrounding parameters for some time.

Then a friend brought a cat named "Skits" and dropped it off at the farm because she was unable to keep it, and friends of hers had an unsuccessful attempt at acclimating him to their premises. Now Skits is a beautiful cat, neutered and accustomed to human company, but decidedly an outside cat. Or so the family of Certain Man had been promised.

There was at least a week when they saw neither hide nor hair of Skits. It was assumed that he wasn't favorably impressed with Shady Acres and its large array of barn and chicken house cats and had moved on to more friendly territory. There is a neighbor of Certain Man's family who will sometimes take in errant felines, march them off to the vet and deprive them of their abilities to reproduce and then bring them back -- sometimes to let them go again, but often to attempt to tame them and keep them domesticated. In the week that Skits was absent, there was much speculation that maybe neighbor Mrs. G. had taken him in, finding him already neutered, and that he was enjoying a life of riley there.

No such luck.

There came a day when Skits presented himself at the door of the sunroom, on the newly renovated deck. He was noisily and insistently announcing his presence and Certain Man was not impressed.

"He better find somewhere else to meow!" he said darkly, "or I shall help him find somewhere else to be and it won't be any fun for him!"

So Middle Daughter and CMW shooed and "encouraged" and tried to make "being on the deck" as unattractive as possible. Though Skits really is a beautiful cat, it is disconcerting to the family at Shady Acres to see him stalking birds at the bird feeder, and parking his very beautiful body directly in line with nests full of fledglings, and in general, standing sentry over the bird population.

In addition, it seemed like every evening, Skits would present himself outside the windows on the front deck, directly in line with Certain Man's La-Z-boy and meow away. This was not met with anything that was even remotely close to approval by the man of the house. In these instances, there was more than "gentle" encouragement for the cat to move on.

Over the last few weeks, there have been some improvements made at Shady Acres, one of which was a set of stairs going up to the "upper deck" that Middle Daughter designed on top of the sun room. One evening, after Certain Man had been especially disgruntled with the obnoxious meows, we were relieved to note that Skits had seemingly disappeared from the deck. It was our hope that he had retired to the barn or the pavilion (or even the middle of the busy highway out front).

Certain Man and his wife retired to their bed, and scarcely had Certain Man's Wife gotten into bed when suddenly, right outside her second story bedroom window was heard, "Meow."

"Meow."

"Meow."

Skits had found and appropriated the new steps leading up to the deck. From there, it was an easy hop over to the roof and on to the interesting windows where he deemed there may be human companionship.

It was nearly impossible to see outside, but CMW peered through the screen, and sure enough, there was Skits, directly outside the screen. He was standing on his hind legs, with his feet up to the window, looking in and calling out for the attention he so desired.

Certain Man's Wife was not impressed. "GIT!!!" she intoned sternly.

"What???" asked a very sleepy Certain Man.

"That cat!" Said Certain Man's Wife. "He's right outside this window."

"He better find someplace else to be!" Said Certain Man, "Or he isn't going to live!"

Well, that was encouragement enough for Skits to drop onto all fours and pad over to the window that is directly in front of Certain Man's head. CMW headed over to the bathroom to fetch a large glass of water to throw out through the screen, but in the meantime, Certain Man had pulled himself up onto his elbows and was looking out into the dark of the garage roof. Skits was plastering himself up against the screen. CMW set the tall glass of water on the end table and poked her head up over the pillows to see what was going on. At the very same instant, Certain Man decided that he was going to exercise his manly strength and send that cat flying with a punch through the screen, and his fist caught CMW on the left cheekbone as it went by.

Wowser! That smarted. CMW got out of the way. Fast. And Skits took himself on down the roof to the far end. Certain Man, unaware that he had even connected with CMW's face kept a sharp lookout out the window, and soon the cat was back. Certain Man picked up the glass of water and flung it through the screen at the hapless victim. There was a great splashing noise and Skits took himself hurriedly down the length of the roof to the far end, and Certain Man complained loudly concerning the fact that his bed was wet, his pillow was wet, and life in general was greatly in a mess.

Then he looked out the darkened window and ascertained that Skits was very much out of reach and wasn't in any mood to visit the window again, and that made him certain the cat was distracted long enough for him to get into dreamland, so he turned over, pulled the covers up and promptly fell asleep. CMW, on the other hand, had a most touchy red spot on her cheek, and was completely awake, and unsure that Skits had any intention of settling down for the night

When Friend Liz had asked about bringing the cat, it was Middle Daughter who had given permission. Certain Man's Wife decided to disturb her evening's quiet solace to ask for assistance. So she traipsed across the landing to tell Middle Daughter the woeful tale. Middle Daughter was inordinately amused at the situation and willingly agreed to come and help.

So, CMW, clad in her blue nightie, and Middle Daughter, also in her jammies, ventured forth into the night. Middle Daughter had a flash light, and CMW armed herself with a garden hose with the great high pressured sprayer end attached. And whilst the neighborhood slept, including Certain Man, the two fearless ladies did battle with the elusive Skits. There was a copious amount of water wasted while the wily cat jumped from flashlight beam to darkness and CMW attempted to propel a stream in a somewhat effective arc. Great were the giggles and whispered shouts of instruction. CMW was finally able to score a direct hit with the water, causing Skits to go flying across the roof, down onto the deck, back up on the opposing roof where she hid behind the edge of the house where CMW could not reach her, even with the fifty foot stream of water.

But that was okay, because Skits had appeared to learn her lesson. Down the steps she flew once the dangerous females had returned to the house and there have not been anymore nocturnal visits to the upper roof.

Oh, Them Green Beans!!!

The garden at Shady Acres (planted in a sunny spot) is quite an interesting undertaking to say the least.

Certain Man plants it. Weeds it. Sprays the bugs and digs the potatoes and picks up ground cherries. He cheers on the asparagus and rhubarb, and he examines and exclaims over the carrots and carefully stakes up the tomatoes so that there is no problem when it comes to picking them. He loves yellow summer squash and he picks those carefully and expertly. He has been known to help pick up the butternut squash, but not because he likes to. He does not pick beans. Of any kind. He does not cut asparagus; he does not usually pick tomatoes unless it is to eat one of his beautiful little ones on his way to the chicken house. His involvement with the peppers is to the extent that he tells CMW when they need to be picked and how they are getting out of hand.

But he weeds and rotor tills and strings up the wires and string for my beloved pole limas and usually his garden is picture perfect.

This year, most of the garden has been exactly right most of the time. But the weeds got away from him in the potatoes and lima bean rows and it has been discouraging. Especially since we aren't getting enough lima beans to even bother with. We can about throw the picking's handful into a soup or eat them raw. It's been discouraging for Certain Man's Wife, too.

At the beginning of the summer, he decided that this year he was going to have a row of peas and a row of green beans. I don't often argue with him, but I REALLY didn't want green beans (or peas, either, for that matter!) But he went ahead and got the seed and planted a row of green beans. I was secretly just a little upset. Green beans are not that expensive, people often have them for the taking, and besides. I have to bend way over to pick those green beans and the hot sun and the way they hide is a great aggravation to this farm girl's heart. I just didn't want to have them on my conscience. Middle Daughter had pretty much said that she didn't feel called to pick green beans for us, and I just knew I would be out there in that patch picking green beans and feeling misunderstood.

They didn't come up! I secretly rejoiced with exceeding great joy!

But then Certain Man came home one day with this lumpy envelope and when I investigated, I found it almost full of bean seeds.

"What's this with these seeds?" I asked him.

"Oh, those," he said. "Gary said I ought to try them and he gave me that pack."

"I don't want green beans in our garden, Daniel. They are hard to pick and Deborah said she would pick them last year and after a time or so of picking them, she got busy and I had to pick and they were nasty and I don't want green beans in my garden."

"I thought I might just try these and see," he insisted. "Gary says they are really nice green beans. There aren't all that many, and the first ones I planted never even came up. It's kinda' late for them anyhow. They probably won't make much, but I'd sorta' like to at least try them and see how they do."

I could tell it wouldn't do me any good to say any more, and I was gratified to see that lumpy envelope around for a very long time. Long enough that I forgot about them. Then one day, he mentioned that his green beans were up.

"Did you plant those beans that Gary gave you?" I asked.

"Yep! And they came up good!"

Oh, well.

We were working on Deborah's library and he wasn't spending much time in the garden and his weeds were fast taking over. I decided that I wouldn't worry too much about it. With all those weeds out there, those beans didn't stand much of a chance. But then his part of the work on Deborah's project came to an end and he got after those weeds with a vengeance and since he started at the edge of the garden that everyone sees first, he weeded the row of marigolds that we plant next to the tomatoes to keep the bugs off. Then he weeded his tomatoes, then his -- you guessed it! his bean row. I came out one night to check on my pole limas and I saw a healthy row of green beans about 2/3 the length of the garden. I decided that I was going to ignore them.

I fought the thistles and the butternut squash to go over my two rows of pole limas and got about a five gallon bucket on the first picking. I was really worried, though, because there were no more viable pods hanging on the vines. I proceeded to pray and sing over them, and tried to keep after the other garden things, but at least two weeks later I went over the patch again and got -- two handfuls of shelled beans. This made me a little cross. Certain Man was steadily weeding the rows of pole limas, he was watering faithfully, he was doing all he could to help the pole limas grow, but it was all to no avail. And I was still ignoring those green beans. Occasionally, Certain Man would lament that "those green beans don't seem to be making anything of themselves, either," but I was still not paying attention. You see, I was afraid that if I looked at them and there were beans there, I would feel OBLIGATED to pick them.

One Tuesday night, when the neighbor kids came to eat supper and play, I went out with them and thought that I would work in the garden while they rode bikes and worked off some energy. When they saw that I was in the garden, they all three came pounding across the grass and wanted to help. They wanted to pick tomatoes and they were pulling the green ones off at an alarming rate. I looked down and happened to see that there were quite a few green beans hanging on the first bush of the row, so I thought long and hard (at least five seconds) about asking them if they wanted to help pick the green beans and sure enough! They did!

So we set to work with a 2½ gallon bucket and before I knew it, that bucket was getting full, and I hadn't picked more than a fourth of the row. Then the kids were tired of it already (they had worked under that scorching evening sun for at least twenty minutes and it was getting to be too much for them, I guess). So they went back to picking tomatoes and peppers that they threw all into the same bucket with the green beans. I picked a few more green beans before Jeffy started sneezing and getting really, really tight in his chest, and we gave up gardening for the night.

I had this wonderful bucket, though, of the nicest green beans I have ever picked. They were long and slender and crisp and green. I looked at those green beans and after feeling so pleased with them, I felt heartsick at how many bushes that I hadn't even touched, and how the week ahead was so very packed with lots and lots of stuff to do. The evening got late before I could do anything with the nice bucket I had picked, so I decided that I would take the fresh green beans to my Sweet Mama's house the next day and we would have them for lunch. I talked to Mama, and she seemed delighted to think that I would bring them. I had also made Chicken-etti for the kids for supper (their favorite meal!) and Mama likes that, too, so we had our lunch all planned.

Eldest Daughter and Love Bug went along out to Sweet Mama's that morning and while I worked on other things, Christina snapped those green beans and Mama fetched out some bacon and between the two of them, they made a big pot of fresh green beans and bacon. Talk about good! Those beans were wonderful.

But now I had a dilemma. There were terribly many beans left out there, and I was coming down with the biggest guilt complex over them that I had experienced in a while. But there was no time to pick those beans. I came home from Sweet Mama's and did some paperwork for the ladies, and then fed them and got ready for small group. After small group, Certain Man and I remembered that his office was having breakfast the next morning and he had told them that I would make sausage gravy to send in. They were celebrating Certain Man's birthday and also the secretary's and the gravy was by special request of the two birthday people. The only trouble was, I was out of sausage. So at eleven o'clock on Wednesday night, I made a mad dash for the grocery store for supplies.

And lest you think that Certain Man was just taking it easy through all this, HE WASN'T. Our chickens went out on Tuesday night/Wednesday morning and the hours and hours of work that lead up to that and then follow it are enough to keep two men busy. And he almost always does it all by himself. I really did not expect him to pick beans. Even if it was something he did, which it isn't, he wouldn't have under these circumstances. I did discuss their presence with him.

"Hey, Mr. Yutzy. Did you know there are a WHOLE LOT of green beans out there?"

"They aren't any good any more, though, are they?"

"They are beautiful, Daniel. Just gorgeous!"

"I saw some time ago-" (probably when he was weeding) "that there were quite a few hanging on out there. I just figured when no one picked them, that they were too hard."

"Well, they aren't. And someone really needs to pick them. I guess I will have to see what I can do." And then I made the mistake. "I really didn't want green beans in the garden."

"Well," he said darkly. "I can take care of those green beans for you in about 15 minutes."

"What do you mean?"

"I'll just go out there and pull them all out and throw them over the fence to the cows."

"Daniel, you can't just throw those beans away."

"Just watch me!"

"No, I don't want you to throw them away. I'll try to do something with them." The thing is, I was pretty sure he had no intentions of throwing those beans over the fence (though he has been known to do such things!) I suspected that he was going to try to somehow pick them himself in his overcrowded, over-committed schedule. He was so tired already that I was worried about him. I decided to not say another word about picking green beans to him.

Thursday (that was yesterday) we were beginning to have lots of warnings concerning the hurricane that was coming and I began to realize that I needed to get as much garden produce off as possible. I had an early appointment with Audrey in Dover, needed to pick up some material to make a trial dress for Love Bug for a wedding, and had a case manager coming for a home visit and Eldest Daughter was having a "31" party here in the evening. There was going to be NO TIME to pick beans. I really didn't want to all that much, anyhow.

And to be honest, not only did I not WANT to, I was pretty sure that it wasn't beneficial for a particular health issue that I've been dealing with. When I had a hysterectomy a couple of months after I turned forty, and at the same time, they did an abdominal hernia repair and put in a stainless steel mesh, I thought it would solve all my problems in both departments. And it seemed to be okay for a decade or so, but the last couple of years I've realized that I need some additional repair done. And bending over, picking produce is not comfortable at all. But I don't like food to go to waste and I don't like to complain. AND, I kept remembering how wonderful those beans had tasted at my Sweet Mama's table.

So this morning, before it got too hot, I decided I would go out there and try to make short work of that bean row. Of course, there is no such thing as short work in a bean patch. I pondered the mysteries of gardening. (Why are these beans doing so well in the same garden as the unproductive Limas?) I prayed for grace under the hot sun. I prayed for a breeze. I prayed that the cloud cover would move over the sun. I prayed that the sun could just go behind a cloud. I stood up and looked at the long row. I took off my glasses and wiped my sweaty face on my sleeve, and remembered that people on Furosomide are not to be out in the sun.

And through it all, I picked green beans and picked green beans and picked green beans. Oh, and I sang some of my favorite storm songs and thought about all the possibilities of the hurricane and looked at my tomato plants and decided that I should take all of the ripe tomatoes off before the storm and that made me think about the peppers and so I checked them and picked them, too. Middle Daughter had been busy getting things put away before the storm, but she came out and helped me just when I thought I could not make it any longer and her good conversation and helping hands saw me through those last difficult moments.

Then Middle Daughter's friend, Abi, came over and the two of them snapped the beans for me, and there is such a hearty, healthy amount. I have a big pot of tomatoes cooked up, ready for juicing out, and those beans almost ready for the blancher. Certain Man and I got Shady Acres about as secure as we possibly could and it is all good.

I'm not ready to say that I am glad he planted all those green beans, and I think I will give away at least the next picking if there is anything left after Hurricane IRENE makes her way across Delmarva, but I am so grateful for these beautiful green beans, and I suppose I will be even happier next winter. Methinks I will cook up a pot of them tomorrow with some bacon to eat while we are weathering out the storm.

And that is the news from Shady Acres, where Certain Man will probably continue to plant whatever he wants to plant in the garden. Certain Man's Wife will probably continue to pick green beans if they are there to pick, and both will gladly accept any help from in that particular department from any of the offspringin's.

Good night, all. This gal is going to bed!

CM & CMW Make Christmas for the Kids

It's no secret that I love buying Christmas presents for children. As our children have gotten older and harder to buy for, we've substituted cash for the gifts. It isn't as personal, no. but for some reason, when the envelopes are opened, not once have I heard anyone threaten to return it!

This year, our lives have been rather involved in those of the three kids that go to Sunday School with us. So I began to think about Christmas months ago, and over the last while, I've been astounded to find little buys here and there that were "perfect" for them. I would tuck these little finds into a secret hiding place upstairs in the guest room, thinking that we would fill stockings with the little items. I had specific plans for the "bigger" gifts. I wanted a Bible, a special toy, and a warm, colorful throw for each child. I was so incredibly blessed on every hand. There were stockings, filled with fruit ropes, candy, chapstick, socks, small toy items like paints, yo-yos, puzzles, as well as incredible buys on the toys, throws and even the Bibles. It felt like God put things into my way over and over again.

The kids knew that we were going to get them some presents. They were almost out of control in their excitement. The three of them have not been in school since before Thanksgiving, and the lack of structure has to be wearing for their poor mother. Diagnosed with Thyroid cancer, she had surgery the Monday after Thanksgiving, and it just isn't a good situation. Even so, I can't understand how she has money to do her hair and nails, but no money for the things these kids need.

"They can't go to school," she said in her lifeless sort of way. "The school district says they can't come until they have uniforms. They have to have Khaki pants and a maroon, white or gold shirt. I can't afford any of it." She pursed her lips and swallowed like she had a bad taste in her mouth.

"Doesn't the school have some provision for them?" I asked. "Did they tell you where you could get some things for them? Have you checked at Salvation Army or some of the thrift stores? I'm almost sure they can have other colored pants, at least, because the neighbor child wears other colors and he goes to Milford."

"Nah, they have to have Khaki pants." she said again, "and I just ain't got the money for that." I should have known that she was looking for someone to give her school clothes, but I was too troubled by the fact that these children haven't been to school. I shopped unsuccessfully for school clothes for the three of them, and when it came to khaki, especially, there was absolutely nothing. I finally went online to check what the restrictions were and found that she had been seriously lying to me. Not only were the kids allowed to wear other things, (Black, navy, and khaki pants, and navy, black, white, gold, maroon shirts) but they were given at least a week after enrolling, to come into compliance with a (very) long suffering dress code. I knew it was all excuses.

I had promised the children an excursion to Chuck-E-Cheese's for good behavior and had said that I hoped to take them sometime before Christmas. With Christmas bearing down on us, and the church going caroling, I thought the last week would be a good week to squeeze some things in. I tried and tried to call her but her phone was off and the voice mail box "hadn't been set up yet" (as in NEVER BEEN SET UP in the last couple of months). It was the Wednesday before Christmas, and it was a blustery, rainy day. I had printed out the guidelines for the dress code and had called and called with no success. I finally got into my car and drove the eight and a half miles to their place and knocked on the door. Jeffy pulled aside the curtain, and looked out. Back went the curtain.

"It's Ms. Mary Ann," I heard him hiss. Then complete silence. I stood on the stoop for a long time, thinking someone would come any minute. Finally, I knocked again. He must have been standing right inside the door because he opened it immediately.

"Hey, there, Jeffy. Is your Mama here?"

"Um, Yeah." He let me in, but went over to the kitchen table where he had some breakfast waffles on a plate, and began working with them. He ignored me.

"Jeffy, I need to talk to your Mama. Can you get her for me?"

He left the table, and went back into the back of the house. Standing in the kitchen, it is impossible to see beyond the doorway of the living room and everything is beyond that. So I stood in the kitchen and waited. And waited. And waited.

Then he came back and went back to his waffle without saying anything to me. Maddie appeared on the scene. So I talked to the two of them about caroling that night and about whether or not they should go. Maddie said she had been to the doctor and had an ear infection. Jerry said that he had one to. I said, "Well, Kids, I really need to talk to your mama, so I can decide what we are doing about caroling tonight and Chuck-E-Cheese's tomorrow."

"She's not feeling good," said Maddie.

"Well, then, maybe we should just plan that you aren't going tonight," I said. Jeffy hopped off his chair and disappeared. I was feeling more than a little frustrated by this time, and didn't know if they would go the next day, either. (Especially not if I had any say!)

He came back. "We ARE going tonight," he said.

"No, you are NOT going tonight," I said.

"Why not?" He asked plaintively.

"Because it is cold and wet and Maddie said that she had an ear infection, and you said you had one, too, and I am just not taking you out in this weather."

"What about tomorrow?"

"I don't know about that, either. I NEED to talk to your Mama to make some arrangements, but if she won't talk to me, how can I know what I'm doing?"

About this time, Maddie had had enough. She went flying back to the back of the house and came out and said, "Mom said she was going to call you."

"That may be, Maddie, but I need to know some things NOW. Wait a minute. Do you have a pen? I can write her a note on the back of these guidelines."

She disappeared again, then came back out. "Mom said she is going to call you."

"That's fine, but do you have a pen? I am going to write her a note so she knows what I need to talk to her about."

She went again, and came back with a pen. I sat down at the kitchen table and began a rather direct note to the mom. Stating that I felt that she had had enough time to get the kids in school, and that if she didn't do something about it, I was going to report her.

About the time I got three sentences down, I heard her male friend, tromping through the house. (He is probably 6'6 and weighs about 300 pounds at least). "Where is she?" he asked the kids in the living room.

"She's out there in the kitchen," I heard someone say. "She's writing a note."

"What's she think she doin'?" He asked. "What's goin' on. What she doin'?"

He came around the corner, and maybe I should have been scared, but I was so MAD that I couldn't see straight. I had been in the house almost 20 minutes, and I had had just about enough.

"Whas' goin' on, Ms. Mary Ann?" he asked, not very friendly-like at all.

"Well, Sensei, it's like this. I went online to check on the clothing requirements for the kids, and the truth is, the dress code is very lenient. What you guys are doing here is illegal. These kids haven't been in school since before Thanksgiving, and I hate to do this, but unless you do something to get them into school, I am going to report you!"

Wrong thing to say. (Duh!) All kinds of exclamations broke forth concerning the fact that she had called, and she had tried, blah, blah, blah!"

I finally interrupted long enough to say, "Listen, Sensei, it isn't good for these children to be out of school. Maddie already told me that her last report card was bad, and they NEED to be in school. I would think you would want them to be in school."

"Wait, wait, wait ----" He disappeared into the back of the house again, and this time, finally, the mom put in an appearance. She looked at me through sleepy, thick-lidded eyes, while Big Sensei hovered angrily behind her.

"Listen, Dee, I am not here to *cause* trouble, but you guys could *be* in really big trouble here. The kids haven't been in school since before Thanksgiving, and that's against the law!"

"Well, I called them and they haven't called me back." She was defensive and angry.

"Well, they've probably tried. It's impossible to get a hold of you. I can try and try and try, and your phone is turned off. And you have it setup so that no one can leave a message. I can't tell you how often I've tried to get up with you and there is no answer. That is why I am down here now. I told you about caroling tonight and that I might want to take the kids tomorrow, but I need to discuss things with you, but you never answer your phone."

"Well, they can go tonight . . ."

"I don't think it's a good idea. Maddie said she has an ear infection, and Jeffy said he does, too."

"Maddie did have one, but it wasn't bad and she's been on her medicine, and Jeffy doesn't have an ear infection."

Big Sensei turned his wrath on poor Jeffy "Jeffy, why you say you got an ear infection? You ain't got no ear infection.

"Yes, I do. I mean I DID. I mean--. No. I don't."

"An' Maddie, what you runnin' yo mouf fo? You say you got a bad report card. You ain't got no bad report card. What you mean by runnin' yo' mouf like dat, sayin' you got a bad report card?"

Maddie was nonchalantly eating her waffle. She paused long enough to put both hands up in an expression of uncaring indifference. "Well," she said, "I didn't know what "S" meant."

He paused in his tirade against the kids and started in on me. "Ain't none of dese kids got a bad report card. Dese kids is all honor roll kids. Ever' one of dem. What you tryin' to cause trouble for? She been doin' da bes' she can. Da' school jus' ain't callin' her back!"

Dee said to me, "Maddie didn't get a bad report card. She got all "S's. And the other kids did fine, too. Milford School District is just slow. It took three weeks for my kids to get on a bus when we moved from Harrington to Milford."

I said, "Dee, I am not saying that it doesn't take time, but I just talked to a friend today who told me that she was taking her kid out of one school and putting her into Milford. She made one call, and within two days it was a done thing. Finished. You need to be on this, you need to be pushing to get them enrolled. It is something YOU need to do, you can't wait on them."

"Well, I signed the papers at (the old school) and so it is up to them to transfer the paperwork. They said I need their shot records and stuff, and a copy of their birth certificates, and the old school just ain't released them. Besides, my kids were in school since Thanksgiving."

"No, Dee. they were not."

"Yes, they was. They went to school the week of Thanksgiving."

"Yes, they went to school the week of Thanksgiving, but they had off Thanksgiving day, and then the day after. Then you moved. Then you had surgery, and they have not been back since."

She hung her head and looked at the floor.

"Dee, listen to me. I am not here to cause trouble. I am here to help. You could be arrested for keeping your children out of school. This could really go against you. It's illegal to keep your kids out of school, and it will go against you as a parent. Do you want this on your record as a parent?"

She looked uncomfortable and said in a very small voice, "No."

I said, "Listen to me, Girlie. I want to do all I can to help. I think that you cannot doubt that. But Dee, there needs to be some mutuality in our relationship. You and I need to be able to talk, to dialog about the kids. I feel like I'm only good for when you need diapers or gas or food or something for the kids. I would like some friendship, a sense of respect between us. If I am going to do anything for your kids of lasting importance, we need to have a relationship. And putting your kids into school would be good for you. You are still recovering from surgery. If the kids were in school you would have some time to rest, some time to yourself. It would be in their best interest and in yours."

She continued to look at the floor, and I decided to weigh my options. "I am not going to take the kids caroling tonight. It is wet and rainy and I think it is in their best interest not to go. However, would you be able to go in to the school tomorrow and see about getting them enrolled?"

"Well, yes, I could do that. I guess I will just have to go up there to the superintendent's office in person after two and a half weeks and see if I can sign them up." (This is where I had to exercise great resolve to not tear my hair out. What she was saying again was that the kids hadn't been out of school nearly as long as they really were. It was actually FOUR WEEKS that afternoon that they were out of school -- and that business of going up to the superintendent's office in person? Well, duh! What did she think she was supposed to do??? But I decided to let it slide.)

"Do you need the kids for that?"

"Um, no. I have the paperwork. I can go do it."

"Okay. Then I am going to pick up the kids around 9:30 tomorrow morning and we are going to Chuck-E-Cheese's. I can't keep them all day because I have a lot of things going on. But I will try to get them home around 1:30 or so. Will that give you enough time?"

"Yeah, that will be enough time."

"Do you want me to take Little Sensei with me, too? Would that be helpful?""No, I can make it okay with him. Big Sensei will be with me, and he will help me."

"Alright! Kids -- I'll see you in the morning."

And so I went down there in the morning, and knocked on the door. Finally Jeffy came out and said that Lexi had to do Maddie's hair. She'd be out soon. He came on out and we waited and waited. Then Maddie came, and eventually Lexi. And so, we got on our way.

They were in great spirits, and we had a wonderful day. I had coupons for Chuck-E-Cheese's and got a wonderful deal. They were happy, cooperative and their eyes were shining. They told me about the presents that they were getting from their parents. It was a fun, fun, day. They traipsed along with me to pick up a few things at Sam's Club and then we stopped at Kohl's. I had a 30% off EVERYTHING coupon there, plus there were wonderful sales going on. We picked up a few things for their parents, and a nice toy for their little brother. They discussed with me whether they should take the items home to wrap but they were pretty united in the fact that I should take them home and wrap them and bring them on Sunday. We stopped for ice cream at the Dairy Queen on the way home because I had promised them that they could have ice cream if they were on their best behavior. And we got home to their house around 2:30.

I was concerned about things at home. I had started trying to call Dee around 1:30, but there was no answer. I was relieved as I pulled into the driveway to see that her vehicle was there, so I knew someone was home. The kids tried and tried and tried to get in, but the door was locked. I finally said, "They may open up sooner if I'm not here. I'm going to go on home, and I am sure that they will let you in. Mr. Daniel and I will be here on Sunday morning a little later than usual because church doesn't start until 10:30. I really need to get home, now, though." They all insisted that they were fine, and that I should go.

So I aimed my trusty minivan towards home, and prayed for the kids and the whole sordid situation. I found out later that she didn't go -- but she got a letter that day that gave her a number to call and she DID call it -- but it was the last day before Christmas break, so she said they said she had to wait until after Christmas. We shall see how this turns out! I am serious about not letting it go anymore.

220

Middle Daughter wrapped and wrapped and wrapped on Saturday until all the presents were ready. Certain Man and I discussed and discussed about how we should handle things. I thought maybe the kids should just come here to open their presents, because I really wanted to watch them open them. But then I thought that maybe we should just take them down there and leave them, and not even worry about taking the kids along to church. There was no Sunday School, and I knew they were going to be keyed up. That didn't feel right to me, either. Just before we left for church, I decided that I was going to take the presents along to church, give them each their Bible before Church and then take them home after church and leave the rest of their presents there in the keeping of their mom. I packed their stockings and the smaller items in a big wash basket and began to carry things out to the van.

Certain Man looked at me in surprise. "What made you decide to take them down there?"

I was ashamed of myself, but I decided to be honest. "Because I'm a selfish old coot!" I said.

"What do you mean?"

"Well, I just don't feel like having the hubbub, mess and noise at our house this afternoon. Our kids are going to be home, and I just don't feel like dealing with it."

"I don't blame you," he said, making relieved tears spring into my eyes. "I think this is much better." He carried the packages out and wondered aloud at the amount of them, but didn't complain overly much.

We drove down to pick up the children. Again, they straggled out, tired and groggy, but soon left it all behind in their excitement over their new Bibles. They were so pleased with their names on the front, and the fact that they were almost alike, yet all different. They exclaimed and paged and chattered things among themselves that bespoke of such a dearth of knowledge of things Biblical that Certain Man and I were amazed.

Making conversation on the way to church, I turned around in my seat and said, "Well, how did things go at your house this morning. Did you open presents?"

Jeffy looked like someone had hit him. I couldn't see Lexi, but both Maddie and Jeffy turned their heads to look at their oldest sister with stricken looks.

"Um. . ." she fumbled around with her words, then said, "Um, yeah. We opened our presents this morning."

I KNEW something was terribly wrong, and I pretended that I hadn't really heard what she said, and I said, ". . . or are you waiting until you get home from church to open the presents from your mom and dad?"

"Yeah, that's what we decided to do." she said, sounding relieved. "Wait until we get home from church."

"Yeah," said the others. "Wait until we get home from church." I had a sudden sick feeling somewhere in the pit of my stomach. I felt certain that there had been no Christmas at that house that morning. At all.

The three of them suddenly started looking for stuff in their Bibles. I suggested that they look up the Christmas story of how Jesus was born. Lexi asked where it was found, and then somehow found Luke 2, and read us the Christmas story on the way to church. I sat there, listening to the timeless words coming out of the mouth of this child who is so old beyond her years, who has learned to lie and cheat and steal to protect her family's secrets as well as to save her neck and I could have wept.

"Do not be afraid. I bring you good news that will cause great joy for all the people. Today in the town of David a Savior has been born to you; he is the Messiah, the Lord. This will be a sign to you: You will find a baby wrapped in cloths and lying in a manger."

The car was quiet after she finished. Once again, I had to wonder what difference all this would make. I kept thinking about the Savior, who is Christ the LORD, the Messiah, and prayed again that somehow, someway, somewhere, someday, the truth of this would soften their hearts and they would BELIEVE.

Just before church started, I took Maddie into a hug. "There weren't any presents at your house this morning, were there, sweetie?" I whispered into her ear.

She looked at me, her brown eyes sad and wary. "No," she said. "None." I hugged her again, and let her go. Suddenly I was so glad for that big pile of presents behind the back seat of our minivan.

We had a wonderful service on Christmas Sunday Morning at Laws Mennonite Church. Music and Scripture, along with the annual candy bars and oranges for everyone. Three little kids on our bench wriggled and laughed and caressed their bibles and helped to sing. It was finally time to go home. Certain Man and I got everyone loaded and their gifts from their Sunday School Teachers that excited them beyond words, and we were finally on our way.

We pulled into the driveway, and things looked dead as a tomb at their house. Lexi went running in and got the door open. Someone had made sure she had a key. The other kids wanted to stay behind and help carry gifts, but we finally convinced them to go on in. Both of us expected one of the adults to come out and tell us where to put things, or to help carry or something, but we saw neither hide nor hair of anyone.

"She's resting," one of the kids said. Certain Man and I stood in the kitchen holding the wash basket full of presents, and the stack of things that wouldn't fit in.

"Can we just bring them on into the living room?" I asked. "Mr. Daniel and I can set them around the tree, if you want us to."

222

Maddie didn't wait for anyone's permission. "YES," she said her little chin sticking out defiantly. "You CAN bring them in."

We didn't wait for anyone to stop us. We walked right on in -- a first for both of us. The Christmas tree stood there in nice array -- but not one single gift anywhere. Nothing to be seen. Certain Man and I separated things out with the help of the children. There was sweet camaraderie, conversation and companionship with the excitement of little people, almost unable to contain their joy at the sight of the growing pile of things that was each of theirs.

And then, the basket was empty. The presents all given out and built into piles and Certain Man and I looked at each other and wondered what to do next.

"Well, Kids, I guess we'll be going," we finally said. They only had eyes for their presents as they lovingly arranged and rearranged and adjusted. They didn't ask to open anything. They didn't shake or rattle a single thing. They just looked and gently touched and in hushed tones, discussed.

Certain Man picked up the basket and we let ourselves out, leaving them there in the living room, shutting the kitchen door behind us.

"Well," said Certain Man. "You would have thought their parents would have at least come out!"

"You would think so, yes," I said, half to myself.

We got into the minivan and came on home. Home to our house that was full of warmth and light and love and the adult children we love so much. And once again, I had to wonder about how God chose me to go to Mark and Alene Yoder's house that long ago day when He was making that decision. I wondered at the Grace that has caused the lines to fall in such pleasant places. I am so grateful for parents who taught me about this Good News -- a Savior, which is Christ the LORD"

And I'm more aware than ever that "from those who have been given much, much will be required." I refuse to entertain thoughts of "deserving" because I know that if I got what I deserved, I would NEVER get Heaven. And so, when it seems like what we do is but a drop in the bucket against the tide of headlong destruction, I want to believe that the end of this story will only be told in Heaven. In the meantime, I pray for grace to be faithful to the calling. And, once again, someday when we are THERE, if even one of these kids makes it safely home, it will be MORE than worth it.

Ah, LORD Jesus. May it be so!

www.ingramcontent.com/pod-product-compliance
Lightning Source LLC
Chambersburg PA
CBHW031836090426

42741CB00005B/258